The European Union and the South

Relations with developing countries

Marjorie Lister

ROUTLEDGE

London and New York

First published 1997
by Routledge
11 New Fetter Lane, London EC4P 4EE

Simultaneously published in the USA and Canada
by Routledge
29 West 35th Street, New York, NY 10001

Phototypeset in Times by Intype London Ltd
Printed and bound in Great Britain by Redwood Books, Trowbridge,
Wiltshire

British Library Cataloguing in Publication Data
A catalogue record for this book is available from the British Library

Library of Congress Cataloging in Publication Data
Lister, Marjorie
    The European Union and the South / Marjorie Lister.
    Includes bibliographical references.
    1. European Union – Developing countries – History. I. Title.
    HC240.L554   1997
    337.1′42 – dc21   96–36572

ISBN 0–415–16098–7 (hbk)
ISBN 0–415–16099–5 (pbk)

Contents

List of figures and tables   vii
Introduction   1

1 The European Union and foreign policy   6
What the EU can offer   25
Selected EU multilateral and bilateral relations   27

2 Europe's colonial history: the problem of the 'other'   42
Europe and Africa: the first links   43
African history   45
The age of colonialism   47
The 'other'   49
Women and colonialism   51
The economic explanations   53
The triumph of technology?   58
The scramble in and out of Africa   60
The colonial legacy   62
Europe and the 'clash of civilizations'   64

3 Europe and the Mediterranean   70
The Mediterranean ideal   71
Issues of dependency   74
Mediterranean relations with the EU   77
Morocco and the EU   90
The Union of the Arab Maghreb   91
The Mediterranean environment   95
Migration   99
The Conference on Security and Cooperation in the Mediterranean   103
Conclusion   106

4 Europe and Africa: the Fourth Lomé Convention   108
Negotiating Lomé IV   112
The results of trade preferences   122
Lomé: the record of project aid, Stabex and Sysmin   125
Lomé: the reply to critics   129
The mid-term review of Lomé IV   131
The Lomé Convention: Horizon 2000 or Horizon 0?   136
Conclusion   141

5 Lomé IV and the breeze of change   143
Lomé in context   143
Sources of marginalization   146
Sources of stability   148
The fallacy of transposition   158
Enlarging Lomé   161
Conclusion   168

6 Conclusion: the EurAfrican construction   170
The EurAfrican construction: the spiritual dimension   176

Notes   178
Index   194

Figures and tables

FIGURES

3.1 Mediterranean states which have preferential trade
     agreements with the EU   78
4.1 The Lomé Convention, 1996   110–11

TABLES

3.1 Mediterranean exports to the World and the EU,
     1981 and 1991   74
3.2 Mediterranean states' GNP, 1990 and 1980   83
3.3 EU aid to the Maghreb, the Mashreq and Israel   88
3.4 Major destination countries of migration   99
4.1 EU aid to the ACP countries, 1958–91   113
4.2 ACP trade with the EU   123
4.3 EU imports from and exports to trading partners   124
4.4 Contributions to European Development Funds –
     Lomé IV   134

Introduction

The European Union (EU) has a vast network of relationships with countries and organizations in all parts of the world. This book undertakes to examine in particular its relations with the developing countries – the 'South'. As a region the South is no better defined than its equally amorphous counterpart, the developed countries or 'North'. Nevertheless, the 'South' is a near-ubiquitous term used to refer to the former colonies of Europe and other poor countries such as Liberia and Ethiopia.

Among the developing areas of the world, European interest has concentrated first and foremost upon Africa. The present text, too, concentrates its attention on European relations with Africa while also recognizing the importance of connections with the Caribbean, the Pacific, Latin America and East Asia. Within Africa, European interest has traditionally concentrated on the sub-Saharan part of the continent, but, as Chapter 3 demonstrates, this situation is changing.

This book is intended to introduce the subject of the EU's relations with developing countries to readers with some knowledge of or interest in the contemporary process of European integration or with a specialism in international affairs. Students of European Studies, International Relations, International Political Economy or Development Studies will find many themes of interest. *The European Union and the South* delves into a relationship which is of central importance to the future of Europe, to the future of the developing countries and to the position of both parties within the global international system.

Before dealing specifically with the European Union's development policy, Chapter 1 situates this policy in the context of the Union's place in the world at large. Chapter 1 raises the question of whether or not the EU has a foreign policy as such. It examines how the theory of foreign policy analysis has been applied with limited success to the EU. Despite over three decades of effort at integration, the EU is neither a state nor nor even a unified voting bloc in the UN. Nevertheless, many European-minded leaders foresee Europe's taking up a global role commensurate with its great economic strength. The structure of the European Commission, which is frequently reorganized, reflects the divisions of responsibility for different aspects of Europe's external relations.

The EU's development policy, one sub-field of foreign policy, is one of its earliest common policies. However, it is still far from unified and each member state maintains its own approach to development. The EU has built up a considerable experience of development policies, but their success is often called into question.

Chapter 1 assesses the development of the internal and external policies of the EU and looks at how Eastern and Central Europe as well as the African, Caribbean and Pacific countries have developed a relationship of 'dependent interdependence' with the EU. The issue of what a politically more powerful Europe could offer to the international system comes under scrutiny. One possible answer is that Europe could use its understanding and history of relations with the South to promote the South's interests in the international arena. Neither the USA – which has traditionally had minimal interest in Africa – nor Japan – whose interest in Africa is growing – is as well suited to this role as the EU. Finally, Chapter 1 probes the EU's bilateral relations with its major partners, the USA and Japan, as well as its multilateral relations with developing countries in Asia, Latin America and Africa.

The external relations of the EU with developing countries of the modern-day South are still built on the foundations of the colonial empires. Chapter 2 delves into the colonial past, a past that still affects, moulds and shapes the present. Because of the strong bonds that France and the UK in particular have with their former colonies, these relations remain important for the contemporary EU and the countries of the South.

Chapter 2 begins with Europe's earliest links to Africa. It examines the views of nineteenth-century European scholars and modern cultural conservatives. The little-known, egalitarian period of European–African relations in the sixteenth century gave way to the age of colonialism. This was 'the rule of the people, by other people and for other people'. Even today, the commemoration of Columbus' 'discovery' of America is fraught with difficulties over the excesses of European conquest.

Chapter 2 investigates Europe's problem in dealing with those who are perceived as 'other' or different to itself. The role of women in the colonial enterprise, the various explanations of colonialism, the scramble in and out of Africa – and the legacy of the colonial empires – are examined. Up to the present, Europeans have not solved the problem of building relationships with less developed countries. The fashionable argument that Europe today faces a near-inevitable 'clash of civilizations' with other cultures is explored and its policy implications are spelt out.

Chapter 3 looks at a specific region with which Europe has longstanding ties: the Mediterranean. The two shores of the Mediterranean Sea are closely linked and aspire to an ideal of greater cooperation. Nevertheless, the different levels of economic development between the northern and southern shores of the Mediterranean mean that relations are better characterized as dependent rather than equal. At the end of the Cold War, Europe is trying to fill the security vacuum in the Mediterranean left by the reduction of activity of the two superpowers.

The EU (formerly Community) has been constructing a Mediterranean policy since 1957. But the development of the policy has been sporadic, reactive rather than progressive. Since 1989 the EU has given increased priority to its relations with the countries of the Mediterranean region. It even aims to create a Euro-Mediterranean free trade area.

Chapter 3 also examines Europe's often disappointing relations with Morocco and with the five-member Union of the Arab Maghreb (UMA). The UMA was meant to replicate the experience of European integration on the southern shore of the Mediterranean, but so far it has produced few results. Environmental cooperation in the Mediterranean region, migration and the prospects for creating a permanent Conference on Security and Cooperation in the Mediterranean are analysed in the final sections of the chapter. The conclusion argues that Europe needs to take a sustained and positive role in the Mediterranean to create a zone of prosperity rather than an 'arc of crisis'.

In Chapter 4, the most ambitious of Europe's development

policies, the Lomé Convention, comes under scrutiny. This chapter examines the political economy of the fourth Lomé Convention, signed in 1989 by the then twelve members of the European Community and sixty-eight countries of the African, Caribbean and Pacific (ACP) Group of States. The negotiations for Lomé IV, including the controversial support for structural adjustment policies, are analysed. Chapter 4 covers the results of Lomé's trade and aid provisions, its Stabex, Sysmin and emergency aid programmes.

Following the 1995 mid-term review of the Lomé IV provisions, the balance of power in the Lomé relationship shifted in Europe's favour. There has been increased speculation that the present or fourth Lomé Convention will be the last. Chapter 4 further investigates the effects that the fall of the Berlin Wall have had on European–developing country relations and argues that these spill-over effects should not be allowed to disrupt the *acquis* (the acquired rights and benefits) of the Lomé relationship.

Chapter 5 analyses the Lomé Convention in its political context. It identifies three principal 'sources of marginalization' for the Convention and juxtaposes these against the Convention's 'sources of stability'. The latter include the functioning of the Lomé Convention as an alliance and as an international regime. Chapter 5 investigates the Lomé Convention as an example of regional cooperation and finds that the 'fallacy of transposition', which argues that developing countries cannot replicate the experience of European integration, is itself fallacious.

Finally Chapter 5 explores the possibility of expanding Lomé to new developing country partners. The current negotiations between the EU and the 'new South Africa' are broadly welcomed, although the proposals for free trade in industrial goods between the EU and South Africa give cause for concern. Once South Africa is admitted to partial or limited membership of the Lomé system, Chapter 5 argues that a similar arrangement for the Caribbean island state of Cuba could be possible and desirable.

Chapter 6, in 'conclusion', surveys the long history of linkages between Europe and Africa. It reviews the evolution of Europe's post-colonial relations from the Treaty of Rome up to the Lomé Convention. It envisages Europe's entering a new phase of relations with Africa, with the African, Caribbean and Pacific states, and with developing countries in general. Europe is currently engaged in the pursuit of internal integration, the 'European construction'. But Europe requires a further project, a 'EurAfrican construction' to complement its integration. This wider project could ensure that peace and prosperity are not limited to Europe, North America, Japan and the newly industrializing countries of Asia and the Pacific Rim. By taking up such a 'EurAfrican construction', Europe could avoid the aimlessness and lack of spiritual purpose which have been identified by Czech President Vaclav Havel, Professor Stanley Hoffman and others as being among its chief problems.

Like the Nigerian-born poet Ben Okri, Europe needs to take a positive look at the future of Africa and the developing countries in general, and to make great, concrete efforts to bring about a positive future for them. Like 'destiny' in one of Ben Okri's poems, the EU should continue to take a positive interest in the peoples of the South:[1]

We are the miracles that God made
To taste the bitter fruit of time.
We are precious.
And one day our suffering
Will turn into the wonders of the earth.

. . . Destiny is our friend.

Chapter 1

The European Union and foreign policy

This chapter begins by introducing the question of whether or not the EU has a foreign policy. Arguing that it does not, the chapter then assesses the potential for the EU to develop a unified foreign and security policy in the future. The tools of traditional foreign policy analysis add relatively little to our understanding of the EU. The EU is best understood as a unique type of institution rather than an embryonic state. Chapter 1 examines also the divided nature of decision-making in the European Commission. The vision of Europe's political power and world role is explained, and contrasted with the widespread perception of Europe as a 'political dwarf'. But despite the higher growth rates of other areas, Europe is still an economic superpower.

Analysing the EU's longstanding development policy, the chapter concludes that the record of achievement has been mixed. Security policy is another area of controversy. Arguably, constructing a common European defence and security policy will be even more problematic than a common foreign policy. Next the chapter compares the development of internal and external policies of the EU, finding different rates of expansion in recent years. This part of Chapter 1 concludes by asking what the EU could offer to the international system by taking on a greater world role.

The last section assesses selected multilateral and bilateral relations of the EU with other regions. The interactions between the EU and Central and Eastern Europe, South East Asia, Latin America, Japan and the USA are investigated. Although Europe has an impressive array of external relations with these and other areas, they do not amount to a unified foreign policy.

Conflicting images of a powerful 'superstate Europe' and of a pathetic Europe unable to cope with local instabilities in the Balkans co-exist in the 1990s. The confusing status of the EU and its foreign policy at present recalls the debates of the 1970s. In the early 1970s it seemed that all the old bets or predictions about the future of Europe were off. Political science had failed to foresee the course of development of the European Community. Johan Galtung characterized Europe as an emerging superstate bent on world mastery while another scholar, Andrew Shonfield, depicted the European Community as a group of states or a 'bag of marbles' only loosely united by inefficient decision-making structures.[1]

The question not only whether the objective or goal of a European foreign policy would be met but also of the means by which this might be accomplished came under scrutiny. In a forceful article, Stanley Henig identified two possibilities for developing a common European foreign policy: first, through organic growth, that is, through the development of internal integration; or, second, through the Community's need to respond to external events. Henig opted for the latter – for the need for external shocks to jolt Europe into further integration. In an extraordinary vision of the world as existing in order to provide a backdrop for European events, Henig argued that 'Dealing with the economic problems of Upper Volta or even Nigeria does not really pose that much of a challenge to those who make common policy and whatever the amount of "spill-over".... such successes hardly make a major contribution towards European integration.'[2] At the end of the twentieth century, it is apparent that dealing with the problems, for instance, of Burkina Faso (formerly Upper Volta) or Nigeria remains a challenge in its own right, and not only for Europe.

More recently, some academics have tended towards the view that the EU has developed a common foreign and security policy (CFSP). Hazel Smith even argued that we should consider that the EU has a foreign policy so that we can apply our knowledge of foreign policy to this otherwise inexplicable phenomenon.[3] But the attempt to fit European realities into the theory of foreign policy analysis has dismally failed. Despite the theoretical and quantitative efforts of hundreds of US and European scholars, there is no general theory of foreign policy and little agreement on methodology or on which theoretical paradigm (state-based, interdependence-based, dependency, neo-functionalist) to apply to which actual case.[4] We might consider this as the 'rise and fall' of foreign policy analysis. The classic foreign policy models of Graham Allison, for instance, have been revised and refined, but neither alone nor together can they fully explain the events they were designed to explain, namely, the Cuban Missile Crisis.[5]

Still less is the theory of foreign policy able to deal with the unusual *sui generis* case of the EU. Susan Strange noted the tendency of international relations theorists to adjust facts to fit into theories rather than to question the adequacy of their theories. The case of European 'foreign policy' supports her contention that the facts of European foreign policy are more complex than the theories so far admit.[6]

Even the broader charge that political science as a whole has failed to produce any worthwhile results from its methodology is not falsified by the experience of explanations of European 'foreign policy'.[7] Political scientists are little better now at predicting the evolution of the EU than they were two decades ago, however enjoyable and fulfilling their theorizing may be. As a prominent analyst painstakingly explained, one of the main analytical distinctions for theories of comparative foreign policy is that '*internal* refers to theories related to domestic factors of a given nation state, and *external* refers to those related to the systemic structure of the outside world'.[8] If this is one of the main analytical contributions of this sub-field, the emperor of comparative foreign policy analysis has very few clothes indeed.

Nikolaj Petersen distinguished three possibilities about how the foreign and security policy of the Community might be conceived: first, as an extra dimension to the foreign policies of the EU member states; second, as a separate policy parallel to national foreign and security policies, i.e. a thirteenth foreign policy; or, third, as an independent expression of the Community's foreign and security policy 'which in some respects is superior to the national policies'.[9] Professor Petersen chooses the third option, the maximalist position. In fact, there is little evidence that the Community has gone beyond the second option, although its foreign policy is intertwined with, rather than separate from, the national policies of the member states. Professor Petersen admitted that a CFSP cannot be compared with true European policies on fisheries or tariffs but, basing his view more on hope than evidence, sees it moving in that direction. In fact, it is even harder to argue that the EU has a common foreign and security policy than a common foreign policy alone. Security is very much a junior area of cooperation. A joint EU foreign policy could become 'superior' to national foreign policies in a legal sense, but, as discussed on pp. 19–20, some EU member states do ignore legal strictures. The idea that an EU foreign policy would be 'superior' in the sense of being better or more effective in achieving its goals remains to be proven.

In fact, relatively little attention has been paid to the quality or content of the foreign policy that the EU could produce.[10] In order to secure the assent of the now fifteen EU member states, any foreign policy initiative would have to be safe and uncontroversial. An EU foreign policy would be a conservative, lowest-common-denominator policy. It could be a policy without clear objectives. Like the EU policies regarding Yugoslavia and Chechnya, discussed on pp. 19–20, EU foreign policy would tend to be passive rather than active. Of course a conciliatory, conflict-avoiding European policy would be preferable to a Europe bent on world domination, but it might not be better than the sum of the individual foreign policies of the member states. It might be a neo-mercantilist foreign policy, neglecting the ties of affinity, culture and empire which have been important in particular to the UK, France, Belgium, Spain, Portugal and Italy.

Professor Soetendorp, also proposing the theory of an emergent unitary European foreign policy, expounded the view in 1994 that the Community was becoming a single foreign policy actor. He maintained that in fact this transformation 'has been a continuous goal of the member states'.[11] Although admitting that some member states wanted to retain their foreign policy sovereignty, Soetendorp saw an inexorable, functionalist progression into joint foreign policy making. Not only was a joint foreign policy almost inevitable, it led to a morally superior type of policy: 'actors involved in joint decision-making change from self-interested actors into joint problem-solvers and from self-maximizers into joint maximizers.'[12] Foreign policy élites and bureaucracies within the member states would abandon their 'egoistic self-interests'. However, to the outside observer, the pursuit of European rather than national-level interests might look just as 'egoistic', and possibly more dangerous.

In addition to examining the foreign policy – or lack of it – of the EU, many scholars have tried to define the nature of the EU itself. Is it an inter-governmental organization, a nation state, a federation in the making or a *sui generis* international organization?

The EU as (almost) a state?

One of the characteristics of statehood is the ability to participate in the international state system, to act as an equal in the society of sovereign states. The Union does not have all the attributes of a nation state, but it does participate intensely in the inter-state system – even playing a central role in important processes such as the successive negotiating rounds of the General Agreement on Tariffs and Trade (GATT). The EU has a vast network of external relations, but not a coordinated or coherent foreign policy.[13]

The European Union (in place of 'Community' since November 1993)[14] is more than an inter-governmental organization, but less than a sovereign state. It has no one head of state, no single written constitution, no common language or currency, no power to raise taxes directly from its citizens. It suffers from a 'democratic deficit'; its directly elected Parliament is widely seen as a second-class form of representation, without the legislative and other powers possessed by the legislatures of the member states, while the unelected Commission has a powerful role in legislation.[15] One way to look at the European Union is as the inverse in structure of the United States of America. The individual states of the USA are not sovereign although they have considerable legislative and judicial power, but the federal level is a sovereign state. In the EU, the individual states are sovereign states, but the 'federal' level is not, although it has considerable legislative and judicial power.

Nevertheless, the EU has become more like a nation state, inseparably linked to many aspects of national policy-making in its member states. In the agricultural, industrial, security and environmental sectors, it is impossible to understand the policies of any member state without reference to European-level legislation. The Treaty of Maastricht established a common citizenship of the 'European Union', proposed economic and monetary union including a single currency, and envisaged 'a common foreign and security policy including the eventual framing of a common defence policy'.[16] Still, many political scientists have doubts about the ability of the Union to frame a common foreign and security policy or to achieve economic and monetary integration, at least in the short or medium term.

As noted above, possession of a foreign policy is generally conceptualized in terms of statehood. K. J. Holsti described foreign policy as actions or ideas designed to solve a problem or promote some change in the policies, attitudes, or actions of another state or states.[17] A state has an official foreign policy pursued by its government, although its international corporations, social groups such as trade unions or political parties may pursue different or conflicting policies. In the EU's case, members primarily pursue individual foreign policies in keeping with their history and national interests while the Union tries to coordinate them with greater or lesser success. But the prevailing view was expressed by Elfriede Regelsberger: despite the Community's efforts to harmonize member states' policies through European Political Cooperation (EPC), and the undoubted intensification of consultations, the participants remained of the view 'that foreign policy is the domain of the sovereign state'.[18] The attachment of governments to their foreign policy prerogatives can be intense. The UK and France, for instance, reacted with little enthusiasm to Italian Prime Minister Andreotti's suggestion in 1990 that the permanent UK and French seats on the UN Security Council should be replaced with a single Community seat. (Although the USA initially liked this idea, it later supported the proposal to add Germany and Japan to the Security Council instead.) States, foreign ministers and ministries are not likely to give up much of their power to the EU willingly. As Professor Geoffrey Goodwin noted, 'In certain limited respects the Community may come to be deemed an "it", but the realities are of a collective "they".'[19]

In some cases the EU does act for the member states in a foreign policy context, negotiating on their behalf. The Community could even be party to a treaty while the member states were not. In other instances the Commmunity and the member states can all sign an international treaty, known as a mixed agreement. According to a strict interpretation of the Treaty of Rome, the Community could only make international treaties where it had express powers to do so. But the Community's foreign policy competence was considerably developed through cases in the European Court. The Court decided in 1971 that if the Community had adopted measures binding on the member states in a particular field, it thereby derived powers to act externally in that field.

In the case of the Lomé Conventions, mixed agreements between the Community, the now fifteen member states, and the seventy members of the African, Caribbean and Pacific (ACP) Group of States, this mixing of levels is especially apparent. But in other instances, such as the international conventions on aircraft noise and waste dumping at sea, the member states have specifically prohibited the Community from acting on their behalf, clearly showing the limitations on Community-level foreign policy competence.[20]

In the 1950s, political scientists began to examine voting records in the United Nations General Assembly as indices of inter-state cohesion.[21] Developing countries, especially those from Africa, were widely perceived as voting in a uniform bloc in the UN General Assembly. That is, the developing countries appeared to US conservatives, among others, to vote together and in opposition to the interests of the industrialized North. This was often considered to be a precursor to a global 'third world union' or a 'third world wide' Organization of Petroleum Exporting Countries (OPEC). US Senator Daniel Moynihan believed that 'world political parties' were emerging in the UN General Assembly.[22]

With hindsight, the challenge of 'third world' bloc voting was more illusory than real. In the first place, a unified 'bloc voting' pattern never really existed. Hovet found that even after the formation of the African caucusing group, African votes in the General Assembly from 1958 to 1962 were identical only in 36.7 per cent of cases.[23] Alker and Russett determined that only the Soviet bloc was consistently (but not always) united in its General Assembly voting.[24] Even where the 'third world' displayed considerable voting cohesion, its unity remained fragile and temporary; in effect it was no more than 'an overlapping coalition of interests'.[25]

In the second place, the importance of the UN General Assembly receded after the 1970s as the Security Council became more active. The ideological, political and economic (at least in oil) challenge of the new post-colonial UN member states to the US-led capitalist system has dissipated. The UN General Assembly is often described as quasi-legislative, but since it has only the power to make recommendations without the power to enforce them, this assessment is on the generous side.

Although the UN General Assembly no longer has as high a political profile as it did during the 1960s and 1970s, and the analysis of voting in that forum is no longer fashionable, voting trends there may still be considered significant. And a unified voting record in the UN General Assembly could be evidence of the converging interests and foreign policies of the member states of the EU. If we apply the General Assembly voting cohesion test to the EU, it looks as though European unity remains elusive. European 'party discipline' in UN voting has not increased. The high point of concordant voting in the UN General Assembly took place in the 1970s, when as many as 65 per cent of Community votes on resolutions concurred. In the mid-1980s, concurring votes happened in nearer to 30 per cent of cases, remaining below 50 per cent up to 1990.[26]

We can conclude that the EU does not operate a unified foreign policy, but something more like fifteen national foreign policies, plus one (at EU level). Nevertheless these foreign policies, like policies in the areas of agriculture, fisheries, and the environment, are increasingly intertwined. If we demote the Community or Union from an actor with foreign policy to one with external relations, these are still far from unimportant or uninteresting. The Union's external relations include political, economic, trade, development, environmental and security issues.

The structure of the European Commission

One of the problems for the EU in constructing a foreign policy is the division of responsibilities within the European Commission. Alternatively, one might say that the separation of external affairs responsibilities in the Commission shows that the member states do not want any single Commissioner to appear as 'European foreign minister', hence becoming too powerful.

There are twenty European Commissioners – the President and nineteen others. The appointment of the President and Vice-Presidents and the share-out of the portfolios is the subject of intense and sometimes bitter political wrangling among member governments and the Commissioners themselves. In the EU, responsibility for external relations is divided into three main parts, as well as the President's role as overall coordinator. (In addition, other portfolios such as fisheries and environment also have international aspects and implications.)

In January 1993, there was a considerable reorganization of the Commission. Leon Brittan became responsible for external affairs and trade while Hans van den Broek received responsibility for external political relations and enlargement negotiations. The effectiveness of this arrangement depended upon these two Commissioners dividing and coordinating their activities, but was marred by a degree of mutual hostility. This was a less than desirable administrative structure, but the portfolios are distributed with regard to personal and national influence as well as administrative efficiency.

While the external affairs portfolio was divided in 1993, the development portfolios were unified. The development portfolio was previously divided into two: development (for Africa, Caribbean and Pacific countries) plus fisheries; and relations with the Mediterranean, Latin America and Asia within general North –South relations. Development specialists were broadly pleased to see that fisheries policy was handed to the environment commissioner, Ioannis Paleokrassas, while the two development portfolios were combined in the hands of Manuel Marin (although some observers were later disappointed with his actual performance).[27]

In January 1995 the European Commission was again reshuffled and enlarged to take account of the new EU member states of Austria, Sweden and Finland. The new Commission President, Jacques Santer, a compromise candidate from Luxembourg, followed President Delors' model and retained overall control of foreign and security matters. The uneasy division of responsibilities between Hans van den Broek and Leon Brittan was altered by giving the former the plum job of relations with Eastern Europe while the latter had to be satisfied with relations with other developed countries and multilateral trade matters. On paper, the situation for developing countries seemed set to improve, with Commissioner Marin allocated the portfolio including the Mediterranean, the Middle East and Asia, plus the Latin American countries which he was said to have put at the top of his agenda. At the same time Commissioner Pinheiro, a former Portuguese foreign minister, took on responsibility for Africa, the Caribbean and Pacific developing countries, a sphere which urgently needs more EU attention. To coordinate the external activities and views of the EU Commission, the External Relations group of Commissioners is chaired by M. Santer, and includes Commissioners Marin, Brittan, van den Broek and Pinheiro, as well as de Silguy (financial affairs) and Bonino (humanitarian aid).

Although the EU has not developed a fully-fledged foreign policy, it would be wrong to consider that the EU's external policy has been in any way stagnant. It has been developing and growing, not just relying on the habits of the past. On the one hand the Community has been working since the 1970s, through European Political Cooperation (EPC) and through the external affairs Commissioners, towards achieving the Delors goal of a common external policy which is coherent and firm. But, on the other hand, the attachment to national interests and the fragmentation of policy-making between the European Council, the Council of Ministers and even between different Commission portfolios has so far militated against a unified external or foreign policy.

However, despite these obstacles, the EU is not without self-confidence. A Community document asserted in 1991: 'It is inevitable that the Community, with the degree of internal and external commercial, economic and monetary cohesion it is acquiring, develops a corresponding international political dimension. A global foreign policy is a necesssary adjunct to global trading and economic interests.'[28] Students of history and political science will realize that in fact little is 'inevitable' in politics and that a number of things turn out to be surprising, such as the fall of the Berlin Wall, the rise of political democracy in Latin America and Africa, or the wish of Russia to join NATO's Partnership for Peace. Still, there is indeed considerable impetus for the EU to develop a common foreign policy, although most national governments remain anxious to keep their prerogatives in this area. States go along with European policies in so far as it suits their national interests, even for the most communautaire-minded countries such as France.

French Prime Minister Beregovoy argued in 1992 that France did not sacrifice its sovereignty through participating in European-level security measures because these were controlled by inter-governmental bodies, the European Council and the Council of Ministers. These bodies in turn were responsible to national parliaments. 'Sovereignty is intact while cooperation multiplies our power. It is this simple idea which, in this area and others, justifies my conviction that the pursuit of the construction of Europe coincides with the interest of France.'[29] At the end of 1994 there was speculation that France would choose to turn away from Germany's devotion to greater European integration and opening up to the east, and instead form stronger links with Spain and the Mediterranean. This change was envisioned to foster French political interests and to counterbalance Germany's power. However, so far the Franco-German axis within the EU remains strong.

Despite the obstacles in the path of a common European foreign policy, many European policy-makers have propounded the view that Europe should take on an increasingly important international political role.

The vision of European political power

Jacques Delors, European Commission President from January 1985 to January 1995, is widely credited with reviving the fortunes of the European Commission, making it 'the genuine motor of integration' in the Community.[30] Supported by President Mitterrand of France, he presided over the passage of the Single European Act and the Maastricht Treaty. Delors certainly did not lack a powerful vision of Europe and its place in the world. It is generally agreed that no other European had as much influence on the development of Europe in this period as did he. With his high political profile, Delors acquired the image of 'Mr Europe'.

Delors envisaged a popularly-based Community with a universal vocation. He described its role in a variety of geographical areas, ranging from Africa to Latin America and the Pacific:[31]

> The Community, by its success, is solicited in all quarters. It can't be deaf to all these pleas without renouncing its universal vocation. . . .
>
> History doesn't wait for the full realization of the Single Act to knock at our door.
>
> The countries of Africa, the Caribbean and Pacific worry that the Community focuses too much on the larger Europe and neglects the cooperation at the heart of future Lomé Conventions.
>
> Our neighbours of north Africa created the Union of the Arab Maghreb in the image of the European enterprise and plan to recall how they need an active partnership with the

Community. A purely demographic perspective brings us, besides, to a profound reflection on the conditions of coexistence between the two shores of the Mediterranean.

Latin and Central America turn to the Community, not only as a point of reference for the relations between these countries and the continent – but also to reclaim a more active presence from the Europe whose blood is mixed with that of their peoples.

In Asia and the Pacific, the Europeans are asked for, probably with less insistence, but to neglect these countries – as we have a tendency to do – is it not to bypass economic opportunities, and more gravely still to allow dangerous imbalances in terms of influence?

Arguing that European states singly could only cultivate nostalgia for their past grandeur, Delors proposed that a united EU should take up a global role, if not as world policeman as the US had sometimes been, at least as a major world presence. But to realize these ambitions the EU would have to give itself greater powers.

President Delors identified the USA as the leading world power and wanted Europe to undertake 'a global partnership with the United States, the only way to better understand the upheavals that shake the world. To combat the disorders of the international economy, and require that new great power, Japan, to share with North America and Europe the burden of world responsibilities.'[32] With his conception of the Community's sharing world responsibilities, Jacques Delors took the view that the old two-superpower world of the USA and the USSR should not become a one-superpower world, with the USA as its unchallenged leader. Neither was he prepared to leave the Asia–Pacific region to the care of the USA and Japan, in a system of bigemony (dual hegemony). The Commission President wanted Europe to participate fully in all regions of the world.

Nevertheless, even President Delors stopped short of predicting the development of a common European foreign policy. At the end of May 1994, he remarked, 'I have never believed that our different nations, taking account of their traditions, their interests or their geopolitical situations, could ever have an entirely common foreign policy.'[33] His successor, Jacques Santer of Belgium, adopted a more emollient and pragmatic approach to

European integration, but still based his activities and aspirations upon the Delors edifice. President Santer agreed that the EU lacked a foreign and security policy. He lamented the lack of political will of the member states to work together as a union, and to share the costs and responsibilities of joint action.[34]

In the run-up to the 1996 inter-governmental conference, designed to revise and review the operation of the Maastricht Treaty of 1992, pressure from the Commission and some member states to strengthen EU foreign and security policy could be intense.[35] While the UK in particular can be expected to resist the drive for greater European integration and to try to maintain its own status as an international power, the themes raised by Jacques Delors continue to be carried forward by other European-minded politicians.

Political dwarf?

The problem of whether the EU is a superpower, whether it can effectively translate its economic resources into political influence, is similar to the problems of Germany and Japan. Both of these states, like the EU, lack military might. Like the Union (but from different causes) they lack the historical legitimacy to function as leading powers in the international system.

The reasons for the EU's lack of clout are different from those of Japan: the divisions within the Council of Ministers and their wish to retain national sovereignty; the separate currencies, financial institutions and policies; the cumbersome decision-making process within the Community; and the dearth of any military dimension.[36] Despite its importance in policy-making, the Union's budget amounts to under 5 per cent of its members' total public spending.

In general, the EU is far from a political pygmy and its international successes – such as negotiating GATT – have been more than minimal. Nevertheless, the EU, like Japan, does not have the political status which its economic power might merit. The European Commission asserted in 1992 that the two entities were at a similar stage of development. Whether or not Japan, a nation state, and the EU, a multinational organization, are at a similar developmental stage, they do have some similar problems: 'Japan because it is searching for ways of translating its economic power into political influence, the Community because it is adopting through the European Union institutions and mechanisms to enable it to play a stronger foreign policy role.'[37]

But this stronger foreign policy role foreseen by the Commission has not yet materialized. France, one of the founder members of the European experiment, has vigorously supported the idea of greater European cooperation in foreign policy. But its actions have been rather different. In January 1995 France announced that it had opened a French-interest section in the Romanian embassy in Baghdad. The insensitivity of this act, establishing low-level relations with Iraq – a country with which its European partners had recently been at war – was considerable. France had not even consulted its EU partners in advance, showing that where France perceived an important economic interest (in this case here in trade with Iraq), the rhetoric of cooperation would not stand in the way of unilateral action even when France was in the chair of the Union.

In the crisis of former Yugoslavia, the Community was accused by the USA and others of being ineffectual, and of being dominated by German policy. The Community certainly did not prevent the widespread bloodshed and the dislocation of over 2 million persons from the former state of Yugoslavia. By acceding to German demands at the end of 1991 and so recognizing Croatia and Slovenia, and then the other former Yugoslav republics (except Macedonia), the Community may have fuelled the civil war. Community observers and peace-making missions have not solved the crisis on the Community's own doorstep. Alain Lamassoure, then a French MEP, and later minister for European affairs, wrote contemptuously of a Community which, faced with the Yugoslav crisis, could do nothing but 'ring the doorbell of the UN'.[38] It was, finally, US pressure through NATO in 1994 which led to the temporary lifting of the siege of Sarajevo, and in 1995 to the Dayton peace accord. When France offered in 1995 to put its national nuclear deterrent at the service of the EU, the other national delegations roundly rejected the offer – seeing it not as an effort to strengthen Europe's defence but merely as a disguise for France's unpopular nuclear testing programme in the Pacific.

Even small powers such as Greece have caused tensions regarding the EU's foreign relations. Greece's suspension of diplomatic ties with and imposition of economic sanctions on the Former Yugoslav Republic of Macedonia in February 1994 (under the Greek Presidency of the EU) have not been replicated by the rest of the Community. In fact, President Delors warned Greece that its actions were illegal under EU rules. In early 1995 the Greek government made it clear that whatever the decision of the European Court of Justice in a case brought by the European Commission, Greece would not lift the blockade which was costing Macedonia an estimated $US500 million annually. It was US-led negotiations in late 1995 which persuaded Greece to agree to recognize the Former Yugoslav Republic of Macedonia (FYROM) and finally to lift its blockade.

Not only the Balkans but also Russia has been a challenge to European determination. In late January 1995, the UK, France and Germany overrode the desire of the EU Commission to see stronger action taken against the Russian Republic in its re-conquest of the breakaway region of Chechnya. While Chechnya is not as close to Europe or European interests as the former Yugoslavia, Europe seems again to be unable to influence developments in a troubled region.

Economic superpower

As long ago as 1973, the Norwegian peace researcher Johan Galtung foresaw the emergence of Europe as a 'third superpower', competing with the USA and the USSR. Galtung argued that the Community would become more and more like a nation state, with a single head of state able to deal on equal terms with the US President or Soviet General Secretary.[39] The present international environment is far different from the two-superpower one described by Galtung, but the question of the Community's taking its place alongside the one remaining superpower, the USA, is still relevant. To Galtung the Community was likely to become a non-military superpower, but even this view may be too limited for a Europe which is considering a common defence policy.

Otto von Habsburg, an influential and well-known German member of the European Parliament (MEP), argued in 1991 that the Community had already become a superpower. It had only to exercise the will to take on a greater political role:[40]

Europeans should finally understand that, like it or not, they have become a superpower, if only because of sheer economic circumstances. If a superpower wants to fulfil its role, it must have global political dimensions. There are only two super-powers left in the world: the United States and the European Community. Now that the economic tasks have mostly been fulfilled, it is the duty of the latter to turn to its essential political task. This is in the interest not only of Europe but also of the whole world.

As well as the voices of those who want the EU to share superpower status with the USA – to act as a 'world partner', as the Community put it – there are some indications that Europe could go further. It could become, in fact, number one. Based on its huge population (larger than that of the USA) and its wealth, the Community has liked to note that it is the world's largest trading bloc. A surprising adherent to this view was the UK's Conservative agriculture minister, John Gummer. In 1992 he indicated that he wanted the Community to become 'the most powerful grouping in the world'.[41] Lester Thurow of MIT argued that just as the nineteenth century belonged to the UK and the twentieth to the USA, the twenty-first century was likely to belong to the world's largest economy with its best-educated population, an integrated Europe.[42]

Whatever the aspirations of the EU to greater power or world leadership, its economic might is undeniable. The Community is the world's largest trader, accounting for 15 per cent of world exports in 1989. This compares with the USA's 12 per cent and 9 per cent for Japan. The Community is one of the world's biggest exporters of manufactures and is the biggest importer of agricultural products, many of which come from developing countries.[43] With only 6.5 per cent of the world's population, it produces a quarter of the world's output. Even if projections showing Europe's proportion of world GDP declining from 22 per cent in 1990 to 17 per cent by 2010 are correct, Europe will remain a formidable economic force.[44] Its economic impact on both developed and developing countries will be extensive.

In summary, the EU has an enormous economic and political importance to the rest of the world; however, it has not always translated that importance into power.[45]

Development policy

Many of the textbooks on the EU focus on its internal organization and neglect its development policy. Nevertheless, the
Community's development policy was one of the first common
policies and from the late 1950s until the early 1980s it was
ubiquitously described in Community literature as a 'cornerstone'
of European integration. In comparison to the lack of coordination and independent identity of EU foreign policy, the Union's
development policy is relatively well coordinated and established.
Part IV of the Treaty of Rome was devoted to the overseas
dependencies of Europe and formed a substantial part of the
original Treaty. The Community's common development policy
has operated for almost forty years and built up a complex set
of ideas and principles, most notably in the four successive Lomé
Conventions. These Conventions have not replaced the bilateral
aid policies of the member states, but they have gradually become
an independent and important set of policies.

Nevertheless, development policy, a sub-field of foreign policy,
has a mixed record of cooperation and achievement. The stated
objective of the EU has not been to create a single development
policy, but to make the policies of the Twelve (now Fifteen)
consistent.[46] The Maastricht Treaty (Title 17, Article 130u) spoke
of a Community-level development policy, that is, a thirteenth
policy, which was not to conflict with the other twelve: 'Community policy in the sphere of development cooperation, which
shall be complementary to the policies pursued by the Member
States'. In practice, EU member states retain their own development priorities in addition to those of sustainable development,
integration of developing countries into the world economy, and
poverty alleviation laid down in the Treaty of Maastricht. The
Dutch are especially concerned with the problems of women and
the environment; the British emphasize economic and political
reform and population control; the Germans focus especially on
human rights, AIDS and drug abuse.

The development ministers did agree common goals for EU
relations with Rwanda in late 1994, and they supported a pilot
project in Bangladesh, Côte d'Ivoire, Costa Rica, Ethiopia and
Mozambique to improve coordination of member states' aid projects. This cooperative approach seemed to support the contention
that European governments can collaborate in areas of 'low poli-

tics', such as development, or relations with Rwanda, but this cooperation does not spill over to areas of greater political concern.[47]

But even cooperation in development policy has had big set-backs. In early 1995 UK Foreign Minister Douglas Hurd publicly announced his lack of confidence in European aid and a reduction in the UK contribution to the European Development Fund. European aid was too haphazard and diffuse for UK tastes. 'We have to eliminate the erosion of bilateral aid,' Hurd maintained.[48]

Security policy

The EU's intention to frame a common foreign and security policy incorporates two difficult aspirations in the same phrase. If anything, constructing a European security and defence identity (ESDI) is even more problematic than the objective of creating a common foreign policy. On the one hand, in a memorable phrase, Helmut Kohl has emphasized that no new divisions should be created in Europe. Security in Europe, he said, 'is indivisible'.[49] But at the same time Germany is participating in building up the Western European Union (WEU) which not only excludes non-EU countries, but is only half-heartedly supported by EU members such as Ireland and Denmark. In another instance of divergent EU defence policies, in 1994 France increased its defence spending by 5 per cent while other EU member states were reducing theirs.

Dr van Eekelen, the former WEU Secretary General, made heartfelt pleas that

> For the want of a foreign and security policy there is a real risk of Europe's becoming a spectator on the sidelines of history and being reduced to a 'regional non-power'. The time has come for a choice in favour of a reactivated WEU with a credible operational role, whatever the differences may be between its member countries regarding the long-term evolution of European security structures.[50]

But even if the EU fails to integrate its foreign and defence policies further, it will be far from a non-power. At present the WEU does not have a credible military role and its ability to coordinate European defence policy is questionable. The wisdom of creating a European defence identity without a solid political consensus to underpin it is also dubious.

European external and internal policies compared

Despite their continuing efforts at political cooperation in external policy, the Union's member states have never adopted a unified foreign policy. The Maastricht Treaty of 1992 calls for the development of a common foreign and security policy as an objective, but member states such as the UK are far from enthusiastic. Even communautaire-minded states such as France are still able to take unannounced, unilateral initiatives on foreign policy such as M. Mitterrand's visit to Sarajevo in June 1992. The failure of the EU to resolve the civil war in Yugoslavia has frequently been cited as an example of the Community's foreign policy impotence. A. M. Rosenthal in the *International Herald Tribune*, put it succinctly: 'Every day now, the new Europe shows it can be strong, united and independent of the United States – but only until a real crisis comes along.'[51] The overall weakness of the EU's external policy in comparison to its economic power as the world's largest trading group has led to the widespread perception of the organization as politically impotent or, as Christopher Hill put it, to the existence of a wide gap between the foreign policy capability of the EU and others' expectations of it.[52]

It is interesting to note the differing trends and rates of development of the Community's internal and external policies. From the late 1970s to the mid-1980s the Community seemed to stagnate in its internal development or integration. The Irish Prime Minister Garret Fitzgerald even accused the Community of devoting effort to its security policy in order to avoid facing its intractable internal problems such as the Common Agricultural Policy's surpluses. In the 1980s Europe was relatively stable internally (except for two expansions including Greece, Spain and Portugal, and one minor contraction – Greenland). Jacques Delors, president of the European Commission, put an end to the period of 'Eurosclerosis', of economic, technological, demographic and cultural decline, in 1987 with the ratification of the Single European Act.

The *Single European Act* of 1986 gave the Community a greater impetus to integration. It regularized Political Cooperation within the treaty and set out a programme which included endeavouring 'jointly to formulate and implement a European foreign policy' as a long-term goal. Surprisingly, development policy as such was not mentioned, but this was subsequently rectified in the Maastricht Treaty. The Treaty on European Union (Maastricht Treaty) of 1992 proposed greater coordination between the member states' development and aid programmes, empowering the European Commission to initiate such coordination. The Treaty made no mention, however, of the thorny issue of untying bilateral aid from purchases of goods and services from the donor state. Currently, the proportion of tied aid ranges from under 8 per cent for the Netherlands to over 40 per cent for the UK.

The UK, never very enthusiastic about the Community's development policy, was not in favour of mentioning the Lomé relationship in the Maastricht Treaty. But, at French insistence, a gesture in the direction of the Lomé Convention was included. This stated that provisions in the Treaty 'shall not affect cooperation with the African, Caribbean and Pacific countries in the framework of the ACP–EEC Convention'. (Title 17, Article 130w).

While the 1970s and early 1980s saw the Community stagnating internally, its external policies – especially with the developing countries – were rapidly developing and expanding. However, with virtually all of sub-Saharan Africa adhering to the Lomé Convention by 1990, and a network of relations with other developing countries in Latin America and Asia already in place, further expansion of the relations with developing countries will be slower while cooperation inside the EU and cooperation in its relations with other European states may well develop more rapidly.

WHAT THE EU CAN OFFER

The EU has grand plans and ambitions for its world role, but often lacks the means and unity to carry them out. Does the Union have anything useful to offer if it takes up a greater world role? In terms of the international system, the EU could be a counterweight or moderating influence on the USA. It could continue as a European pillar of the Atlantic Alliance to support the West against general instability, uncompromising religious fundamentalism or a rising Asia. During the Cold War the Community offered itself to the developing countries as a benign partner. It was to be a middle way, an alternative to the domination of the USA or the USSR.[53] This last role is no longer available as the Union has moved closer in its development thinking to US, International Monetary Fund (IMF) and World Bank policies.

Yet because of its geographical location on the Mediterranean and its almost four decades of special arrangements with the African, Caribbean and Pacific states, the EU may have a greater sensitivity to North–South issues than the USA or Japan. The viewpoint of continental bilateralism – where the USA is the natural partner of Latin America and Canada in the North Atlantic Free Trade Area (NAFTA) and Organization of American States (OAS) while Europe is the natural partner of Africa through the Lomé Conventions and other agreements – is still a tenable one.

Europe could have a new role to play as a champion of the developing countries in a world which has largely marginalized them. At the meeting of the Group of Seven industrialized countries in Tokyo in July 1993, the 108 developing country members of the non-aligned group were not permitted to present their views directly.[54] It was left to Japan to listen to and represent their concerns. This is a role which Europe could take up. The EU could decide not just to have a different or *sui generis* foreign policy in terms of its component parts and decision-making apparatus but to give its foreign policy a different and positive, development-oriented focus.

Christopher Hill argued that Europe in fact should not seek any particular international role as this would lead inevitably to the rise of nationalism, the desire for world leadership or other undesirable effects.[55] He further contended that Europe already had a series of functions in the international system, including 'Principal voice of the developed world in relation with the South'. This is certainly an overstatement: during the Cold War period the principal actors affecting the South were the USA and the USSR. In the 1990s, Europe has not taken a pre-eminent role. Japan may take on a leading role; Japan is a larger aid donor than any European country. When it comes to destabilizing crises in the developing world, it is currently to the USA that the concerned parties look. The Mexican peso crisis of 1995 threatened the whole international financial system. It was the

IMF, backed by the USA, which provided a $US50 billion loan to keep Mexico solvent. Closer to Europe, in the Algerian civil war, it is the USA and NATO which are guaranteeing that the war does not spread, not the Europeans. Even in the context of the Lomé Conventions, European decision-makers accept that they are now largely following the policies of the Washington-based institutions, the IMF and the World Bank.

Christopher Hill characterized Lomé I and Lomé II[56] as 'unusual and imaginative'. But if the EU does not seek any world role, only a 'series of tedious (sic) compromises',[57] it will not create any more imaginative external policies. Instead, the EU will concentrate on reorganizing its institutions and maximizing its commercial potential.

The following section analyses the ongoing relations between Europe and some of its major international partners.

SELECTED EU MULTILATERAL AND BILATERAL RELATIONS

In general, the Union's external relations fall into two groups – those with multilateral bodies and international organizations, and those with single countries (i.e. bilateral). Because the EU's own internal decision-making process is something of an international negotiation, it is very experienced in this type of interaction. It is particularly well-suited, and even sympathetic, to dealing with other multinational organizations. By and large the Union is skilful, practised and well-resourced for negotiations at the multilateral level. In fact, the EU's high level of resources and expertise makes it hard for under-resourced developing countries to match it when discussing or negotiating the Lomé Convention or other agreements.

The EU has participated extensively in GATT trade negotiations, in the Organization for Economic Cooperation and Development (OECD) – the developed countries' trade union – and in the UN and its specialized agencies, although it is not technically a member or contracting party of any of these organizations. After some initial accreditation problems, the European Commission was also active in the first post-Cold War global summit, the UN Conference on Environment and Development (UNCED), popularly called the 'Earth Summit', held in Rio de Janeiro in 1992.

Cooperation with Central and Eastern Europe

Cooperation with the Central and Eastern European states which were formerly members of the Warsaw Pact is developing particularly swiftly. To developing countries, the EU's interest in its near neighbours has been a source of considerable concern. The developing countries fear that aid and investment will be steadily diverted from them to Eastern Europe. The modest results of the Lomé mid-term review and the cloud over Lomé's future suggest that developing countries may be correct in some of these fears. In 1991, the ten Eastern European countries in receipt of EU Phare programme aid were each allocated an average of 77 million ecus while the seventy ACP states were each allotted an average of 34 million ecus for that year. Thus, the ACP received only around 44 per cent of the aid given to the newly de-aligned countries of Eastern Europe.

Obviously, there are vast differences between the candidate members of the EU in Central and Eastern Europe and the Lomé 'partners' of the EU. However, cooperation with Central and Eastern European countries has followed an interesting course, with some parallels to the Lomé relationship.

In both cases, 'temporary' aid has become institutionalized. For Lomé, aid has continued since 1958; for Eastern Europe aid from the Community budget was originally supposed to end in 1992, but is still continuing. For both aid relationships, some resources are directed via the European Investment Bank in Luxembourg (so far, the EIB is unable to operate in the former Soviet Union). Eastern European aid is heavily directed to the private sector; Lomé aid is becoming more so.

There are also similarities in the treatment of ACP and Eastern European trade. For both regions, the trade regime is not as liberal as it is portrayed by the EU. In both cases the treatment of industrial goods is more liberal than that of agricultural products. Sensitive Eastern European products such as iron, steel and textiles are highly restricted in their access to the EU market. Strict rules of origin for ACP products have often been criticized as a factor restraining ACP–EU trade; they are now also regarded as hampering trade between Eastern Europe and the EU. (See Chapter 4 for more details of Eastern Europe's trade prospects.)

Immigration is another area where the EU has feared an exodus from both developing countries and Eastern Europe.

There is no free movement of workers from Lomé countries, the Mediterranean or Eastern Europe into the EU. In fact, as described in Chapter 3, the EU has adopted some rather dubious policies to promote family planning in North Africa in order to stem the tide of potential immigrants.

Finally, both the developing countries and Eastern Europe have a relationship of 'asymmetric interdependence' with the EU. Both groupings depend more heavily on Europe for aid, markets and political support than Europe depends on them. For the developing countries, this unequal relationship is likely to continue almost indefinitely, whereas much of Eastern Europe (excluding the former Soviet Union and former Yugoslavia) is moving towards integration into the EU.

Europe–ASEAN relations

In theory, the EU and the Association of South East Asian Nations (ASEAN; comprising Brunei, Indonesia, Malaysia, Philippines, Singapore, and Thailand) make excellent companions. Both are regional groupings with a strong interest in trade. When the EU–ASEAN dialogue was established in the 1970s as an aspect of European Political Cooperation, the neutral, civilian Community seemed to the Asians to be less controversial than the former colonial powers in the region. EU–ASEAN relations have since been seen as a model for inter-regional cooperation. Dialogues developed in the 1980s between the Community and Central America and with the African front-line states have followed similar lines to the ASEAN dialogue.

However, despite the ongoing process of talks, South East Asia (as Jacques Delors admitted) remained low on the EU's list of priorities. The outputs of the dialogue often comprised routine expressions of concern over the situation in Afghanistan, Sri Lanka or Vietnam while issues of human rights abuses within ASEAN were overlooked. Political Cooperation meetings on Asia were often attended by officials rather than foreign ministers. Large powers such as France and the UK preferred to keep their relations with Asia as a 'reserved domain' outside the framework of a common European approach under EPC. But both sides of the dialogue have benefited from the support of the other, enabling each one to bolster its international role. For Europe, there is the prospect of ASEAN's acting as a moderating influence on the North–South relationship, while for ASEAN Europe's support enhances its role as a political speaker for the region.

However, as the network of Community relations with the world has proliferated since the 1970s, ASEAN has not maintained its preferred position. European foreign ministerial meetings with Central America, for instance, occur more frequently than with ASEAN. Although the EU and ASEAN have benefited from their mutual interactions, the low priority of Asia in the thinking of European governments and publics has mitigated much deepening of the relationship. Direct investment from the EU lags behind that of Japan and the USA. Problems over exports of textiles and footwear, agricultural goods, the operation of the Generalized System of Preferences and air transport rules interfered with trade. In the two decades following 1970, Community–ASEAN trade doubled, but remained a relatively small proportion of total Community trade – at just 3.4 per cent.[58]

European Commissioner Leon Brittan lamented the lack of European interest in Asia despite the latter's potential to surpass Europe economically.[59] As Elfriede Regelsberger noted, 'there is a certain discrepancy today between the solemn declarations of the Europeans on the importance of Asia in general and ASEAN in particular and the steps the Europeans take to demonstrate their belief in it.'[60] At present, disputes between the USA and the People's Republic of China over trade and human rights have made life in Asia more uncertain. This uncertainty could propel East Asian countries to look beyond the USA and towards Europe for reliable partners.

EU–Latin America

Unlike the new decade in Africa, in Latin America the 1990s ushered in a new era of optimism. 'What a difference a decade makes,' enthused a US brokerage firm. 'Burdened by debt, scorned by international financiers and written off by most multinational corporations, Latin America was considered an economic basket case just ten years ago.'[61] Now Latin America is popular with overseas investors and widely regarded as the home of the latest batch of Newly Industrializing Countries (NICs) such as Brazil, Argentina and Chile.

The 1990s have seen a dramatic shift in European policy

towards the region. The traditional neglect of South America by Europe and its concentration on Central America have been reversed: today the EU is trying to build up relations with the growing economies of the Southern Cone countries while it lets its involvement in the problems of Central America decline. Europe enthusiastically acted as peace broker in Central America's conflicts in the 1980s, starting the San José dialogue of European and Central American foreign ministers in 1984. Esperanza Duran argued in 1985 that, unlike South America, 'Central America has entered the mainstream of European foreign policy'.[62] However, after the resolution of the Central American conflicts, ending with the El Salvador peace settlement in 1992, Europe turned its interest to more important trading partners. Central America, with some of the Western Hemisphere's poorest and most indebted countries, and with less than 1 per cent of EU–developing country trade, attracted little attention. The 1993 EU trade agreement with Central American countries offered only most-favoured-nation treatment, with limited access to the Generalized System of Preferences.

The small amount of European aid directed to the region, often to political projects, has increased substantially in recent years. It rose from 73 million ecus in 1985 to over 150 million ecus in 1994. But the 120 million ecus scheme agreed in 1990 to help Central American countries with balance of payments deficits was abandoned in 1992.[63] Compared to the billions of ecus spent on aid under the Lomé Conventions, this is still a drop in a bucket. At the end of the 1980s, the Lomé Convention countries received 30 ecus per caput while Latin America got only nine.[64]

Until the 1990s, the pattern of EU–South American relations was one of neglect, misunderstanding and even hostility. The lack of cooperation between the two regions seemed 'almost mystifying' to World Bank Executive Director Enzo Grilli. He concluded that the outstanding characteristic of the two regions' relations in the field of development cooperation 'is their near absence, after more than two decades of attempts made on both sides'.[65] The major obstacles to cooperation included the operation of the Common Agricultural Policy which virtually closed Europe's markets to many of Latin America's most important exports while destabilizing and depressing world market prices for commodities by as much as 25 per cent.[66] In addition to restrictions on agricultural exports, quantitative restrictions were applied to textile exports from Argentina, Peru and Brazil and to iron and steel exports from Brazil. A further obstacle to the relationship was the resentment caused by the discriminatory trade preferences given to the Caribbean, Pacific and especially the African members of the Lomé Convention.

During most of the twentieth century, Latin America has been inward looking, following economic policies of import substitution and self-sufficiency rather than export production. In political terms Latin America has been firmly within the US sphere of influence, with governments looking north to Washington rather than east to Europe for their friends and supporters. The USA had mixed feelings about European activities in Latin America. It saw European economic activities as supportive of the US free market approach, but it objected to any European political interference.[67]

Despite this background, there have been a number of attempts at Community–Latin American cooperation. These included the Brussels dialogue of the 1970s; a series of bilateral trade agreements starting with Brazil and Uruguay in the 1970s; an agreement with the Andean Pact in 1983 (leading to the EU becoming its major external donor); the San José dialogue with Central America mentioned on p. 31 and the 1990 ministerial dialogue of the Rio Group (Brazil, Mexico, Uruguay Paraguay, Argentina, Chile, Bolivia, Colombia, Peru, and Venezuela). Most recently, and potentially most significantly, the EU has taken an interest in Mercosur (*Mercado de Sur*), also known as the Southern Cone Common Market. This organization comprises Brazil, Argentina, Paraguay and Uruguay, with Chile and Bolivia as potential new members.

EU–Mercosur

Stimulated – or frightened – by the plans for other free trade areas, the EU has been seeking counterpart deals for itself. The North American Free Trade Agreement (NAFTA) was approved by the US Congress in late 1993, thereby creating a market of some 360 million consumers in the USA, Canada and Mexico. It is thus the world's largest economic grouping. In addition, APEC, the Asian Pacific Economic Cooperation organization founded in 1989, including the USA, has plans for a Pacific free trade region in the twenty-first century. European plans include the TAFTA

(Trans-Atlantic Free Trade Area) between the USA and the EU, which was proposed by the German foreign minister in 1995, and an EU–Mercosur (*Mercado Commun de Sur*) agreement. The latter has been particularly strongly supported by Spain.

The EU has been surprisingly open about its political intentions towards Mercosur. Europe stressed that its interests in Mercosur are both economic and political. It aims at trade liberalization and the consolidation of democracy in Latin America. The EU notes with interest that Mercosur has an internal GDP which is fourth in size after NAFTA, the EU and Japan. The EU openly argues that its influence will serve to balance or counteract US influence on the Southern Cone region.

Latin American economic growth is predicted by the World Bank to reach as much as 6.3 per cent by the end of this century.[68] The Mercosur countries are set to be at the centre of this good fortune. In trade terms, the EU–Mercosur relationship stands to boom: the EU is traditionally Mercosur's largest trading partner. Community exports to Mercosur increased by a massive 40 per cent from 1992 to 1993, forming Europe's fastest growing export market.[69] In addition, 70 per cent of European direct foreign investment in Latin America is directed to Mercosur.

The EU has been engaged in a political dialogue with Mercosur since 1992 and plans to strengthen and intensify the relationship. The EU has already committed 17 million ecus to transferring its integration expertise and to supporting various cultural and training programmes in Mercosur countries. It is, however, ironic that Europe proposes to transfer its 'expertise' in agricultural cooperation to Mercosur. It was Europe's own restrictive policy towards agricultural imports, embodied in the Common Agricultural Policy, which has largely prevented Latin America from capitalizing on its natural comparative advantage in food production.[70]

The provisions envisaged for future EU–Mercosur cooperation include a free trade area in industrial products (but not agricultural ones), the liberalization of trade in services and capital, the joint financing of regional projects, and cooperation in many sectors such as transport and telecommunications.

However, several caveats to the EU–Mercosur relationship should be noted. One is that democracy in Latin America may not be as stable as Europe hopes. Since the whole of Latin America became democratic in 1991, there has been considerable backsliding. Authoritarian governments suspended constitutions in Guatemala and Peru; there was a coup in Haiti; there were attempted coups in Venezuela, and corruption scandals in Brazil. These events have shown that the democratic edifice in Latin America is still shaky. Would the EU try to impose sanctions on Mercosur if one or more of its members abandoned the democratic path?

Trade disputes among Mercosur members could also lessen the region's attractiveness to Europe. The customs union established by Brazil, Argentina, Paraguay and Uruguay in January 1995 has already experienced problems. Brazil imposed quotas on Argentinian car exports, and many observers fear that other trade problems could erupt.[71]

Another caveat relates to President Clinton's long-term plans to expand the North American Free Trade Agreement into a Western Hemisphere Free Trade Agreement (WHFTA). If this were to happen, the Mercosur organization might well be superseded by a larger and more powerful grouping, and so all of Europe's efforts to make a political impact in Latin America would be dwarfed by the power of the WHFTA association. For the Mercosur countries, care should also be taken that their current political salience to Europe does not decline if their growth rates diminish. They might then fall like a stone from the top of the European foreign policy agenda, just as Central America has done in the 1990s.

Whether or not the EU, as a latecomer, can rectify its years of neglect of Latin America remains to be seen. Without tackling the restrictions of the Common Agricultural Policy, or trying to address the indebtedness problems of Nicaragua and Venezuela, Europe's devotion to the cause of Latin American development remains unconvincing. The EU has little claim to being more than a commercial partner for Latin America if it does not commit itself to real development strategies in the poorest countries of the western hemisphere, such as Nicaragua, Guyana and Haiti, and to trying to solve the political problem of Cuba (see Chapter 5 for a discussion of current relations between the EU and Cuba).

Bilateral relations

In the Community's own estimation, its bilateral relationships are most intense with the other major economic powers, the USA and Japan. EU officials meet regularly with these powers at the highest levels. The importance of these industrialized country relationships is shown in the relative levels of representation at industrialized and North–South meetings. Whereas the Western heads of state and government such as Bill Clinton, John Major and Helmut Kohl attend the annnual Western economic summits of the Group of Seven (the USA, UK, Canada, France, Germany, Japan and Italy), meetings with developing countries rarely receive such high-level attention. The signing of the 1989 Lomé Convention between the Community and the then sixty-eight ACP developing countries, for example, was not at head of state and government level. Although the French Prime Minister was present as President of the Council of the European Communities, no heads of national governments participated. The French and Belgians were represented by their development ministers, the Germans by a deputy minister, while the UK sent only a government whip.

EU–Japan

Despite the existing and potential tensions between the USA and the EU, they have traditionally had better relations with each other than either has had with Japan. Since the Second World War the USA has had a 'special' if not always harmonious relationship with the Japan it occupied and helped to reconstruct after the war. The Americans gave the Japanese a liberal-democratic system, including such non-traditional provisions as equality for women. The Japanese took with enthusiasm to many aspects of American culture from baseball to jazz.

The Europeans, by contrast, played only a minor role in post-war Japan. Jacques Delors recognized that Community relations with Japan in the cultural and political spheres were weak. Mutual deprecations and incomprehension were common. A 1979 European Commission report, for instance, referred to the Japanese as workaholics living in rabbit hutches.[72] Fairly open trading relations existed between the USA and the Community and even between the USA and Japan, but not between the Community and Japan.[73] Considering the difficulties in US–Japanese relations over automobile exports and Japanese buy-outs of flagship American enterprises such as Columbia Pictures, the view that Community–Japan relations were still worse than those between the USA and Japan is gloomy indeed.

Community–Japanese relations have centred on trade. Trade is a particularly sensitive issue and the Community considered that Japan did not always 'play fair'. It has technical and administrative barriers to European imports, structures and attitudes of production and habits and structures of consumption which tend to keep imports out, giving Japan sizeable trade surpluses with the Community, the USA and others. The Community has tried to open Japanese markets, to monitor Japanese exports closely, to foster scientific, technical and industrial cooperation, and to open a foreign policy dialogue. Despite the Community's desire to improve its relations with Japan, visits from the President of the European Commission – in 1986 and 1991 – have been relatively infrequent and the Community's tendency to neglect Asia and the Pacific has not been overcome. Professor J.-P. Lehmann summed up the problems by noting that 'the Euro-Japanese relationship remains especially ill-defined'.[74]

Since the mid-1980s the USA has encouraged Japan to become more active and to take on more international responsibilities. Despite the internationalist outlook of many young Japanese, Japan has so far been a 'reluctant superpower'. Less publicized (but arguably more important) than its financial support for the Gulf War is Japan's role in giving aid to the developing countries. Since 1988 Japan's total aid disbursements have been only slightly less than those of the USA, with the USA giving $US11.26 billion compared to Japan's $US10.95 billion in 1991 (OECD figures). With an additional pledge of $US1.4 billion per year made to the Rio Summit in 1992, Japan became the world's largest aid donor. It remained in that position until 1995. Japan's most recent annual disbursements of $US13.34 billion represented an increase over the previous year of 16.3 per cent, owing to the rise of the yen against the dollar. But this figure still amounted to only 0.29 per cent of GNP.[75] Japanese aid is less tied (over 70 per cent untied) than the aid programmes of the USA, France, Germany or the UK but the grant element is lower. Japanese aid has been largely devoted to economic infrastructure and production projects, but scope exists for a more 'human resource' or poverty-focused approach. New intitatives on AIDs and population growth, as well as environmental problems, have recently been introduced.[76] There have also been concerns over unfair practices in giving out contracts which were uncovered by Japan's Fair Trade Commission in 1994. Traditionally, Japanese aid has been concentrated on Asia, but it has also become a major source of funds for countries such as Kenya, Zambia, Ghana and Nigeria.[77]

Japan has used its aid spending to address other problems in US–Japanese relations such as the Japanese trade surplus. However, as Japan settles in as the world's largest aid donor it may look less to the USA for guidance on aid policy and increasingly develop its own style and priorities. It might even become a reference point or model for US and EU aid programmes.

EU–US relations

The shape of US–European relations underlies the structure of the post-Cold War international order, just as US–European relations were a crucial part of the Cold War system. An increasing part of these relations involves the EU. This section will briefly highlight some of the main features of EU–US relations, and the issues now surrounding them.

In the period of the Cold War, there was no doubt as to whose side the European Community was on. It was seen as a bulwark of capitalism and freedom by the USA; Europe – especially the Community and NATO member countries of the UK and Germany – were the much-needed second pillar of the Atlantic Alliance. Trade disputes and other misunderstandings did often arise but, in the words of the Community, 'these have never been allowed to undermine the basic relationships'.[78] The Community view was that Community–US relations have been more harmonious over the past three and a half decades than the publicity about a variety of trade disputes might suggest.

René Schwok rightly considered that a multidisciplinary perspective incorporating historical, economic and strategic factors was necessary to assess the future of US–Community relations. He posed the question of whether there will be a US–Community partnership or a series of conflicts.[79] But this dichotomy is too simple a formulation. In the post-war period the Atlanticist partnership of the USA and Europe was punctuated by a series of crises. The Suez crisis, the withdrawal of France from the military arm of NATO, the disputes among the allies over Vietnam, the USA's unilateral floating of the dollar in 1971, all called into question the basis of the relationship. Certainly from the 1960s on, the 'perennial crisis' of Atlanticism has spawned a voluminous literature.[80]

Nevertheless, the Atlantic alliance survived into the 1990s and proved stronger than the tests and challenges it faced. Indeed, NATO has been seen with justification as the most successful alliance the world has ever known. In the mid-1990s it is the only fully functioning major military alliance. The question of its future might be better phrased so as to ask whether the underlying perception of mutual benefits from the Atlantic Alliance will prove stronger than the undoubted challenges and conflicts it will face. After the fall of the Berlin Wall, NATO underwent considerable internal and external soul-searching about its future role. But in view of the continuing instability in the East and the call by leaders such as Eduard Shevardnadze and Vaclav Havel for NATO to expand its activities in the East, the organization found a renewed role.

Whether or not the old pattern of US–Community solidarity will continue is an unknown question. Schwok identified as many sources of divergence, ranging from strategic objectives to GATT, as of convergence. These are both geo-political – a shift of interest to the Pacific basin – and domestic – as the US population shifts to the south and west and as the presumed ascendancy of non-European minorities causes the USA to re-orient its foreign policy towards Latin America and the Far East. However, this latter scenario remains highly speculative.

In addition, the continuation of the relatively harmonious scenario of US–Community cooperation and of US support for European integration could decline as these two economic super-powers vie for markets and influence. Or, it might be that serious misunderstandings are prevented by their common commitment to the values of human rights, political democracy and free trade (free trade being a virtue that both sides profess, but neither fully practises). Professor Henry Nau has even envisaged the US and Europe as potential joint leaders in the formation of a global community of shared democratic values.[81] But certainly the Atlantic partnership will continue to experience tensions, as it has in the past. The USA may find that a Europe which is

challenging its leadership in the twenty-first century is less con-
genial than the old second pillar.

Complicating the context of US–Community relations is the
multiplicity of images that the USA has about Europe. C. M.
Kelleher identified three images of Europe as being, first the
prize of superpower conflict; second, the object of a mission for
the USA – to make Europe and its integration successful; and
third, the old, corrupt imperialists.[82] To these we could add the
NATO strategists' Cold War view: Europe as a theatre of war or
locus of conflict. As well as considering which image is paramount
to US policy-makers at a given time, we can also ask how
important the EU now is compared to more traditional avenues
of US–European relations.

So far the USA has not shown that it would rather deal with
a superpower Europe than with its foremost European ally –
Germany. A US State Department document leaked in 1993 listed
countries in order of their importance to the USA. Germany was
first, followed by France and then the UK. No other Community
country appeared in the top ten, and the EU was not included
among these 'major players'.[83] President Clinton said in Tokyo in
July 1993 that the USA's partnership with Japan was America's
'first international economic priority'.[84] This caused particular
concern among Europeans, despite the President's obvious desire
to tailor his address to appeal to his Japanese audience and the
possibility that Europe remained a political priority.

Nevertheless, the USA recognized the increasing importance
of the Community's role in European politics. As James Baker
put it in 1989, 'As Europe moves toward its goal of a common
internal market, and as its institutions for political and security
cooperation evolve, the link between the United States and the
European Community will become even more important.'[85] In
order to further their joint goals of democracy, peace, security,
and prosperity, the Community and the USA issued the 1990
'Declaration on EC–US Relations'. It called for cooperation in
fields such as medical and environmental research, energy, space,
nuclear safety, education and culture. The declaration also set up
an institutional framework to enhance consultation between the
two sides. This included consultations involving the presidents of
the USA, the European Council and the Commission down to
those between the European Commission and US Cabinet.

A US Defense Department document widely leaked in March

1992 proposed that the USA should remain militarily predomi-
nant in the world, both to deter aggressors such as Saddam
Hussein and to prevent friendly powers such as Germany and
Japan from becoming military superpowers, 'to discourage them
from challenging our leadership or seeking to overturn the established political and economic order'.[86] Although the leaked
document was withdrawn, suspicion remains that the USA wants
to maintain its pre-eminence as the only superpower.

In his early 1994 tour of Europe, President Clinton made all
the right noises about European–American cooperation. He
envisaged 'a new day for our transatlantic partnership'. Clinton
exhibited a more Atlanticist perspective than he had on his
Japanese tour and a revived American leadership role. He called
for more European integration between East and West to prevent
the old iron curtain from being replaced by a new 'veil of indiffer-
ence'.[87] He called for Western Europe to reduce trade barriers
to the East and he commended the new Partnership for Peace to
improve links between Eastern Europe and NATO. In a concrete
gesture, Clinton committed the USA to keeping at least 100,000
US troops in Europe.

Given Europe's rising aspirations to a world role commensurate
with that of the USA (and the possiblility of more competititive-
ness between them) and the USA's rising interest in Asia, it seems
unlikely that there is soon going to be an intensified relationship
between the EU and the USA. The Americans' efforts at the
end of 1994 to persuade the Europeans to adopt a more bellicose
policy in Bosnia, while refusing to commmit US troops there,
made the USA an unpopular back-seat driver in the conflict.
Some of the debates from the early 1990s about the continuing
usefulness of NATO in the post-Cold War world were resurrected
in the press. But despite these continuing problems, the old
EU–US partnership is still in the interests of both parties and
still has considerable mileage left in it. The proposals, now finding
favour with the French, Germans and British, to supplement
the original NATO military treaty with economic and political
provisions could work to enhance US–European relations.

In summary, the future content and direction of the EU's
external relations are difficult to predict using the existing tools
of political science and foreign policy analysis. The EU is an
important international actor, but one whose role is unclear. At
present, the external policy of the EU is best considered as the

sum of the many parts described in this chapter. Among these parts, there is now considerable scope for the EU to expand and improve its relations with developing countries.

Chapter 2

Europe's colonial history
The problem of the 'other'

In considering the current relations between the EU and the countries of the South, it is impossible to avoid noticing that these are still largely based on the ties established during the colonial period. France has close links with its francophone former colonies; the UK has developed its relations with former colonies within the fifty-member Commonwealth, and Belgium, Italy, Spain and Portugal similarly maintain special interest in their previous dependencies. In fact, because post-war relations between Europe and its former dependencies still resemble those of the nineteenth-century era of colonialism they are often termed 'neo-colonial'. Thus, in order to understand the contemporary pattern of trade, aid and political links between Europe and the South, the colonial period is an almost inescapable starting point for students and scholars.

This chapter examines the question of how Europeans have traditionally dealt with people who were perceived as 'other' or different to themselves. It first addresses the earliest links between Africans and Europeans. The Europeans' view of African history, the egalitarian but little known 'Kongo model' of relations between Africa and Europe, and the subsequent 'age of colonialism' are explored. Mannoni's classic study of colonialism and the often neglected role of women in the colonial enterprise come under scrutiny. Economic explanations of colonialism, including the dependency school, have been at the forefront of efforts to explain the phenomenon of colonialism. But neither they nor the 'technology' explanation can fully account for the Europeans' colonial expansion. The European scramble in and out of Africa has left the continent with an extensive political, economic, technological, cultural and social legacy.

British Foreign Minister George Canning told the House of Commons that, by recognizing the Spanish colonies and Brazil in 1824–5, 'I called the New World into existence to redress the balance of the Old.'[1] Canning wanted Britain to distance itself from its old allies, Austria and Russia, and at the same time to take on a global role. The Foreign Minister's statement was met with great applause in the House of Commons, but it reflected the Europeans' lack of understanding that the Latin American ex-colonies already had – and would continue to have – an existence independent of Europe. By the late 1940s the Europeans had lost the ability to shape and dominate the international political system which had arisen out of post-Reformation Europe. Most of their colonies became independent by the 1960s. The early 1990s saw sweeping political reforms in Eastern Europe and many developing countries. Western Europe has still not completely resolved the problems of how best to deal with other, 'less developed' societies, and what kind of political, economic and social relations to have with them. Following the end of the Cold War, a pessimistic 'clash of civilizations' theory has become popular. According to this, there is a clear dividing line between West and non-West, and conflict between the two sides is almost inevitable. The final section of this chapter argues that seeing the world as 'the West against the Rest' is unjustified. Europe, for instance, already has a more positive relationship with the developing world than such a thesis admits.

EUROPE AND AFRICA: THE FIRST LINKS

Since Roman times Europe has had territorial ambitions in Africa. But the earliest links between Europe and Africa go back still further to the dawn of humanity. The dominant modern theory of the origin of human life is that it emerged in Africa. The fossil and genetic records suggest that we human beings are all descended from Africans. The earliest recognized human remains come from the Rift Valley in Kenya. Modern genetics finds more differences between peoples in Africa than between Africans and others, suggesting that Africans are the oldest group, from which other peoples diverged many millennia ago.

There are alternative theories of evolution which propose a marine origin for modern humans or an origin in a variety of continents as put forward by scientists such as Dennis Eetler.

However, the most widespread belief, espoused by sources as respectable as *Time International* and the Secretary General of the Commonwealth, is that Europeans are directly descended from Africans.[2] For Africans, being the fount of human life has been a source of pride, rather like Ireland's claim to be the origin of ten US presidents. For Europeans, this evidence of a close biological relationship with the Africans whom they had long denigrated and mistreated produced some discomfiture.

Many early Europeans' views of Africans were severe. In the seventeenth-century Dutch settlements of the Cape, Jacobus Hondius described the Hottentots: 'They are thus very dissolute and in every way like animals, for they are wild, rough and unclean in their habits.'[3] This kind of view was very useful to settlers to justify both their taking of the Africans' land and participating in the very lucrative black slave trade. In fact, from this point of view, sending the Africans into slavery was doing them a favour as it gave them their only chance to become 'civilized' and saved in a Christian sense.

The increasingly sophisticated views of European scientists three hundred years later were not substantially different from those their predecessors expressed. Dr Carothers of the World Health Organization declared in 1954 that the African was the physiological equivalent of a European who had had a frontal lobotomy. They thus needed punitive re-education. When faced with impressive architectural achievements such as ancient Zimbabwe, Europeans simply denied that Africans had constructed them. In the words of one explorer, 'Whoever these people were, they have long since vanished.'[4]

From the African side, the Europeans' lack of respect for them and their cultures was a tragedy. It led to a long history of violent and unequal relations, including the slave trade, the loss of Africans' cultural artefacts and suppression of their cultures. The poet Ben Okri described this desecration:[5]

Lament of the Images
They took the masks
The sacrificial faces
The crafted wood which stretches
To the fires of natural gods
The shrine where the axe
Of Lightning

Releases invisible forces
Of silver.

They took the painted bones
The stools of molten kings
The sacred bronze leopards
The images charged with blood
And they burned what
They could not
Understand

... The land
Has almost
Forgotten
To chant its ancient songs
Ceased to reconnect
The land of spirits ...

It is interesting here to note Okri's critique of Europeans who separate the real from the spiritual, feeling from mind, who 'desacralize' the world. This is in many ways similar to the views of contemporary feminists who criticize the West's excessive reliance on abstract forms of thinking without feeling.[6]

AFRICAN HISTORY

The nineteenth-century political philosophers reflected the Europeans' lack of understanding of Africa, just as the Spanish and Portuguese had failed to understand and respect indigenous cultures in the Americas in the late fifteenth century. Hegel and then Marx argued that in fact Africa had no history. That is, it had nothing civilized or worth mentioning as history. Based on the reports of European explorers such as the Victorian Richard Burton who, it is said, saw everything and understood nothing, Europeans dismissed Africa's achievements. This view was completely wrong. The intricate history of ancient Egypt was African history. Africa also had other developed civilizations. The Ethiopian kingdom of Axum flourished near the Red Sea from the first century AD. Its rulers traced their descent back to Solomon. Axum became christianized and had a literate culture with fine manuscripts and architecture, and a feudal system of agriculture. The ancient African empires of Mali, Songhai and Ghana have become well known. The empire of Ghana flourished from the fifth century AD and reached its peak between the ninth and eleventh centuries. It had advanced skills in iron-working, mining, agriculture and trade. The modern states of Ghana and Zimbabwe take their names from these sophisticated ancient African empires.[7]

'Cultural conservatives' such as the Nobel Prize winning author Saul Bellow like to stress the primacy of European culture. They stress its unique contributions to democracy, law, individual rights science and art. Yet when we examine the contributions of Africa to art, music, and early Middle Eastern religions, this Euro-centric view becomes less attractive. When we look particularly at Europe's own history of violence towards Africa, its internal problems and wars, the oppression of women, or the persistence of anti-semitism, then the superiority of Europe, the so-called triumph of the West, is less apparent.

The Kongo model

So far we have described a set of Euro-African colonial relations which have been unequal, often violent. But there is an alternative model. Adda Bozeman described the first, egalitarian contacts between Portugal and the African state of Kongo in the fifteenth century.

The King of Kongo and the King of Portugal were regarded as equal sovereigns, equal in their subservience to the universal Catholic Church. Alvare I of Kongo felt free in 1572 to express his intention to become a vassal of Portugal, but Portugal refused the offer. The two states became nearly equal actors in the European system – Kongo was seen as weak, but able to progress intellectually, spiritually and politically. Kongo even took on a pro-Dutch policy from around 1622, showing its diplomatic freedom to manoeuvre. It established a permanent embassy at the Vatican in 1613, and was involved in many complicated dealings with the Holy See. But from the mid-seventeenth century links between Portugal and Kongo weakened. By 1700 the Kongo lost its status as an 'Afro-European state'. Kongo–Portuguese relations could have been a more humane and egalitarian model for Afro-European relations, but ultimately they came to little or nothing. These near-equal dealings were forgotten and replaced by formal colonialism.[8]

THE AGE OF COLONIALISM

The theories and practices of European colonialism, from forced labour to floggings and apartheid, are nowadays generally horrifying and repugnant to Europeans themselves and to other peoples. Yet the propositions that other races were inferior and should be ruled by whites seemed perfectly acceptable to most nineteenth-century Europeans. As the great liberal thinker John Stuart Mill observed, each generation finds some of the practices of the previous generation to have been not only wrong, but absurd.

Most scholars acknowledge that Europeans' justifications of their empires, of keeping them in peace and orderliness, could not vindicate the genocide of groups such as the Hereros in South-West Africa. In some cases the more exalted justifications of a civilizing *paix française* and so forth were dropped to reveal raw considerations of power. The German Gustav Frenssen wrote, 'The world belongs to the stronger and the more energetic. That is God's justice.' Another German writing in the early twentieth century explained the colonial enterprise in terms of a struggle between the races: 'Do not forget that between the white man and the coloured there can never be peace until one is the master and the other his servant. It is a question of "them" or "us".'[9]

But a revisionist school emphasizes the benefits of colonialism, its legacy of transport infrastructure and culture, law and even parliamentary democracy. Europeans and some Africans and Indians recall that the trains, the production of cocoa or the administration worked better under colonialism. Africans themselves engaged in the slave trade and committed atrocities in battle. Therefore, the revisionists argue, we should not require higher standards of the Europeans in their behaviour than we do of the Africans.

Nevertheless, modern-day Europeans, such as the French regarding their treatment of the Jews during the Second World War, or North Americans, with regard to their treatment of the native American peoples, are not quite comfortable with the history of colonialism. Imperialism has aptly been called the rule of the people, by other people and for other people. Neither the quest for 'God, gold and glory' in Latin America nor the 'civilizing mission' of Europe in Africa sounds to modern ears like a convincing defence of the colonial empires. Scholars such as Basil Davidson have pointed out that European enslavement of Africans was in fact more brutal than traditional African and even European forms of slavery. Although Europe has not taken the step of making a formal apology for the age of colonialism, it is not completely reconciled with its own history.[10]

The cinquecentenary of Columbus' voyage to America in 1492 showed the Europeans' dilemma. On the one hand, Spain in particular wanted to celebrate its achievement, its imagination in 'discovering' the New World. On the other, the indigenous peoples of the Americas protested that they had been self-aware long before the Spanish visitors and for them the legacy of the conquest was not that of civilization but, in many cases, extermination. As Hazel Waters noted, 'for those who benefited from the exploitation he opened up, Columbus is the harbinger of progress and prosperity. For those who did not, he is the bringer of catastrophe on an exponential scale.'[11] The achievements of Columbus were based on the 'ethnic cleansing' of Moors and Jews from Spain. His motivations included a quest for profit and a messianic desire for fame and power. On some readings he was verging on insanity. His explorations led to a long and miserable history for the Americas, including slavery and colonization:

> He was the instigator of transatlantic slavery, who shackled to his deck six unsuspecting Taino people after the first landfall on the Bahamas in 1492, eventually carrying them back to Spain. He was the prototypical colonist who first 'pacified' the Caribbean by countenancing the *encomienda* allocation of slaves to settlers, and oversaw the erection of 340 sets of gallows across the island of 'Hispaniola'. He was the self-proclaimed 'messenger of a new heaven' whose brief rule as a governor of the same island accounted for the deaths of some 50,000 of its people, whose lust for gold and profit made him decree that every Taino man, woman and child over the age of 14 must deliver, every three months, a hawk's bell crammed with gold – those who failed were to be hanged in groups of thirteen, 'in memory of Our Redeemer and His twelve apostles'.[12]

Many Europeans have felt a sense of shame or revulsion at the actions of Columbus and his successors. Pope John Paul II, in his August 1993 tour of the Americas, expressed his solidarity with the indigenous peoples who had a right to their lives, culture and societies. The pontiff stressed the positive role of missionaries who had opposed the atrocities of the *conquistadores* rather than the Church's role in supporting the colonial enterprise and its forced conversions of indigenous peoples to Catholicism. Despite his defence of the Church's role, the Pope recognized that many indigenous peoples have lost their lands and many still today 'suffer from great poverty. For this, the world cannot feel at ease or satisfied.'[13]

Both sides of the Atlantic saw a variety of ceremonies and celebrations of the 500th anniversary of Columbus' first voyage, notably the World's Fair in Seville and the Olympic Games in Barcelona in 1992. The campaign against the celebrations had some moderating or dampening effects and the term 'discovery' of the Americas has largely been replaced by the more anodyne 'encounter'. During his rule, Franco used the celebration of the landing in America to rally nationalist feeling in Spain. More recently the new democratic Spain has used the 1992 celebrations, now termed *Hispanidad* (Spanishness), to celebrate the spread of Spanish culture and its meeting with other cultures.

As an EU and NATO member, Spain now desires to play a more active world role and has portrayed its past overseas explorations in the best possible light. To the president of Spain's *El Pais* newspaper, for instance, 'The journey of Columbus was the first great adventure in the era of communications, in which the mass media, with the diffusion of knowledge, contributed to the understanding of peoples and the progress of humanity.'[14]

However, what the debate about Columbus has made clear is that his explorations and conquests say as much about the failures of humanity as about its progress. And about these failures, about the extermination and exploitation of the native peoples of the Americas, human beings 'cannot feel at ease or satisfied'.

THE 'OTHER'

The theories and practices of colonialism are examined in Otare Mannoni's classic study, *Prospero and Caliban*, written in 1956. Mannoni points out that Shakespeare's *Tempest*, a seventeenth-century play, can be seen as an allegory of colonialism. The colonist is Prospero, a misfit in his own land, who rules the island he colonizes by magic (cf. technology). He seldom speaks to

Ariel, the 'good' native, without reminding him of how grateful Ariel ought to be. Ariel reminds Prospero that he was promised self-government but Prospero, like later colonialists, does not think the natives are ready for it. Caliban, the bad native, is consistently treated harshly, like a mission boy who has not made good and is degraded by being taken away from his background.

The term 'calibanization' came to be applied generally to indigenous peoples brutalized and degraded by their experience of colonialism. Caliban expressed his own bitterness and disappointment in his treatment, saying to Prospero:[15]

> This island's mine, . . .
> Which thou tak'st from me. When thou
>   camest first,
> Thou strok'dst me and mad'st much of me;
>   wouldst give me
> Water with berries in 't; and teach me how
> To name the bigger light, and how the less,
> That burn by day and night:
>   . . . You taught me language; and my
>   profit on't
> Is, I know how to curse;

The *Tempest* here correctly foreshadows the problems of indigenous peoples who are educated in and have to use the colonizers' own language to express themselves and their wish for freedom. It also accurately portrays the colonialist as a misfit in his own society – a prototype for real exemplars such as Cecil Rhodes. Tellingly, what both Prospero and the colonialist lack is an appreciation of, awareness of and respect for the world of 'others', for anyone who is different.

Based on his experience in colonial Madagascar in the earlier part of the twentieth century, Mannoni considered that the Europeans were baffled by the behaviour of the indigenous peoples of Africa. Pierre Sorlin pointed out that the French were simultaneously well disposed, afraid and hostile towards the natives. The French settlers had an underlying fear of the colonized people, but they were never precisely aware of the reasons why they had this fear.[16]

The colonizers resorted to two extreme attitudes: one was to give up the attempt to communicate and to declare communication impossible; they thought that only rule by force would succeed. The second attitude was to assume that all persons are equally endowed with reason and intelligence, but then to try to impose their own rules and institutions on the colonized – to practise assimilation – as the French tried to do. Both camps believed that their way of thinking was the only right one and that they should impose it on the rest of the world in the interests of reason and morality. But neither the approach of indirect rule nor of direct assimilation ultimately worked, and the colonial empires dissolved. The Europeans did not develop a consistent, humane and successful policy for dealing with what they saw as the 'other'.

The Europeans regarded the colonized as faulty and inferior beings. The native peoples were in need of European help in terms of religion, education and civilization. Yet many of the colonized peoples failed to be grateful for the benefits they received from European rule. Although Europeans regarded the colonized as inferior, paradoxically some like Baudelaire desired to identify with and associate with them. They wanted to inhabit their lands, and to look upon their contacts with the native peoples as a romantic search for a lost paradise – perhaps for their own innocence. The less innocent overtones of this quest are examined in the next section.

WOMEN AND COLONIALISM

One aspect of colonialism and its aftermath was largely over-looked until recently: the role of women. As described in the following section, there have been many attempts to explain colonialism in terms of economic factors, but the role of women in colonialism and the post-colonial period was little analysed. Many contemporary accounts of colonialism still neglect this field.[17] Recent studies, such as Barbara Bush's *Slave Women in Caribbean Society 1650–1838*,[18] are valuable in rectifying the problem of the neglect or 'invisibility' of women in historical and academic studies. Bush, for instance, points out that enslaved women in the Caribbean were far from the passive creatures of the traditional stereotype but worked to ameliorate their conditions. Elizabeth Stone's volume on *Women and the Cuban Revolution* describes the very active role of women in overthrowing the Batista regime in Cuba.[19]

As we approach the end of the twentieth century, more recognition of the importance and variety of women's experiences under colonialism and its aftermath is still needed.

To a large extent colonialism was a male enterprise and reflected male aspirations and behaviours. European colonialism was primarily carried out by men, for the benefit of men.[20] It was based on the decisions of male leaders in European capitals and in negotiations such as the Berlin West Africa Conference. Sjoo and Mor characterize the patriarchal tradition in general in terms of 'rape, genocide and war'; this 'unholy trinity' certainly formed a substantial part of the colonial enterprise.[21] Colonialism was an outgrowth of the Western patriarchal society and state. But women interacted with colonialism in a wide variety of ways, sometimes supporting it and sometimes – like Margaret Cousins and Olive Schreiner – questioning it.[22]

In many cases, women were discouraged from visiting or residing in the colonies, and a number of theories blamed them for the problems there. Everything from preventing the 'natural' mixing of male white colonialists with the female colonized, to arousing the sexual appetites of the indigenous males, to distracting colonial administrators from their jobs was blamed on European women. Despite the many prejudices against them, women did manage to participate in the colonies in a variety of roles. Sometimes they found a greater freedom of activity in the colonies than they had experienced in their home country. Women in the colonies were mothers, wives, anthropologists, teachers, and sometimes social and political reformers. But they remained a subordinate group within the male-dominated colonial society.[23] Women such as Margery Perham, though having some influence on decision-makers, did not rise to the top rank of colonial officials despite their undoubted administrative abilities.[24]

Another strand of post-colonial thinking points out that the colonial conquest – especially in terms of Africa – was expressed in near-sexual terms. One cannot go very far in the literature of imperialism before encountering phrases about the domination, penetration and possession of virgin territory. According to Freudians, all human activities are motivated by unconscious, sexual desires. The colonial enterprise is certainly not immune from this interpretation. The direct desire to associate with native women, as Cortez did, or the sublimated desire to control territory can be associated with colonial expansion. As Rebecca Stott noted,

The discourse of imperialism clearly expresses anxieties other than directly imperialist ones. The discourses of entering into, penetrating, colonizing, conquering and the dominating of colonized peoples draw upon sexual discourse for the expression of supressed sexual and imperial anxieties. Imperialist fiction of the late nineteenth century illustrates the complexity of the relations between sexual and imperialist discourses.[25]

The colonial enterprise, then, very much caught the male imagination, from the novels of Kipling to those of Rider Haggard. Africa, in particular, was almost unbearably attractive to such male imperialist imagination. This imagination motivated not only the writers and readers of popular fiction but also the colonizers themselves.

THE ECONOMIC EXPLANATIONS

The twentieth century has seen a variety of attempts to explain colonialism. A number of them have tried to concentrate the complexity of the colonial era into only one or two causal factors. The most popular theories of causation have been economic. Untypically, the eminent sociologist Joseph Schumpeter saw imperialism, the objectless disposition of a state to unlimited forcible expansion, as being opposed to economic concerns. Only a people who were not living off their own labour could exhibit a continuous imperialist policy. Otherwise, Schumpeter argued, they would submerge the instinct for conquest into economic concerns. For him, capitalists and bankers were not good imperialists.

The leading twentieth-century explanations of colonialism have been economic ones. Scholars tried to answer the question of whether colonialism (the flag) came first and was followed by trade, investment and migration or whether trade, investment and migration came first and were then followed by the flag of colonialism. J. A. Hobson's influential 1902 study, *Imperialism*, set out to explain the most powerful contemporary movement in Western politics. To Hobson, the British empire was not about trade or the export of surplus population; it was about protecting British investments. Finance fuelled the empire and turned other interests such as patriotism and philanthropy into its instruments. The British empire was thus essentially but not exclusively about economics. Hobson foresaw the ultimate decay of British imperialism, like Roman imperialism before it. To him the system was based on depravity and greed; it never rendered services to the conquered that were equivalent to what it took from them. Despite its moral tone, however Hobson's analysis was marred by references to the 'lower races' and by anti-semitism.

Lenin used Hobson's work to create his own theory of the capitalist imperialism he deplored. Lenin saw contemporary imperialism as a system whereby a small number of capitalist states plundered the whole world. The imperialist stage of capitalism was characterized by the export of superabundant capital to Europe and to the colonies. The export of capital by the financial oligarchy would lead to the rise of international cartels controlling trade and to the territorial division of the entire world among the capitalist powers. Socialist revolutions in Europe or revolutions in some colonies themselves could lead to the end of the system. However, modern analyses of the colonial powers' investment flows give little support to the theory that the flag followed investment or trade – or even, in many cases, that these relations followed the flag. The tropical African colonies that were rushed into the British and other empires at the end of the nineteenth century were not in the mainstream of trade, investment or migration patterns before or after colonization.[26] In the late nineteenth century independent Latin America received more British investment than all of the dependent empire. Some sectors of the British economy – mainly the agricultural, extractive, and some public utility sectors – and some élites did benefit from British imperialism, but not the economy as a whole.[27]

The search for an economic explanation for European colonialism was in keeping with the positivist mood of the early twentieth century. It de-emphasized the political, racial, and violent nature of the enterprise, stressing the rationality of economic processes underlying colonialism. Creating single-factor explanations, however misleading, was very attractive to those inclined either to economic determinism or to reductionism and simplicity.[28] But by the second half of the twentieth century economic interpretations of colonialism were no longer seen to stand up – no general theory sufficed to explain all the variety of colonialism. The French scholar Hubert Deschamps considered, in despair, that there were a thousand and one reasons, and often no reason at all, for colonization.[29] But the notion of a thousand reasons was closer to the truth.

The dependency school

The most recent outgrowth of the economic explanations of colonialism has been the dependency school. Dependency theory radically challenged liberal capitalist theories of development. The dependency theorists (or *dependentistas*) saw capitalism as failing to produce economic development in the poorer countries. In the 1950s influential writers such as Baran and Sweezy questioned why 'second echelon' capitalist countries such as Brazil and Argentina failed to modernize and to achieve the full economic development of Western Europe and North America.[30]

Most of the dependency writers, such as Cardoso and Faletto, and Andre Gunder Frank, argued that the only way out of poverty for the dependent countries was to turn to socialism. The Chilean economist Raul Prebisch had written from the 1950s about the problems of developing countries in a world where they could not get ahead through traditional methods such as trade. But Prebisch argued that capitalism could be modified to benefit the poor countries more.

Like many other schools such as 'Marxism', 'liberalism' and 'conservatism', the exact origins and confines of the dependency school are hard to pin down. Later authors revised and refined the tenets of earlier writers. The inspiration of the school lay in the complex and sometimes ambivalent writings of Marx, Engels and Lenin about colonialism and imperialism. Like Marx, the *dependentistas* believed that the point of studying society (here mainly Latin American underdevelopment) was not just to understand it, but actively to change it. In this way dependency theory was a major challenge to the 'hands off' approach to policy of liberal academics.[31]

Western writers have principally understood Karl Marx as a dogmatic theorist, or political agitator, rather than as a careful empiricist who warned against 'super-historical' theories. On the one hand, Marx saw colonialism as a modernizing force, the only way for non-European societies to progress. He thought that the UK brought to India unity, the telegraph, a national army, a free press, private property, European education, railroads, irrigation and steam. On the other hand, Marx recognized that it must be 'sickening to human feeling' to see how the British had destroyed the ancient Indian civilization and way of life. Despite seeing colonialism as necessary to progress in 'Asiatic' countries, by 1882 Marx accepted that the primitive communal land ownership of the Russian people might lead them directly to communist development.[32]

Lenin shared the assumptions of Marx and Engels about the superiority of Western over non-Western societies. Whereas Lenin referred to Russia as an 'Asiatic' country in 1912, by 1916 it had the more progressive term 'feudal' or 'semi-feudal'. Lenin's 1916 study, *Imperialism: the Highest Stage of Capitalism*, observed the creation of a world market. The 'superprofits' from the workers of the world were added to the profits that capitalists derived from their own workers. Lenin prefigured the dependency school in arguing that there were transitional forms of dependence, such as Argentina's dependence on British capital, not just full colonialism. He also noted the close relationship between British capitalists and the Argentine bourgeoisie.

Dependentistas divided the world into the Centre (the developed capitalist states) and the Periphery (the countries which were apparently capitalist but failed to modernize). The Centre thrived and prospered by exploiting the Periphery. Theorists such as Frank and Dos Santos saw the development of part of the capitalist world system at the expense of other parts. The surplus generated in the dependent countries such as Latin America was transferred to the dominant countries in payments of profits and interest. The dependent states had their production determined by demand from the Centre countries, resulting in unbalanced development. Foreign capital investment in Latin America produced industrialized enclaves amidst general underdevelopment. The developed countries, furthermore, monopolized access to advanced technologies, leaving the Periphery with a second-class industrial capacity. Dependent countries were often trapped into relying on the export of a single crop such as sugar (monoculture). Dos Santos identified three kinds of dependency: colonial – where the colonial power monopolized trade and many sectors of the economy; financial – where the power of foreign capital controlled the economy; and multinational – where huge foreign enterprises dominated production.[33]

Moreover, many *dependentistas* tried to combine a class-based analysis with one which incorporated the recognition of the problem of the domination of one nation by another. Thus, the bourgeoisie of the Centre countries were often seen to share interests with the bourgeoisie of the Periphery. Johann Galtung's structural analysis called this national élite of the dependent country the bridgehead of the Centre in the Periphery. Although all the groups in the Centre could benefit from the system, the Periphery group in the Centre were largely marginalized and secondary.[34]

The most sophisticated and popular expression of dependency theory was Cardoso and Faletto's 1979 *Dependency and Development in Latin America*. In a manner reminiscent of Marx's rejection of the 'super-historical', the authors claimed to look at concrete situations of dependency, not a theory, though of course implicit theoretical assumptions informed their work. They argued that 'a system is dependent when the accumulation and expansion of capital cannot find its essential dynamic component within the system.'[35] But this analysis can be questioned: not only Latin America but also the USA had depended on foreign capital to fuel its expansion.

Robert Packenham, one of the dependency school's most trenchant critics, admitted that in respect of Latin America dependency thinking has influenced every social science discipline – and even the humanities and popular culture.[36] But by the early 1980s dependency theory was on the wane. There were several reasons for this. In the 1970s theorists such as Bill Warren and Colin Leys critized dependency as *inter alia* over-structuralist, insufficiently Marxist, crude, obscure, and stagnant. Even Andre Gunder Frank, one of its founders, pronounced dependency dead in 1974. In 1980 the December issue of the influential Institute of Development Studies *Bulletin* of Sussex University queried the death of dependency ('Is Dependency Dead?', IDS Bulletin 12 (1), December 1980). The authors by and large argued that if reports of the death of dependency theory were premature, the approach was at least in need of substantial modification.

The phenomenal economic growth of the so-called NIC, or Newly Industrializing Countries, in the 1970s seemed to disprove many of the tenets of dependency theory. South Korea, Taiwan, Hong Kong and Singapore grew and prospered not in spite of but because of their integration into the world economy. As Barrett and Whyte observed, a variety of factors such as a strong state 'allowed Taiwan to exploit opportunities for world trade instead of being exploited by them'.[37] They concluded that the Taiwanese situation might not be applicable to all cases, but 'at the very least the case proves that dependency does not inevitably and uniformly lead to economic stagnation and rising inequality. Indeed, it may provide clear benefits.'

Robert Packenham argued that the problem of dependency theory lay in its 'politicized' approach, its unfalsifiability, and the fact that 'the contradictory and ambiguous character of dependency ideas invites distortions and perceived distortions'.[38] A senior OECD economist agreed that dependency theory could be positively harmful. It obfuscated the real causes of Latin America's problems. *Dependentistas* located the causes in the external world, in the exploitative capitalist system. In fact the causes were the corruption, bad government and bad management of the countries' own élites. During the 1980s the 'Washington consensus' in policy-making circles such as the World Bank and IMF was that developing countries needed to put their own houses in order. They needed to have freer markets and export-oriented growth, not to blame their problems on some hostile and amorphous 'world system'.[39]

By the 1990s, dependency was largely out of fashion. Robert Packenham admitted that some propositions of dependency could be interesting and even correct, but many others were not. He claimed that the biggest cost of dependency theory lay in its politicized attacks on scholars who differed with the school. However, if dependency theory failed, it was because it did not account convincingly for the variety of experiences of developing countries, not just because it challenged the thinking of the liberal academic world. Dependency theory did not provide a way to end poverty in Brazil, for instance, or a programme to reduce Cuba's dependence on sugar exports. Thus, its practical value was limited. It is possible that if the 'Washington consensus' on free market economics as the road to development breaks down, dependency theory may be due for a renaissance or re-invention.

THE TRIUMPH OF TECHNOLOGY?

Professor Daniel Headrick pointed out that the two great processes of the nineteenth century – industrial technology and imperialism – are usually considered independently. However, these two phenomena were in fact closely linked. In imperialism, both motives and means were equally important, and it was the new technology which supplied the means for imperialism. Without quinine protection from malaria, advanced firearms such as the Maxim gun, steamships, telegraph cables and railroads, the colonization of sub-Saharan Africa, in particular, might not have occurred. It certainly would have been more arduous. The difficulty of overland travel in the interior of Africa and the appallingly high death rate for Europeans from tropical diseases might have prevented settlement and annexation. Yet the existence of pre-nineteenth-century imperialism in India, Latin America and elsewhere suggests that at least part of the imperial project would have occurred without these technological advances. Headrick argued that,

> The real triumph of European civilization has been that of vaccines and napalm, of ships and aircraft, of electricity and radio, of plastics and printing presses; in short, it has been a triumph of technology, not ideology. Western industrial technology has transformed the world more than any leader, religion, revolution, or war.[40]

This is an interesting argument, but Headrick overstates his case. It is undoubtedly true that these technological advances have had a great influence on the development and life expectancies of humankind – but they have not fundamentally altered the problems of leadership, conquest, and social organization which have existed for as long as recorded history. Technology alone cannot resolve the basic political questions of who gets what, when and how.

The continuing power of fundamentalist religions and ideologies, of old ethnic allegiances is undeniable at the end of the twentieth century. Contemporary wars in south-eastern Europe, in the successor states of the Soviet Union, in the Middle East and elsewhere owe much to ancient ethnic and political divisions. Modern technology may help to disseminate political and religious ideas, and to wage wars, but there is little doubt that modern weapons are the servants of intolerance, nationalism and expansionism, and not the reverse.

THE SCRAMBLE IN AND OUT OF AFRICA

The establishment of formal colonies in Africa occurred much later than in the Caribbean or Latin America. The Europeans' undignified rush for colonies in the last decades of the nineteenth century is generally known as the 'Scramble for Africa'. The leading European powers and the USA met in the Berlin West Africa Conference of 1884–5 and settled the problems obstructing the colonization of Africa. In 1875 less than one-tenth of Africa had been colonized; by 1895 nine-tenths of the continent were under European rule.

The scramble for Africa was largely hasty and ill-conceived. It was, in most cases, also unprofitable for the colonizing powers. The European powers which so eagerly scrambled into Africa in the latter part of the nineteenth century were forced out after the mid-twentieth century. The reasons for decolonization were almost as various as those for the colonial enterprise as discussed on pp. 47–59.

One reason lay in the liberal ideologies of the empire-builders. European doctrines of nationalism, equality, self-determination and democracy were not lost on the leaders of the colonies, from Nehru to Nkrumah. These liberal ideologies – and the example of former colonies in the Western hemisphere – implied that the colonized had a right to determine their own destiny, independent of the colonizers.

The process of decolonization in the twentieth century, fuelled by liberal thinking, accelerated in Europe after the First World War when the great Ottoman, Hapsburg, Tsarist and German empires collapsed and the UK lost most of its Irish territory. The war revealed the European powers as vulnerable. The overtly anti-colonialist ideology of the new Soviet government and of US President Wilson's Fourteen Points gave further impetus to the decolonization movement. After the war Germany's colonies were removed from it on the grounds that they had been treated inhumanely. This established the principle that henceforth colonial rule was to be judged on grounds of humanity as well as mere utility.

The high hopes of decolonization raised in the aftermath of the First World War went largely unmet in the inter-war years. But after the Second World War again embroiled the colonies in the Europeans' conflicts, and the USA and USSR again promulgated anti-colonialist doctrines, decolonization made progress. Decolonization was not foreseen or planned by political theorists or by European leaders such as Churchill or de Gaulle, but, as leaders of weakened colonial powers facing increasingly determined nationalist movements, they had to yield to the inevitable.

The British 'theory of preparation' was the doctrine that the new states of the Commonwealth were carefully and deliberately trained to function as Westminster-style democracies. Unfortunately, this was a myth. The concept of preparation for self-government did not emerge until well after the Second World War. As late as 1950 the legislative council of Uganda was designed not to represent the views of the populace but to disseminate the views of the government to the people. In many cases the democratic training which did occur was only a strategy to delay independence. By the late 1940s it was already too late for the colonial power to build up the necessary social prerequisites for liberal democracy such as secondary and higher education and an independent civil service. Colonial administrators were also confused over the role of local government in the African colonies: some saw it as a path to Westminster-type democracy; others as an alternative to a strong central government.[41]

Thomas Pakenham described the confusion of the British when they realized in the 1950s that they could no longer hold on to their tropical African colonies:

It had been an axiom of the British that they would have decades to turn tropical colonies into nation states. After all, these haphazard blocks of scrub, and desert, peppered with ill-matched tribes, had neither geographical nor political unity. Many had been kept divided, the better to rule them. . . . Now the British found they had gravely miscalculated. In desperation the British launched a crash programme in nation-building. Constitutions were borrowed from elsewhere or hammered out overnight, parliaments thrown up like theatre props . . . elections held, Prime Ministers lectured on the intricacies of British democracy.[42]

Under these circumstances, it was not surprising that the new democratic institutions did not fare well.

The French, too, launched a crash programme of preparing their colonies for independence, or at least some autonomy. The

1946 French constitution was drafted to include not only metro-
politan France but also the Overseas Departments and Territories,
and the Associated States and Territories, that is, the empire. This
French Association arrangement lasted only twelve years until
the revised constitution of the Fifth Republic was adopted in
1958. This time the colonies were given the chance to vote whether
or not to join the newly-organized French Community. However,
this freedom of choice was merely cosmetic. President de Gaulle
threatened the direst consequences for any colonies foolish
enough to reject membership of the French-led system. Only the
Republic of Guinea voted '*non*' to the French Community, but it
rapidly became apparent that the other colonies also wanted
independence and not the constitutional halfway house of the
French Community. By the early 1960s the Community was dead
and the French African colonies were independent.

In addition to the French Community, France had further plans
to establish multinational organizations linking it with its former
dependencies. The Treaty of Rome provided France with another
opportunity. France insisted that the 1957 Treaty must include
provisions for the 'association' of the dependencies of the European signatories (namely, Germany, France, Belgium, the
Netherlands, Italy and Luxembourg; 'the Six'). The other signatories were less than enthusiastic about this venture into colonial
policy, and Adenauer even offered to pay France to drop the
idea.[43]

Finally, France got its way by making the association policy a
pre-condition of its signing the Treaty of Rome. This association
policy, Part IV of the Treaty of Rome, still exists for the dependencies of the EU member states alongside the successor
arrangements for the independent countries of Africa, the Caribbean and Pacific. These successor agreements, the two Yaoundé
Conventions and then four Lomé Conventions, have formed the
backbone of the EU's development policy up to the present.

THE COLONIAL LEGACY

Modern Europeans have dealt with the question of the 'other' in
different ways. In the context of the Lomé Convention in 1975,
they emphasized that this agreement with developing countries
represented a new start owing nothing to the unequal relations
of the past. In the case of the former British empire, now the

Commonwealth, the ties of language and culture rather than the history of political control are cited as the cement of the relationship.

However far from ideal we may consider today's European relations with developing countries, they are a long way from the violence and brute exploitation of the colonial empires. Europe still likes to direct Africa in the way it should go, and tries to keep African markets open for European exports and investments. Political influence is exerted by the West through conditions on World Bank and IMF loans, and there have been more forcible interventions by French and Belgian paratroopers and other foreign troops. Professor William Zartman argued in the early 1990s that 'Africa had simply, finally, awkwardly, taken its security into its own hands',[44] but this view was premature as US and UN troops tried to stabilize war-torn Somalia in 1992 and 1993.

Like Europe's historic relations with the Kongo, the EU's development policy shows that potentially a more egalitarian relationship with Africa and other developing countries could emerge. Europe still bears considerable responsibility for the distress of Africa and other former colonies. The legacies of colonialism can be seen in many aspects of African life: European languages, legal systems, state borders, constitutions, divided ethnic groups, cultural practices, economic distortions and environmental problems resulting from the over-exploitation of resources.

But Europe's efforts to remedy the situation – through aid and trade pacts, guidance, policy dialogues, cultural cooperation and sometimes military intervention – have not so far been successful. Africa remains a dependent, largely marginalized continent. Neither in its treatment of immigrants inside Europe (see Chapter 3) nor its treatment of the developing countries has Europe completely solved the problem of dealing with the 'other'.

How to co-exist is an ongoing problem for different civilizations which meet and interact but do not fully understand each other. The question of contemporary 'civilizational conflict' has been widely discussed and is examined in the next section.

EUROPE AND THE 'CLASH OF CIVILIZATIONS'

In 1993 Professor Samuel Huntington proposed a new grand paradigm or model for international politics. He claimed that with the end of the Cold War, ideological and economic conflicts would be replaced by civilizational or cultural conflicts.[45] These conflicts, he argued pessimistically, would be even more expensive than fighting communism. However, Professor Huntington's analysis is deeply flawed. His efforts to come up with a simple map or model of the post-Cold War world are in themselves misguided.[46] The Cold War world was not the simple three-fold division of First, Second and Third Worlds which Huntington maintains.[47] Neutral developed states, rifts between the USSR and China and among developing countries made this scenario – however desirably simple – also inaccurate. There is even less reason to presume that a post-Cold War world will resolve itself not into greater complexity but into a simple set of conflicting civilizations.[48]

For Huntington's purposes, the West is presumed to be a coherent entity, which clashes with seven or eight (*sic*) other civilizations. The variety in number arises from whether Africa is considered to have any consequence or not. Indeed, not only Africa but also all of the non-West is reckoned to have been marginal to history up to now: 'international relations, historically a game played out within Western civilizations'.[49] This assertion can be refuted by considering the importance of India to the British empire or more recently the effects of the Japanese bombing of Pearl Harbor.

Neither is 'the West' as homogeneous as Huntington argues. After all, the USA was born out of conflict with the traditional values of Europe, a civilization America's founders saw as decadent and corrupt. Contemporary Europe has aspirations not to follow the USA but to be a world actor, rivalling the USA. The commitment of Canada and Australia to a 'European' identity is also changing. The former has removed its troops from Europe while the latter seeks more connections with its Asian neighbours. Professor Huntington rightly notes that US concerns over Japanese investment include a degree of xenophobia; however, he fails to mention that the French have likewise stridently objected to US investment in their country.[50]

As to the European culture which Professor Huntington sees as vital to the underlying unity of the West, it does not exist.

Wilson and van der Dussen described the paradox of European culture succinctly in that it has 'no stable core, no fixed identity, no final answer.'[51] The name 'Europe' dates back thousands of years and encompasses a variety of meanings. The origin of the term, perhaps poetically meaning 'evening land' or 'the dark-looking one', is unclear.[52] Until the nineteenth century there was no unified history of 'Europe' as such. But in the wake of the French Revolution, there arose a nostalgia for the old, idyllic civilization of the Middle Ages, a common civilization which never really existed. From then, the history of Europe was extended backwards to encompass Rome and Greece as well. It seems that Professor Huntington is doing something similar to the early nineteenth-century Europeans. In the confusion and chaos following the end of the Cold War, he is looking backwards for a theme to explain contemporary reality.

The 'clash of civilizations' theme is a very old one. Greek historians such as Herodotus in the fifth century BC began to differentiate between two warring civilizations: the Greek one characterized by political freedom and the Persian one ruled by absolutism. The early nineteenth-century political theorist de Tocqueville contrasted the liberty of the English and Americans with the abject servitude of Russians. In the 1930s the Nazi theorist Alfred Rosenberg saw within Europe a clash of three cultures or races: the Nordic race struggled with both the Roman-Catholic and the Jewish–Marxist elements.[53] In a more reasoned and scholarly vein, Adda Bozeman argued in the 1960s that cultures and civilizations needed to be incorporated into the study of international affairs. However, she refrained from claiming that this was 'a clear projection of new perspectives in the conduct of international relations'. Instead she saw it as the source of further reflection.[54] In 1993, Huntington echoed Bozeman's call for inter-cultural accords and understanding.

As well as reifying 'the West' and 'Europe', Huntington makes several dubious assumptions. He repeatedly refers to the conflict in the former Yugoslavia as 'cultural'. But even a cursory glance at the different living standards which prevailed in Slovenia and Bosnia, for instance, will suggest that an economic interpretation of the conflict is not without merit. Factors such as territorial ambition and power maximizing by leaders also have to be taken into account. Huntington refers to an ancient line clearly dividing Western Christendom from the Orthodox East but he does not explain how Orthodox Greece – from the wrong side of the line – managed to be incorporated into the EU or how Malta and Cyprus can be prospective members.

The Gulf War, in Huntington's view, shows the Islamic world juxtaposed against the West. This thesis would be more believable if Saddam Hussein had attacked Washington instead of a neighbouring Islamic state. In fact, in the Gulf War Arab countries such as Egypt and Saudi Arabia assisted the West. Huntington also mistakes some of the more extreme pro-Islamic rhetoric of King Hussein for a policy statement. Huntington rightly deplores the military build-up of countries such as Pakistan and Iran, but fails to note that Israel and even France – with its defence budget expanding through 1996 and its nuclear testing programme – could be called 'weapons states'. Neither do a few arms deals between China and Pakistan mean that there is a solid Confucian–Islamic (*sic*) bloc opposed to the West.

Islam itself is far from monolithic. Its practice varies from country to country and over time. Olivier Roy, for instance, argues that the political force of Islam has died as it has become increasingly 'social democratized'. States have largely succeeded in controlling Islam as a political movement.[55]

In a well-researched book, *Islam and the Myth of Confrontation*, Professor Fred Halliday points out that the myth of a unified, expansionist and revolutionary Islam is propagated not only by orientalists in the West but also by many Islamic leaders. From Khomeini in Iran to al-Madani in Algeria, Islamic leaders portrayed Islam as a force united in its opposition to liberal–democratic values and locked into a perpetual conflict with the West. After the Cold War, some Islamic leaders eagerly tried to shoulder the fallen mantle of communism as the West's public enemy number one. The Islamic idea of a *jihad* or holy war is often employed to support the idea of an Islamic threat to the West. But, in fact, the main Islamic military threat to the West disappeared in 1918 with the fall of the Ottoman empire.[56] Islamic states are more typically a threat to each other – as in the Iran–Iraq War, the Morocco–Algeria War, the Iraqi invasion of Kuwait – than to the West.

By contrast, Huntington approves of the extreme view that future international conflicts are likely to be between 'the West and the Rest'.[57] In fact, the proliferation of organizations of cooperation is as notable as the proliferation of conflicts in the post-

Cold War world. The Commonwealth has over fifty member states, and even some former non-colonies of the UK, such as Mozambique, are eager to join. Cooperation in Asia is expanding in the Asia Pacific Economic Cooperation (APEC) organization. Membership of the World Trade Organization, established in 1994, is expanding by leaps and bounds. Most of the former Warsaw Pact and USSR members want to ally with NATO's Partnership for Peace. Even Professor Huntington admits the growing cooperation between Mexico, the USA and Canada in the North American Free Trade Agreement.

The clash of civilizations thesis may just represent the West looking for a new enemy, a new 'other' against which to juxtapose its own identity. The 'clash' thesis certainly over-estimates the likelihood of conflict between civilizations and under-estimates the degree of cooperation and inter-penetration between them.[58] One of the main historical events following the Second World War was the desire of the Europeans' colonies, starting with India, to throw off the colonial yoke as rapidly as possible. The new states wanted to distance themselves from their former colonial masters and pursue independent policies. For over three decades, the process of decolonization proceeded in Asia, Africa and Latin America. Nowadays the decolonization process, which once seemed urgent, has little momentum. Non-Western countries are no longer so eager to distance themselves from their colonizers. The Netherlands Antilles (rather than the Netherlands) have shown little interest in their own independence.[59] The Democratic Alternative Party of Suriname, recognizing the country's disastrous post-independence history, seeks stronger ties with the former colonial power. It stops just short of seeking renewed colonial status.[60] In 1980 Anguilla withdrew from independence plans and in the summer of 1995 the population of Bermuda voted to remain a British colony. The clash of North and South – or West and the Rest – is not materializing. The majority of former colonies are not opting for recolonization, but many are continuing to cooperate with the former colonial powers through organizations such as the Commonwealth and the Lomé Convention.

In conclusion, the hypothesis that civilizations are increasingly conflicting and cleaving apart rather than compromising and cooperating is not justified by the evidence presented. If Europe seeks to define itself by reference to an opposed, enemy 'other', it risks creating an enemy out of Islamic, Confucian or other cultures. But to the extent that Professor Huntington is warning policy-makers to pay attention to the possibility of civilizational conflict and thereby avoid it, he is doing humankind a service. Huntington's writings have already inspired Islamic and Confucian leaders in Malaysia, for instance, to enter into a dialogue.

A more political cast was given to the West versus the Third World model by Steven David. He responded to the popular US view that, in the post-Cold War world, the Third World could simply be ignored because it had no strategic importance and lacked both the military might to threaten the USA and the motivation to do so.[61] Instead, David depicted the Third World as riven by internal and external conflicts. It bristled with nuclear, biological and chemical weapons, as well as acting as a spawning ground for terrorism. Third World culture, including Islamic culture, meant that nuclear deterrence would be less effective than it had been in the case of the former Soviet Union, democracy would be hard to establish and Third World governments might try to withhold essential oil supplies from the USA. Like Huntington, David saw the Third World as a real threat, but he considered culture not as the pre-eminent source of problems between the West and the Rest but more realistically as one of the factors making up this situation. However, he overlooked the point that the so-called 'Third World' is internally diverse and exists in its own right as well as being a foil for Western policies. David got so carried away with the idea that the Third World was menacing the USA that he argued that it posed not only the threats he had described but also others endangering American interests 'in ways whose implications are still unknown'.[62]

Like Huntington, David overlooked the possibility that the developing countries (or some of them) might be able to cooperate with the West in mutually beneficial ways. Nevertheless, David's analysis led him to the constructive conclusion that the USA should not ignore the Third World but should positively engage it. Economic development and modernization for the Third World, as well as intense aid conditionality (The problems associated with which are discussed in Chapter 5), were on the agenda. The USA needed to fight an uphill battle against Third World instability, even diverting funds from military expenditure to foreign aid.

In so far as 'the West versus the Rest' models of post-Cold

War international relations refocus attention on the developing countries, they are to be welcomed. But there is an unfortunate tendency to lump dissimilar countries together, as the 'other', and to over-simplify and over-emphasize the prevalence of conflict instead of cooperation. Neo-colonialism or conflict are not the only options for the relations between the EU and the South.

Chapters 3–5 analyse concrete examples of the EU's experience of cooperation (and conflict) with the developing countries of the Mediterranean, Africa, the Caribbean and Pacific.

Chapter 3

Europe and the Mediterranean

The recent flurry of interest from the EU countries in the states of the southern Mediterranean coast might give the casual observer the impression that Europe has only recently discovered North Africa. Intense French interest in the region, the Mediterranean summit in Barcelona in November 1995 and the EU's proposals for a Euro-Mediterranean Economic Area suggest a growing interest and involvement between the two shores of the Mediterranean Sea.

This chapter investigates the history and coherence of the Mediterranean region, and its aspiration to unity. The awkward development of the EU's Mediterranean policy and the inescapable security problems of the region are examined. The chapter analyses the EU's relations with Morocco and with Union of the Arab Maghreb, 'the Union of the Southern shore'. Lastly, the problems of the environment, of migration within the region, and the prospects of addressing these problems through the proposed Conference on Security and Cooperation in the Mediterranean are assessed.

In the post-Cold War re-allocation of political allegiances, Europe is trying to reassert its influence over the whole Mediterranean region in political, economic and military terms. Fostering development in the Mediterranean region through trade liberalization and development aid is a useful spin-off from this new European expression of interest.

However, this most recent phase of European involvement in the region is based on an extensive history. From a long-term perspective, the relations between the European countries and North Africa go back thousands of years. Arab culture has always been the closest 'different' culture to Europe, and over the centuries Europeans have in turn found it attractive and influential, menacing and incomprehensible. A large measure of the ambivalence of the northern Mediterranean countries towards their southern counterparts still influences the EU's development policy. Like the fifteenth-century scholar Dionysius the Carthusian, modern Europeans still desire 'a peaceful discussion rather than armed conflict' with their North African neighbours.[1]

The Mediterranean Sea often appears to form a clear dividing line between Europe to the north and Africa to the south. In many respects, the two shores of the Mediterranean have never seemed so far apart as they are now. The Mediterranean looks like a microcosm of the division of the world into North and South. It is the meeting ground of Orient and Occident; Islam and Christianity; Europe and the Arab world.[2] But the division is much less simple: the Mediterranean is better considered as an overlapping set of cultures rather than a region bisected down the middle. The division of the Mediterranean region into 'Europe' and 'other' is a useful political construct, but fails to reveal the close relations of the two entities.[3] A modernist development perspective would look at the EU's project of 'developing' the southern littoral; from a post-modern perspective, the two sides each have something to offer the other.

At present the northern shore is preoccupied with crisis prevention in the southern Mediterranean region and sees development as an instrument of that objective. For the longer term, perhaps the North would be wiser to concentrate on development in the Mediterranean and reap crisis prevention as a spin-off.

THE MEDITERRANEAN IDEAL

The doyen of Mediterranean scholars, Fernand Braudel, observed two major truths about the Mediterranean.[4] The second was the greatness of the Mediterranean region, which lasted up until the seventeenth century or later. This is largely uncontested. Braudel's first truth is more problematic. He asserted that there was a unity and coherence pertaining to the entire Mediterranean region; the whole area shared a common destiny.

Modern scholars and politicians differ greatly about the nature, desirability and future prospects of Mediterranean unity. Braudel himself noted the many differences in the Mediterranean region:

even the Mediterranean Sea itself can be divided into sub-regions. The Mediterranean region borders on to the desert and the ocean; it has shores, flatlands and mountains, a bewildering variety of peoples, languages, cultures and political units. Nevertheless, basic elements of unity exist as well as differences.

Social organization on both shores of the Mediterranean has much in common. Monique Gadant pointed out the similarities of the family structures of the peoples of the Mediterranean basin. These were characterized by the power of the extended family over individuals, especially over women. The importance of the maternal role for women in assuring their social legitimacy; the dominance of men over women and the virtual exclusion of the latter from political power are common themes throughout the Mediterranean. It fact, she argued, such social similarities 'make a mockery of the barriers constructed by religion and state'.[5] Nevertheless, social roles and ideologies do differ between the more developed countries of the northern shore and the poorer states of the southern Mediterranean.

The Mediterranean idea, the Mediterranean principle or 'entity', the Mediterranean mystique – all these are different ways of referring to the same thing: the ideal of Mediterranean unity. This is conceived of as a unity encompassing both the northern and the southern shores, including poor, Islamic states and developed, Christian ones. This 'ideal' is rarely explictly spelled out; it is usually a vague expression of goodwill and shared history. The ideal involves more than a dialogue among states but less than complete integration. It aspires to a condition of peace, harmony, cooperation and mutually beneficial exchange throughout the region. It bases its hope for the future on the close and productive relations of the past, often the ancient past.

Proponents of this unity refer to the common interests and continual interchanges among Mediterranean states. They frequently hark back to positive experiences in the region under the influence of Greece or the empire of Rome. Thierry Fabre argued that Mediterranean unity was also necessary for geopolitical balance in Europe. Europe should form a Southern European-Mediterranean axis to balance the powerful axis of Germany with Northern and Central Europe. He saw this Mediterranean axis as essential to preserve stability in the region, but the exact form that the Mediterranean axis should take was not spelled out.[6] Similar views have been propounded by former French president

Giscard d'Estaing. However desirable such a balance might be, the prospects for Mediterranean unity, discussed in this chapter, make it an unlikely counterweight at present to the economic and political power of Central and Northern Europe. Another worthwhile political aim for a Mediterranean axis – linking the northern Mediterranean EU countries with the southern shore – would be to anchor the unstable fledgling democracies there to the apparently solid rock of liberal democratic Europe. The EU has already functioned in this way for Greece.

In the 1970s Johan Galtung of Oslo University put forward brief and sketchy proposals for greater unity in the Mediterranean region. These included regional assemblies and functional networks in the area. These institutions were intended to foster unity and protect the Mediterranean area from the encroachment of Northern European culture, which Galtung saw as otherwise inevitable. These brief proposals were among the early attempts to put the modern Mediterranean ideal into concrete terms.[7]

But the value of holding Mediterranean unity as an ideal, even a relatively inchoate one, has been fiercely challenged. Wolfgang Hager argued that the old unity of the Mediterranean could not be re-established in the modern world. Europe ought not to fall victim to a mystique such as manifest destiny or the Greater East Asia Co-Prosperity Sphere (the oppressive vehicle of Japanese imperialism).[8] In the apocalyptic vision of Professor Hager, Europe's political concept of its relations with the Mediterranean could only lead to another crisis similar to the one France had with Algeria in the 1960s. Scholars such as Hager and Hamilton were pessimistic that Europeans would ever have a clear understanding of and a successful method of dealing with the southern Mediterranean region. But in today's post-modern world, more wedded to economic targets than to grand concepts, a transmediterranean war of ideology and race is less likely.

The different levels of development of the northern and southern Mediterranean littorals put any organizations of cooperation in danger of being dominated by the north. Despite these doubts, the attractiveness of the Mediterranean ideal remains. There is little alternative to seeking greater cooperation in the region if one wishes to avoid greater division and potential conflict.

In summary, it is easier to hold some kind of ideal of Mediterranean unity than to develop and implement concrete proposals

Table 3.1 Mediterranean exports to the World and the EU, 1981 and 1991

Country	Exports to the World ($US millions)		Exports to the EU (% of total exports)	
	1981	*1991*	*1981*	*1991*
Algeria	13,296.0	12,314.0	51.0	67.7
Cyprus	562.4	975.2	30.2	44.1
Egypt	3,232.6	3,838.2	44.2	28.3
Israel	5,673.3	11,598.3	35.8	34.4
Jordan	540.8	879.2	1.6	3.1
Lebanon	1,001.7	490.2	4.5	22.7
Libya	15,575.0	10,775.0	52.7	83.8
Malta	449.6	1,140.7	70.4	71.8
Morocco	2,286.5	5,148.8	57.9	67.8
Syria	2,101.9	3,699.8	65.5	45.7
Tunisia	2,463.7	3,826.7	61.4	73.8
Turkey	4,695.6	13,334.9	33.4	50.8
Yugoslavia	10,929.0	16,235.0	23.3	56.0

Source: Tovias, Alfred, 'The Mediterranean Economy', in Ludlow, P. (ed.) *Europe and the Mediterranean*, Brussels, Brassey's, 1994

for cooperation. But having an ideal of cooperation, of shared interests or neighbourliness, is necessary to underpin efforts at creating greater harmony and cooperation in the region. However, given the political problems which are considered here, such an ideal of unity may be achieved only at the margins (say, between the EU and Morocco and Tunisia) or only in the long term.

ISSUES OF DEPENDENCY

There is no doubt that the rest of the Mediterranean region is economically dependent on the EU. The Union is the motor of economic development for the whole region. For small states such as Malta and Tunisia, over 70 per cent of their foreign trade is with the EU. In many cases, such as that of Algeria and Cyprus, the share of exports heading for the EU has been growing significantly over the past decade (see Table 3.1). The importance of the EU as an engine of growth, a source of financial aid, a model of regional cooperation and of domestic political organization can hardly be over-estimated.

In 1974 Professor Wolfgang Hager made the much-quoted

observation that the northern and southern Mediterranean littorals did not have interdependence, but instead two distinct
kinds of dependence. The Europeans mainly had a security
interest, along with some interest in oil, in the south. The south,
by contrast, was economically dependent on the north, but had
no particular security interest in it.

Today, the situation is far more complex. Europe continues to
have security and oil interests in North Africa. Furthermore,
North African security problems might spill over into Europe in
the form of unrest in immigrant communities. In 1995, several
terrorist bombings in France appeared to be connected with the
Algerian civil war. Economically, European multinationals are
interested in investing in North Africa where labour costs are only
a quarter of those in Europe. Europe also has a substantial self-
interest in ensuring that southern littoral countries adhere to the
various environmental measures agreed since the 1970s to preserve the Mediterranean environment.

The southern Mediterranean continues its dependence on the
EU as a market and source of aid. But southern security has also
been affected by Europe; the Community has so far supported
the military regime in Algeria which has suppressed Islamic fundamentalism. Created in 1993, the Franco-German naval
squadron, and more particularly the French, Spanish and Italian
force 'aero-maritime' for use in the Mediterranean (also known
as EUROMARFOR), will have a security impact on the Mediterranean region, enhancing European power there. In the 1995
'Lisbon Declaration' of the ministers of the Western European
Union (WEU), this joint force was declared answerable to the
WEU and open to all WEU states to join. Portugal and then
Greece also indicated their intention to participate.

NATO's decision in 1992 that it can act in out of area situations
(i.e. outside the territories of its members) might bring the question of a NATO action in North Africa into the realm of
possibility. It would not be out of the question for NATO to
consider North Africa as its own 'near abroad'. In early 1995
NATO Secretary General Claes set up a dialogue with North
Africa and Israel. European plans to support and increase its
defence industry, via a proposed European armaments agency
and the establishment of an armaments secretariat in the WEU,
will also affect the interests of North African arms purchasers.

As explained in Chapter 2, the dependency school was a broad movement which arose in Latin America in the 1950s and 1960s to explain the poor record of economic development in that continent. Its principal theorists such as Andre Gunder Frank and Cardoso and Faletto took their inspiration from Marx and Lenin, with an admixture of Latin American nationalism.

They argued that Latin America could never develop under capitalism, but required a socialist alternative. They contended that capitalism, while providing wealth in the Western industrialized countries, simultaneously produced poverty and underdevelopment in Latin America. The international and national bourgeoisies colluded to keep the Latin American workers and the Latin American states poor.

The dependency movement has been criticized for its undeniable vagueness, internal contradictions, lack of clarity, and failure to provide a clear alternative to capitalist development. In their commitment to change rather than clear analysis, the *dependentistas* were seen by Robert Packenham as behaving more like politicians than social scientists.[9] By the 1980s the influence of dependency theory began to wane. The phenomenal economic growth since the 1970s of the Newly Industrializing Countries (South Korea, Hong Kong, Singapore and Taiwan) seemed clearly to refute the dependency proposition that poor countries could not succeed in a world capitalist economic system. Countries such as Taiwan were able to exploit the opportunities of the international economy rather than to be exploited in the way that many countries of Latin America, the Caribbean and Africa seemed to have been.

Theories of dependency have not been extensively applied to the Mediterranean region, and it may be that this Latin American framework is too vague and inaccurate to be readily transferrable. But if we take a loose definition of dependency as 'the reverse of domination, power and influence', then the relationship of the southern littoral of the Mediterranean with the north will qualify.[10] The northern shore countries can readily be conceptualized as the 'Centre' in dependency terms, while the states of the southern shore are the less powerful 'Periphery'. The future shape of Euro-Mediterranean relations will predominantly be decided by the countries of the northern shore, the Centre. But, like the results of the dependency analysis of Taiwan discussed in Chapter 2, the dependency of the southern Mediterranean countries on the northern ones may bring them the benefits of economic growth.

The traditional view of Western scholars or so-called 'orientalists' is that the Arabs 'show lack of coordination and harmony in organization and function, nor have they revealed an ability for cooperation. Any collective action for mutual benefit or common profit is alien to them.'[11] This view is still common today. It appears in the EU's attitude to the Mediterranean: the conception that the EU alone can and should bring about a Mediterranean community of peace and prosperity. The *Financial Times* correspondent David Gardner took up this theme: 'The European Union's strategy to enhance stability on its southern Mediterranean border through an aid and (eventual) free trade agreement with the Middle East and the Maghreb could do more to integrate the region than the past half-century of rhetoric about Arab unity.'[12] It may be that Europeans under-estimate the Arabs' organizational abilities, their political skills and their problems.

MEDITERRANEAN RELATIONS WITH THE EU

To many northern Europeans the southern shore of the Mediterranean is a backward region which holds little of interest. Its Arabic culture, political conflicts, Islamic and Judaic religions seem strange and foreign. As David Buchan aptly remarked, the Community has proximity but no great affinity to the southern Mediterranean. Many people in the EU – including some decision-makers – would like to forget about it altogether.[13] This state of neglect is certainly true for the UK, Germany and the other non-Mediterranean states, but is not the case for Italy, Spain, France, Portugal or Greece.

As with any geographical region, defining the exact limits of the Mediterranean basin is difficult. Like any region it has anomalies. Portugal and Jordan are often considered as 'Mediterranean' although they have no Mediterranean coast. Where 'Europe' departs from 'the Mediterranean' is not clear. Iceland is seen as more 'European' than the countries of North Africa, but it is farther away from Central Europe and less influenced by the classical cultures of Greece and Rome.[14] To many North Africans, the division between Europe and Africa is the Sahara, not the Mediterranean.[15] Despite these difficulties in defining the region,

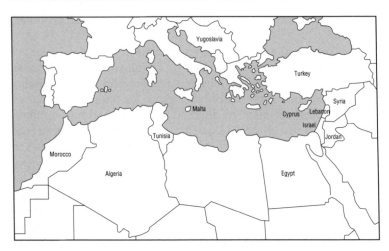

Figure 3.1 Mediterranean states which have preferential trade agreements with the EU

Source: European Commission, *The European Community and the Mediterranean Countries*, Luxembourg, Office for Official Publications, 1991, p. 3

the following Mediterranean countries have had agreements under the Community's Mediterranean policy (see Figure 3.1): Morocco, Algeria, Tunisia, Egypt, Jordan, Lebanon, Syria, Israel, Cyprus, Malta, Turkey and Yugoslavia (its agreement was terminated in 1991 owing to its internal conflicts). For political reasons, the Mediterranean states of Albania and Libya were not included in the Community's Mediterranean policy of the 1970s and 1980s.

The modern history of European involvement in the Mediterranean contained traumatic incidents, especially for the British and France. In 1956 the US navy opposed the Suez invasion by British and French forces. This humiliation for the Europeans marked the end of European influence in the Eastern Mediterranean. The long, bitter war with Algeria, culminating in Algerian independence in 1962, also struck deeply at European sensibilities.

Following such events, Europe was wary of involvement in the North African/Mediterranean region, preferring the better-known quantity of relations with black Africa. During the Cold War, the Mediterranean became a superpowers' lake, with the Europeans having only a marginal role. Their frustration was expressed in the European Commission's 1982 'Pisani Memorandum'. It objected to the fact that: 'Between them the Community's

Member States and special partners stretch along nine-tenths of the shores of a sea whose waters are ruled by powerful outsiders.'[16]

The history of the Community's Mediterranean policy goes back to the 1957 Treaty of Rome which established the European Community. Article 16 of the Implementing Convention declared that the preceding articles applied to Algeria and the French overseas departments – mainly to qualify them for Community aid. Article 237 of the Treaty held out membership as a prospect for Northern Mediterranean countries (such as Greece, Spain and Portugal). A Commission document in 1989 admitted that the early relations of the Community and the Mediterranean were 'tentative', but it cited the reference in the Treaty of Rome to Morocco and Tunisia as evidence of the Community's interest in these two countries.[17] However, the reference concerned was merely a protocol noting that the Treaty of Rome did not require France immediately to change its customs treatment of goods originating in a group of countries including Morocco, Tunisia, Vietnam, and Laos. Ironically, the North African state most openly courted in the Treaty of Rome was Libya. The 'Declaration of Intent on the Association of the Kingdom of Libya' specifically offered Libya the prospect of a convention of association – which was never realized.

Despite these early connections, the Community was far from having a coherent Mediterranean policy in the late 1950s and 1960s. Whereas the Community's policy towards the former colonies of sub-Saharan Africa, based on part IV of the Treaty of Rome (later the Lomé Convention) had a reasonable coherence, the early Mediterranean policy did not. The Community's relations with the Mediterranean were reactive rather than proactive. The Lomé Convention in the 1970s and 1980s was a policy that tried not to look like a policy; it was a 'discreet entente'.[18] By contrast, the Mediterranean policy was portrayed as more coherent than it really was.

The Community's Mediterranean policy has variously been described as 'accidental' or 'just growed' like Topsy. Shlaim and Yannopoulos were particularly scathing:

Given the stakes involved and the existence of unique conditions for regional cooperation, the apparently random and almost absent-minded manner in which the EEC's policy toward the Mediterranean evolved is most striking. Indeed, the importance of these problems was almost matched by the incoherence of the policies.[19]

With hindsight, it is highly doubtful that special 'unique conditions for regional integration' in the Mediterranean existed in the 1960s or 1970s. Furthermore, the Community itself lacked an overall Mediterranean approach which would have fostered such integration. By the 1970s the Community wanted to establish a regional Mediterranean agreement similar in design to the Lomé Convention, using this relationship as its model.

Of course, the Community had no way of predicting events such as the independence of Algeria, the colonels' coup in Greece or the disintegration of former Yugoslavia. Any external policy would be strained or disrupted by such events. But in the Community's vision of three regions, namely, Europe, the union of Europe and black Africa in the Lomé Convention, and the agreements with the Arab–Mediterranean, the latter were latecomers. The Mediterranean agreements never developed the institutional framework or the multilateral character of the Lomé Conventions. The European Commission tried to put this institutional deficit into a positive light, arguing that the Lomé dialogue was 'excessively formalistic' while bilateral relations could be 'more specialized and more intimate'.[20] Dialogue with the Mediterranean countries might have been more intimate, but it was also less broad and deep, and less reliable than the Lomé dialogue.

Even now the EU's Mediterranean policy faces a major challenge in terms of the potential accession of the Mediterranean states of Cyprus, Malta and Turkey to the EU. There is no coherent policy framework or formula to deal with these matters; there is only a piecemeal approach. Periodically, scholars have discerned a renewed European interest in the Mediterranean. In 1977 at the beginning of the Euro-Arab dialogue, in the late 1980s, and again after the Gulf War signs of enhanced European interest in the region emerged.[21] But it remains to be seen whether the current bout of increased European interest in the Mediterranean will be sustained – and whether it will lead to further enlargements. Only if the EU's interest in the Mediterranean region is continuous, generous and adaptable will it have a chance of creating the kind of stable Euro-Mediterranean community it now seeks.

Security in the Mediterranean

The Community has recognized the importance of Mediterranean stability, even though it has often felt at a loss as to how to secure it. As an overtly economic body, the Community reckoned it did not have the means to deal with political questions – although these were often no more separable from economic issues than they have been in the case of GATT. The European Commission recognized 'the stake which the Commmunity has in the harmonious development of the Mediterranean region and the stabilizing role it must play in that area both economically and politically if it is to preserve peace on its doorstep and markets for its products.'[22] By and large, stability has been the goal of the Community's Mediterranean policy. The Community was neither seeking an active 'sphere of influence', such as it developed through the Lomé policy, nor to re-establish the nineteenth-century era of European dominance when North Africa, especially Algeria, was to the French the 'narrow door' to sub-Saharan Africa.

In the Cold War world of the 1940s to 1980s, the Mediterranean region – and the Europeans – played a secondary role. The Soviet navy, with its traditional aspiration for warm water, had bases in Malta and Libya. Morocco and Tunisia provided staging points for the US Rapid Deployment Force. NATO saw the Mediterranean not as a unit but as a mixture of areas of Central importance (France) and Peripheral, out of area regions (the southern littoral).

With the ending, or at least the diminution, of the Cold War since 1989, it has been argued that regional conflicts in the Mediterranean will have more significance in their own right and not just as proxy wars for the superpowers. George Joffe went further and argued that the security issues of the past have been replaced by economic issues, the confrontation of the haves and have-nots on the two Mediterranean shores.[23] There is no doubt that the security issues of the Mediterranean region have changed, but they have not disappeared.

To the North Africans, Europe was always as important or more important than the superpowers. Economically, they were more dependent on trading with the Europe on their doorstep than with more distant powers. The European model of unity and regional political organization has been almost irresistible.

The European political, economic and cultural model has been diffused throughout the Mediterranean by means of trade, education, tourism, satellite television links, and other connections. Eberhard Shein, European Commission director for EC–Arab affairs, noted: 'Europe acts like a powerful syphon, drawing the Arab world into its orbit.'[24]

Lately, relations between the two shores of the Mediterranean have experienced considerable problems. These have included the poor treatment of immigrant workers from North Africa in Europe, for instance by the British in Gibraltar, and the Community's rebuff of attempts from some Mediterranean countries to join the EC. The European Parliament's decision in February 1992 to withold 463 million ecus of aid to Morocco on the grounds of its violations of human rights and occupation of Western Sahara, caused particular friction. Nevertheless, the contention that the Arab Maghreb were turning their backs on the EU was never correct.[25] To the liberalizing governments of North Africa which were desirous of sharing in Europe's peace and prosperity, following the European model or joining the Community, as Greece, Spain, and Portugal had done in the 1980s, was the way forward.

According to the theory of hegemonic stability, having one state act as a dominant power which makes the rules for the other states of the system is a force for international peace. According to this viewpoint, after the Second World War both the USA and the USSR kept stability in their respective camps.[26] Traditionally, the leading or hegemonic power in the Mediterranean region has been France. Rather like the USA's attitude to the Caribbean, France regarded the Mediterranean as its own backyard. US and Soviet activities there were seen as an annoyance, a limiting factor on French hegemony. In 1980, France accounted for 44 per cent of the region's GNP while the largest three economies – France, Italy and Spain – together made up 85 per cent. By 1990 France, still the Mediterranean's largest economy, accounted for 37 per cent of the region's GNP while France, Italy and Spain together made up 85 per cent of regional GNP again owing to Italy's strong performance. (See Table 3.2 for relative GNP rankings.)

France is still the main trading partner of the other Mediterranean countries and the main investor in North Africa. Most of the regional initiatives discussed in this chapter emanated from France (although it has since had cold feet about some of them).

Table 3.2 Mediterranean states' GNP, 1990 and 1980 ($US millions)

Rank	Country	1990	1980
1	France	1,099,750	627,700
2	Italy	970,619	368,860
3	Spain	429,404	199,780
4	Turkey	91,742	66,080
5	Yugoslavia	72,860	58,570
6	Greece	60,245	42,190
7	Algeria	51,585	36,410
8	Israel	50,866	17,440
9	Egypt	31,381	23,140
10	Morocco	23,788	17,440
11	Libya (1989)	23,333	25,730
12	Syria	12,404	12,030
13	Tunisia	11,592	8,340
14	Cyprus	5,633	2,210
15	Jordan	3,924	3,244
16	Malta	2,342	1,190

Source: Alfred Tovias, 'The Mediterranean Economy', in P. Ludlow (ed.) *Europe and the Mediterranean*, Brussels, Brassey's, 1994

But despite France's quasi-hegemonic role in the region, it has not produced the institutional stability provided by GATT, IMF or COMECON. In the light of emerging European military and political cooperation, the so-called European security and defence identity (ESDI), the EU – or at least its Mediterranean members – might take on an increasing share of the hegemonic role hitherto played by France in the Mediterranean. An early foreshadowing of this was given by the Commission in 1989 when it argued: 'The Community is aware of its responsibility as the dominant economic and political power in the area.'[27]

Arriving at the global Mediterranean policy

As noted on p. 79, some links between the Community and the Mediterranean region date back to the Treaty of Rome. The first set of Mediterranean agreements were concluded with aspiring members of the Community in the early 1960s. Greece in 1962 and then Turkey in 1963 signed association agreements with the Community. (Greece was admitted to the Community in 1981, but Turkey which applied formally in 1992 is still waiting.) Following this, Morocco and Tunisia approached the Community for an agreement in 1963, but not until six years later were bilateral preferential trade agreements signed with these two countries. The Community granted preferential access to Israeli and Spanish citrus fruit exports in 1969 and followed this the next year with preferential trade agreements.

In the wake of these latter two controversial agreements (Spain was still a dictatorship and Israel was anathema to pro-Arab interests), the Community offered to give favourable consideration in principle to other Mediterranean applicants for similar agreements. This offer led the Community into an 'explosion' of agreements with Egypt, Lebanon, Jordan, Syria, Malta, and Cyprus, and Yugoslavia.[28] By 1973 the Community had signed agreements with seventeen Mediterranean states.

This proliferation of agreements, which had started slowly in 1962, effectively concentrated minds within the Community. In 1971 the Community had a 'low-key' approach to the Mediterranean, but it began to see the Mediterranean basin as more important, 'as a natural extension of European integration'.[29] That is, the Mediterranean became more important as the troublesome nature of the agreements that the Community had signed became apparent. Some countries received much less favourable treatment than others; the agreements also overlapped in time so that they would have to be constantly renegotiated. The introduction of the Generalized System of Preferences in 1971, the general reductions of tariffs under the GATT rounds, and the prospect of preferences to be accorded to Commonwealth countries after the accession of the UK seemed also to jeopardize the value of these agreements.

By late 1972 the European Commission proposed a reorganization of the bilateral network into a 'Global Mediterranean Policy' (GMP). The Community's heads of state and government discovered at their Paris summit in the same year that the Mediterranean agreements were of vital importance to the Community and should be put on a consistent basis. The 'overall approach' to the Mediterranean comprised compliance with GATT rules, consistency among the agreements, and non-discrimination towards neighbouring countries.

It is tempting to remark that just as the Holy Roman Empire was neither holy, Roman nor an empire, the Global Mediterranean Policy was not global and not even fully Mediterranean (it excluded Albania and Libya). Furthermore, the GMP developed more as a reaction to events than as a policy.

The first-generation Mediterranean agreements ran into many problems over trade. In particular, exports of agricultural products, textiles and processed foods, and restrictive rules of origin were troublesome (although international limitations on the exports of textiles from East Asia may have worked to the benefit of Mediterranean exporters in practice). The effects of the preferences on trade were limited.[30] From 1960 to 1971 total Mediterranean exports to the Community grew by a substantial 250 per cent, while agricultural exports increased by a mere 39 per cent – held back by the Community's restrictive Common Agricultural Policy (CAP).[31]

The Global Mediterranean Policy was designed to improve on this record. It was supposed to create a free trade area in industrial goods between the Community and each Mediterranean country by 1977, except for 'sensitive products'. And it has been argued that the successful industrial development policies of Tunisia were based on the expectations created by the GMP. The Community would also give preferential treatment to 80 per cent of each Mediterranean country's agricultural exports. But in practice the Community's own intractable agricultural problems made any real concessions difficult. The Community took unilateral action against Mediterranean exports such as tomatoes when these seemed to threaten its interests.

The Community originally wanted the Mediterranean countries to accord it trade preferences in return for the GMP. But the USA disliked the European desire for reverse preferences from the Mediterranean states, seeing this as a 'sewing up' of markets. Owing to UK, German and Dutch influence, along with US pressure, reciprocity was abandoned. Finally, the GMP offered financial aid and the prospect of a common approach to immigrant labour.

Negotiations under the GMP framework began in 1974 and culminated in a series of new agreements of unlimited duration, starting with Israel in 1975. But despite its good intentions the results of the GMP were not too different from those of the preceding piecemeal agreements. The disbursement of aid has been useful to the recipients, if not on a scale comparable to the Lomé Convention.

But the value of the trade preferences was again disappointing. Most of the Mediterranean states continued to import more from the Community than they were able to export to it. The margin of preference was eroded as other 'non-associated' developing countries received preferences, the Common Agricultural Policy maintained its protectionist profile and the export of sensitive goods such as textiles continued to be restrained by the Community.

As Greece, Portugal and Spain joined the Community in the 1980s, their exports entered the Community duty-free, while competing countries became worse off. Mediterranean countries' exports of wine, olive oil, citrus fruits and other agricultural products suffered as these three countries took over a large proportion of the Community market. Special arrangements with the Community produced few benefits for Mediterranean countries. The preferential relationship of the Mediterranean countries and Europe was eroded until the 'GMP would soon be giving them a preferential share of nothing'.[32] Moreover, the North Africans were disillusioned with Community threats of restricting migrant workers' entry to the Community, but the prospect of the single market in 1992 did not greatly affect them.

The European Commission was unusually frank in admitting that its 'voluntary' restraints on textile exports, and problems in agricultural trade fell short of what had been envisioned under the GMP: 'the Community has lost some of the credibilty it had previously acquired among its Mediterranean partners. It has ceased to be a source of growth and hope and become an uncertain factor in their development strategies.'[33]

The uncertainty about Community–Mediterranean relations extended beyond the ostensibly economic agreements into the political sphere. After the 1973 oil crisis, in December of that year, the Arab states informed the Community that they wished to expand their cooperative relations with it in all fields on a long-term basis.

However, the development of this relationship has been less than encouraging. Following the first meeting in Cairo in 1975, a joint memorandum was issued and working groups established. After a few more meetings in 1976–8, the Arabs requested that the dialogue be suspended following the Camp David agreements between Egypt and Israel. Abortive attempts to re-start the dialogue were made in December 1983, and June 1988. President Ben Ali of Tunisia called for the revival of the Euro-Arab dialogue in a speech to the European Parliament in June 1993, but further progress remains elusive. The Euro-Arab dialogue is widely seen as in limbo, moribund or dead.

The two sides differed in both their aims and their abilities to pursue them. The Arab League wanted a political dialogue, aimed at influencing European views on the Middle East. The Arab side was weakened by internal divisions. The Community wanted a more economically-based dialogue, leaving issues of 'high' politics to national governments. Thus, the two sides unfortunately ended up having nothing to discuss. Moreover, without US participation, the dialogue also lacked a crucial element.

Following the Gulf War, the Middle East peace process was established in 1991. This conference has been chaired jointly by the USA and the EU. In September 1993, Israel and the Palestinian Liberation Organization signed peace accords in Washington, raising hopes for a wider settlement to follow. Compared to the relative success of this process, the Euro-Arab dialogue looks ineffectual and unlikely to be revived.

The New Mediterranean Policy

The European Council adopted a new framework for relations with the Mediterranean countries in December 1989. In 1990 and 1991 new protocols were signed which incorporated the Union's free market approach to economic development and its support for International Monetary Fund and World Bank policies. The New Mediterranean Policy (NMP) offered 4,405 million ecus in grants and loans over five years to eight Mediterranean countries. Just over half of the aid was allocated to Morocco, Algeria and Tunisia. (However, in mid-1995, France, frustrated by the Algerian civil war, was preparing to cut back its annual aid to that country by 17 per cent.) These funds were to be spent: in support of structural adjustment; to encourage private investment; to increase bilateral and Community financial aid; to facilitate access to the European market; to encourage involvement with progress towards the single European market; to strenthen economic and political dialogue, where possible at the regional level. The New (or Renovated) Mediterranean Policy states its support for economic reform, but its support for political reform is implicit. The enormous increase in aid to Israel (see Table 3.3) is not unrelated to Israel's support for the UN forces in the Gulf War.

Despite its substantial increase in resources (2.7 times greater

Table 3.3 EU aid to the Maghreb, the Mashreq and Israel (ecus per caput)

	1989	1990	1991
The Maghreb			
Libya	1.41	1.31	0.40
Mauritania	67.72	37.33	40.40
Morocco	10.91	12.07	14.54
Algeria	3.00	5.03	7.73
Tunisia	18.99	22.86	29.48
The Mashreq			
Syria	5.32	4.00	8.54
Jordan	14.55	52.39	39.64
Lebanon	18.23	14.28	9.80
Egypt	7.08	10.21	8.41
Israel	21.20	26.95	88.59

Source: Eurostat, Luxembourg, 1994

than the previous protocol) and its more coherent statement of objectives, the NMP still strongly resembles its predecessor. Strict controls on agricultural and textile exports remain in place. The NMP shows, if anything, a shift in power towards a more self-confident Europe. Europe has increased its aid to the region and developed a more coherent picture of the types of economies and polities it wishes to support there.

Euro-Mediterranean relations after Barcelona

The Barcelona Conference of November 1995 brought together 15 EU member states with 11 Mediterranean countries and the Palestinian governing authority. As a reminder of its leading role in the Middle East peace process, the USA was present as an observer. The Conference was designed to be the first step towards a 'Euro-Mediterranean partnership' spanning the region.

The success of the Conference in continuing and producing the 'Barcelona Declaration' was considerable. The political differences between many of the participants such as Syria, Israel, Turkey, Morocco and Spain had to be held in abeyance during the Conference. The Barcelona Declaration called for a regular political dialogue among the signatories, greater EU aid to the southern Mediterranean states (4.685 billion ecus up to the end of 1999), and the control of migration, crime and drugs. It also referred to nuclear non-proliferation, anti-terrorism and self-determination. But potentially most innovative and significant in the medium term is the plan for free trade in industrial products (only) by the year 2010.

Currently, about 10 per cent of EU trade is with the southern Mediterranean region. This could increase, but free trade in industrial products is likely to benefit European exporters more than Mediterranean ones. The EU estimated that 4,000 Tunisian enterprises could be seriously damaged by this free trade regime,[34] while UK consultants predicted that 40 per cent of Morocco's industry would suffer.

Southern Mediterranean commentators have pointed out additional flaws in the Barcelona process. Just as the Euro-Arab dialogue of the 1970s was derailed by questions of terrorism, self-determination, repatriation of immigrants and nuclear proliferation in the region, these subjects could destroy the new dialogue.[35] The Barcelona process was initiated and guided by Europe, which still has a modernist development project on its agenda. Instead of a shared, Euro-Mediterranean vision of cooperation in the region, Barcelona produced a European vision. Criticisms of the leading role of the European Commission, and of the Barcelona pact's imitation of the Balladur pact on stability in Europe – but with fewer resources and less institutional support – have similarly been expressed.

To some in the southern Mediterranean, the Barcelona Declaration was no more than a 'fool's bargain' because it did not provide for free access into Europe for the region's agricultural exports or for the industrial development of the area. Even the aid provided under the Barcelona Declaration appeared limited: in 1994 the EU gave 1 billion ecus in aid to Central and Eastern Europe, compared to 407 million ecus for the Mediterranean countries. A long-running fishing dispute between the EU and Morocco was resolved just before the Barcelona Conference. Morocco had asked for a 50 per cent reduction in Spanish catches in Moroccan waters, but settled for a 25 per cent reduction. As part of the agreement, the EU cut its duty on Moroccan sardines by 1 per cent. When a senior UK official described the fisheries agreement, he observed that the EU had been 'conservative in its generosity' towards the southern Mediterranean countries.

The political problems of the Mediterranean region have already spilled over into the Barcelona process. In May 1996

Greece threatened to obstruct the aid package for the Mediterranean countries as part of its territorial dispute with Turkey.
Greece finally accepted that the aid programme could go ahead,
but indicated that it would still veto aid for Turkey.

Despite the ringing declarations by the Spanish prime minister
and French foreign minster at the Barcelona Conference that a
new era in history was dawning, the non-Mediterranean EU
members such as Germany and the UK remain unconvinced of
the importance of Mediterranean cooperation. Such optimistic
pronouncements are reminiscent of those at the signing of Lomé
I in 1975 that a new partnership between Europe and Africa was
taking shape. More than twenty years later, Europe's attention
has turned away from Lomé and towards the Mediterranean (see
Chapter 4). Whether Europe now has the political determination
and the economic generosity to support the Mediterranean region
during its long transition period to peace and prosperity remains
to be seen.

MOROCCO AND THE EU

As early as 1984 Morocco took a radical approach to its relations
with the Community. It decided that cooperation and trade agreements were not enough. As more Mediterranean countries such
as Greece, Spain and Portugal gained entry to the Community,
their products and their nationals received better treatment than
those of outside countries.

The Moroccan minister concerned with the first entry application, Azeddin Ghessous, was particularly concerned over the
reduction of Community import quotas for citrus fruit and other
products, as well as the second-class staus of more than a million
Moroccans resident in the Community. He argued:

> How can Europe not include Morocco? Spain is only fourteen
> kilometres away. The southern standard of living in the Medit-
> erranean cannot suffer because of the north. In classical terms
> this is a setting for war. How can you make one of the great
> corridors of commerce of history into a barrier, a fortification?
> This could result in conflict.[36]

In 1987 King Hassan II wrote to the Danish president of
the Community Council of Ministers, formally applying to join the
European Community. The reaction, as with the earlier approach,

was cold, even colder than the reception of Turkey's application. In 1984 Brussels treated the application as a joke, much to the mortification of the Moroccans. David Buchan's description of the reception of the 1987 approach was that 'no one in Brussels knew whether to laugh or cry'.[37] While this is no doubt an accurate account of the reaction, it shows a poor quality of decision-making in the Community. Instead of laughing or crying – symptoms of bad decision-making, or groupthink – the Community would have done better to consider the costs and benefits of the application more open-mindedly.

Despite the Community's initial reserve, Morocco's approaches to Europe have borne some fruit. In February 1992 Morocco began a new dialogue with the Community, and Tunisia followed suit with discussions on a *partenariat euro-maghrebin* in May. By November 1992 France announced a new partnership with Morocco. Morocco held relatively fair elections in 1993, and Commission President Delors visited the country in the same year, demonstrating an improved relationship. By December 1993 the European Council of Ministers announced a 'political gesture' from the Community towards Morocco. Morocco would engage in an institutional dialogue at the ministerial, senior official, and parliamentary levels as well as in contacts with the Economic and Social Committee of the EU. Based on 'reciprocity and common interests' the plan is to create a new agreement including the eventual removal of all customs duties from Community industrial products imported into Morocco. Morocco would retain the right to protect sensitive sectors or infant industries and would be allowed to export greater quantities (3 per cent a year for five years) of its quota-limited products to the Community. The possiblity of reciprocal free trade in agriculture for a five-year period is also under consideration. Financial help for Morocco involving EU aid, aid from EU member states and private investment is also being negotiated. This is not yet a Euro-Maghreb partnership, but at least it may be a start to greater cooperation.

THE UNION OF THE ARAB MAGHREB

The idea of a *grand maghreb* dates back to the lost unity of the medieval North African Almohad dynasty. Twentieth-century independence movements also received inspiration from this past unity. The continuing vitality of the *grand maghreb* idea was demonstrated in 1958 when the principal North African liberation movements met in Tangier to affirm their commitment to a common future and to the cause of Algeria's liberation.

Further efforts to put flesh on the ideal of Maghreb in unity were made through the Permanent Consultative Committee of the Maghreb from 1964 until 1975 when the parties' conflicting views over the Western Sahara ended these meetings.[38] Yves Boyer attributed the foundation of the Union of the Arab Maghreb (UMA) to a process initiated by France in 1983, in keeping with its quasi-hegemonic role mentioned earlier.[39] It was a combination of the historical ties among the Arabs and their political aspirations, the diplomacy of France, and the geopolitical challenge of creating a union with the ability to match the Europeans' integration (a challenge also perceived by other regions) which led to the formation of the UMA.

In 1988 the first pan-Maghreb summit since independence which united Morocco, Libya, Algeria, Tunisia and Mauritania took place in Algiers. The result of the summit was that a Maghreb High Commission was established. Following a series of meetings of its sub-committees, the High Commission drew up a Treaty of Union in 1989. Wounds over Western Sahara were smoothed over as King Hassan II received a delegation from Polisario, an organization seeking the independence of the Western Sahara (now controlled by Morocco), in early 1989 and the President of Algeria officially visited Morocco.

In February 1989 the five presidents signed the Treaty of the Union of the Arab Maghreb which seemed to signal a real desire to cooperate and an historic turning point.[40] However, the new UMA ran into problems almost immediately. At the Algiers summit of 1990 a seat for the secretariat could not be agreed. The Gulf crisis saw the five countries adopt radically different positions at the Cairo summit, ranging from opposing a resolution condemning Iraq (Libya) to supporting the resolution and sending troops to Saudi Arabia (Morocco).

Despite the internal problems of the UMA, it briefly participated in a wider dialogue with Europe. The '4 + 5' dialogue included France, Italy, Spain and Portugal plus the five UMA members. In 1991 Malta also joined the European side, making a dialogue of 5 + 5. The group held two summits in Rome in 1990, and one in Algiers in 1991. Discussions covered cooperation, the development of regional financial organizations, self-sufficiency in food, anti-desertification measures, migration, cultural dialogue, transport and communication, technology and the environment. But after 1991 the pace of cooperation slowed as political problems over Libya's involvement in the Lockerbie bombing and Algeria's struggle with religious fundamentalism impeded progress.

Up to the present the contacts between the EU countries and the Maghreb (15 + 5) have been limited. Several reasons can be found for this. One is the northern Europeans' general lack of interest in the Maghreb. Another is their neglect of the UMA or lack of faith in its future. There is also the apparent desire of France to keep the politics of North Africa as a *domaine réservé* to itself.

The objectives and prospects of the UMA

The treaty which united Algeria, Libya, Mauritania, Morocco and Tunisia in the Union of the Arab Maghreb had extensive and ambitious objectives. These included:

- to achieve economic integration;
- to remove trade barriers;
- to create a regional common market by the year 2000;
- to achieve better relations with Europe;
- to diffuse regional tension;
- to set up transport links and common institutions such as a joint consultative parliament, an investment bank and an airline.

Morocco's King Hassan II stated that the ultimate objective 'is to turn the Arab Maghreb into one country, with one passport, one identity, and a single currency'.[41]

Many objections can be raised as to the viability of the UMA enterprise. The UMA has been criticized for including too many countries, notably Mauritania. But most of the UMA's political problems have originated in other, more radical members. Mauritania's involvement with Morocco in the Western Sahara issue makes it a desirable participant in any pan-Maghreb organization.

It has also been observed that the Maghreb is not a viable economic unit. Although the five countries have a substantial population of 60 millions, 3.5 per cent of the world's oil, 3.8 per cent of its natural gas, and 75 per cent of its phosphates, their economies are weak. Most of the North Africans' products are competitive rather than complementary and intra-UMA trade comprises only about 3 per cent of the members' foreign trade. Trade with Community is around 70 per cent of the external trade of the UMA, making cooperation with the EU arguably a more important objective than regional integration. By contrast, when the Community was founded in the late 1950s its internal trade accounted for around 40 per cent of its total foreign trade. Moreover, the members' relative wealth is very different, ranging from Libya's per caput GNP of $US5,310 to Mauritania's of just $US500.[42]

Although the UMA might not immediately seem to have the potential for prosperous unification which had been present in the Community, nevertheless greater integration could produce significant benefits. Increasing trade, political cooperation and stability are attractive in a region where fundamentalist religious challenge is strong, and even wars such as the short Moroccan–Algerian war of 1963 are possible. For EU companies anxious to avail themselves of North African labour costs which are a quarter of those in the EU, the UMA is also a bonus. Reducing tariffs between the Maghreb countries would boost their trade.

Since the 1980s the Maghreb countries have pursued more similar, liberal economic policies, following the early example of Tunisia. From the mid-1980s they have adjusted with the IMF and liberalized their trade under GATT. For Tunisia and Morocco their record of economic growth has been positive: for Tunisia economic growth in 1992 was 8.6 per cent while for Morocco it was a lower but respectable 2.3 per cent, outstripping both Germany and Japan. During 1980–92 Tunisian trade grew at an annual rate of 5 per cent and Moroccan trade by 4 per cent. The picture was less favourable for oil-exporters Algeria and Libya whose trade fell by 2 per cent and 6 per cent respectively over the same period. Mauritania, a least developed country, lost 2 per cent of its merchandise trade over the decade 1980–90 (GATT figures).

Up to the present the UMA has little to show for itself. Richard Pomfret argued that the UMA was almost entirely symbolic.[43] What could be debated is whether it is symbolic of the Maghreb countries' positive desire to cooperate or of their failure to do so. The economic benefits that were foreseen have not materialized and its political problems have so far kept the UMA from making much progress. In early February 1993 President Ben Ali of Tunisia proposed a relaunching of the UMA. However, by the end of the month differences between Morocco and Algeria made relations difficult and a 'pause' in the UMA was agreed.

The politics of the Maghreb and the southern Mediterranean as a whole have been volatile in the post-war period. In view of the dearth of organizations linking the two shores of the Mediterranean basin, Europe should support any efforts at regional integration which, like the 5 + 5 process, may lead to greater stability and inter-regional cooperation. However, the UMA may prove as impermanent as the Permanent Consultative Committee of the 1960s and 1970s. A senior Moroccan official opined in 1993 that in view of divisive political problems, 'There is no Maghreb.' This may be the case in practical terms as North African states look for vertical accords with the EU rather than horizontal ones with their neighbours, but the pan-Maghreb inspiration – and indeed the Mediterranean ideal – is not yet finished.

THE MEDITERRANEAN ENVIRONMENT

One of the main trends of the late twentieth century is the growth of environmental awareness in governments, international organizations and populations. In the wake of the UN Conference on the Human Environment (1972) and the Rio 'Earth Summit' in 1992, protecting the environment is a subject which seems to be on everybody's lips, if not on everybody's political platform. In terms of environmental awareness, the gap between the views of the developed and developing countries has diminished.[44] The EU too shares in the growth of environmentalism. A *Eurobarometer* survey of public opinion in the twelve Community states in 1992 revealed that 85 per cent of respondents considered environmental issues 'an immediate and urgent problem' while only 2 per cent felt that they were 'not really a problem'.[45]

The Community has argued that the external and internal dimensions of environmental issues are inextricably linked. To the European Commission, the cross-border nature of pollution makes it a suitable subject for Community rather than national regulation. The 1957 Treaty of Rome did not explicitly deal with environmental issues, but since the 1970s the Community has expanded its legal competence on environmental issues through judicial cases, internal rules and mixed agreements. The Community has put forward some 280 legal regulations covering pollution of the soil, of air and of water; noise levels; waste disposal; product standards; and nature conservation. In addition, the Single European Act of 1986 and the Maastricht Treaty on European Union of 1992 have given the Community expanded powers in this area.

A clear commitment to environmental standards was issued at the Community's Dublin summit in June 1990. Heads of state and government stated: 'We recognize our special responsibility for the environment, both to our own citizens and to the wider world. We undertake to intensify our efforts to protect and enhance the natural environment of the Community itself and the world of which it is part.' They also committed themselves to developing measures which would guarantee their citizens 'the right to a clean and healthy environment'. For millions of European citizens, this includes cleaning up the Mediterranean Sea and shore.

From 1990 the EU tried to establish a European Environment Agency (EEA) to supply reliable data on the state of the air, water, soil, flora, fauna, coasts, waste disposal, noise, and toxic wastes of Europe.[46] The European Council finally decided in 1993 to establish the agency in Copenhagen, with a staff numbering about fifty. As well as the EEA, the Community has established a series of environmental action programmes. The current, or fifth, is called 'Towards Sustainability'. It runs from 1993 to 2000 and has as its main goal raising public awareness about environmental problems and changing behaviour. How successful this programme will be in practice remains to be seen: governments such as the UK's continue to be reluctant environmentalists and countries such as Italy have a better reputation for passing environmental legislation than for implementing it.

The way in which the environmental commitment of the Community and the other Mediterranean states has affected the management of the Mediterranean Sea is an interesting case. It sheds light on both environmental issues and the problematique of Mediterranean cooperation. To Peter Haas, the international environmental programme for the Mediterranean (Med Plan),

> which was developed under the auspices of the United Nations Environment Programme (UNEP), is widely acclaimed as the most successful example of international environmental collab-

oration, and serves as a model for arrangements for nine other regional seas in which over 130 states, sixteen United Nations agencies, and forty other international organizations take part.[47]

The condition of the Mediterranean, though still badly polluted, has improved since Lord Ritchie-Calder warned in 1972 that the sea could shortly become a biological time-bomb, a danger to humans and surrounding trees.[48] In 1978 over 80 per cent of municipal sewage discharged into the Mediterranean was untreated; swimmers had a one-in-seven chance of contracting a disease from the sea. Most of the pollution came from the developed states of France, Italy and Spain.

To remedy these widely perceived but incompletely documented pollution problems, sixteen Mediterranean countries signed the ambitious Mediterranean Action Plan (Med Plan) in 1975. The objectives of the Med Plan were basically to combat pollution and to protect the marine environment. To these ends the Med Plan called for four main areas of activity: regional treaties; coordinated research and monitoring activities; integrated planning; and administrative and budgetary support. The aim of saving the Mediterranean environment was further bolstered by the Barcelona Convention of 1976 on protecting the Mediterranean Sea as well as many subsequent measures. From a loose framework, the Med Plan developed into a set of specific controls of land, air and riverine pollution by the mid-1980s.

Results flowed quickly from the Mediterranean Action Plan. These included studies of the environment, protocols banning marine dumping and those promoting cooperation in dealing with oil spills. Most notably, the Land-Based Sources [of pollution] Protocol of 1980 restricted industrial, municipal and agricultural discharges into the Mediterranean. Although land-based sources are estimated to account for 70 per cent of marine pollution, there is still no such agreement at the global level. Neither has regional environmental cooperation in the Arabian Gulf been as productive so far as in the Mediterranean.[49]

Within the Med Plan system, the least successful area was the most ambitious one: integrated management. Known as the Blue Plan, integrated management was supposed to construct a variety of possible futures for the Mediterranean region which would inform the decisions of national planners. Inter-disciplinary studies involving everything from fishing, human migration and health to industrialization and tourism culminated in a report in 1988. The plan was not well understood by or popular with officials other than its French originators. More concrete projects were of more interest to Mediterranean governments.

But despite such problems within the system, and the fact that the Mediterranean is still heavily polluted, there is little doubt that the Med Plan made the Mediterranean a cleaner region than it would otherwise have been. Under its auspices sewage plants were constructed, pollution in rivers such as the Rhône was reduced, and national environmental ministries were established.

Haas found that the unexpectedly cooperative behaviour of the Mediterranean states differed markedly from the mutually competitive and antagonistic style of behaviour predicted by the neo-realist school of international relations. He attributed this cooperation to penetration by the epistemic community (of like-minded scientists) into decision-making at national level and in the United Nations Environment Programme (UNEP). But in his excellent study Haas neglects one important aspect of environmental cooperation in the Mediterranean region. It was not only the weight of environmental scientists' arguments but also the shared experience of thousands of years of the Mediterranean community which facilitated cooperative action. Where an issue-area can be shown to coincide with the aspiration to Mediterranean unity – the Mediterranean ideal discussed above – without challenging entrenched national viewpoints, it faces a reasonably high chance of success. Because the environment is an area where southern and northern littoral states had no tradition of opposing each other or defining some states as 'other', they were able to cooperate effectively. The epistemic community, of course, played an important role in tapping or mobilizing this underlying and enabling Mediterranean culture, especially by proclaiming that the much-cherished Mediterranean Sea was dying. But the idea that the epistemic community sucessfully imposed new interests on old states seems wrong; instead it successfully appealed to the states' shared interests in 'mare nostrum'.[50]

But whatever the basis for the environmental progress which the Mediterranean region has made in the past two decades with the help of bodies such as UNEP, this progress has contributed to an *acquis Méditerranéen*, the shared knowledge, experience and accepted working practices of the Mediterranean community. The enhanced *acquis Méditerranéen* can in turn

Table 3.4 Major destination countries of migration (thousands of persons per year)

Destination	Estimates 1985–90	Projections 1990–95	Projections 1995–2000	Origin	Estimates 1985–90	Projections 1990–95	Projections 1995–2000
USA	580	560	550	Mexico	150	150	150
Australia	122	127	102	Philippines	58	58	58
Canada	74	70	68	Lebanon	55	32	16
Saudi Arabia	65	45	30	China	55	51	50
Ivory Coast	59	39	30	Pakistan	51	32	16
France	21	16	14	India	50	50	50
UAE	20	10	5	El Salvador	42	35	30
Hong Kong	15	14	14	Columbia	40	36	25
Kuwait	14	11	8	Sri Lanka	38	36	34
Germany*	10	8	6	South Korea	35	35	35
Netherlands	10	8	6				

Source: G. Gomel 'Migrations Toward Western Europe', *USA International Spectator* 27, April–June, 1992
* Not including refugees from former East Germany 1989–90

contribute to the foundations of further areas of cooperation in the region.

MIGRATION

Whereas the Mediterranean countries have been reasonably successful in recognizing that the Mediterranean Sea is a shared resource, the same realization has not dawned on the northern shore with respect to the human capital of the region. Indeed, human migration in the Mediterranean region is a source of nightmares for many European policy-makers.

Countries of southern Europe such as Italy, Greece, Spain and Portugal were traditionally countries of emigration. But since the 1970s they have become countries of immigration. Ireland alone in Western Europe in the 1990s remains a sending country. Although the world's main receiving countries are outside of Europe (i.e. the USA, Australia, Canada and Saudi Arabia), Western Europe's annual intake of immigrants from Eastern Europe rose dramatically from around 100,000 during the 1970s and 1980s up to 1.2 million in 1989, as over half a million refugees from the Yugoslav civil war added to numbers. But by 1993 applications for asylum were dropping.[51] According to the European Commission, only 2.5 per cent of the population of the Community in 1991 were immigrants. World Bank projections show that immigration to major receiving countries is likely to decline by the year 2000 (see Table 3.4).

Although immigration flows to the Community as a whole so far have been modest, the fear of 'the threat of a sudden influx' of immigrants from Eastern Europe, and especially from the southern Mediterranean is real.[52] The demographic trends in the Mediterranean region indicate that substantial changes are under way. In 1950 two-thirds of the region's population lived on the northern side, but by 1990 the majority lived in the south. With continuing growth, by the year 2025, two-thirds will live in the south.[53] These trends could not only increase unemployment and poverty in the southern Mediterranean but also lead to uncontrollably large cities and shortages of vital commodities such as water there.

Even development aid has been enlisted as a tool to prevent immigration. The European Commission's 'Horizon 2000' document, which outlined its development cooperation strategy following the Maastricht Treaty, was clear about the Community's fear of Mediterranean immigration: 'Mediterranean – here the major problems are political, environmental and social (emigration). Aid should be increased and refocused on family planning programmes.'[54] Another European Commission publication likewise argued that 'Improving the economic position of developing countries is one of the ways of easing migratory pressure.'[55] It went on to note that the Lomé Convention, the New Mediterranean Policy, the Phare programme for Central and Eastern Europe, cooperation agreements with Latin American and Asian countries, and emergency aid were instruments of this migration-prevention policy.

The chief objections to using development aid as a tool for preventing migration are two-fold. The moral case is that aid should be used to benefit the recipients, not for the benefit of the social policies of the donor.[56] The other objection is practical: it will not work. As David Buchan put it, 'It is an illusion to believe that people in the South can be paid to stop them coming to the North.'[57] Despite the lack of evidence for the proposition that European development policies can successfully stem the tide of southern Mediterranean immigration, a great deal of attention has been given to considering what changes in the south would prevent emigration to the north. As well as family planning on the southern shore, such changes include:[58]

- Political measures, such as making aid more conditional on human rights, with the effect that southern countries would treat dissenting views more tolerantly. Dissidents would then have less incentive to emigrate.
- Economic measures such as (a) reducing income differentials of the north and south, (b) stimulating employment in the south by investing in labour-intensive industries, (c) opening Europe's markets to labour-intensive manufactures and agricultural products in order to create jobs in the south, (d) and pressuring southern countries to open their markets to imports to prevent shortages from driving emigration.

What is not explicitly stated is why Europe does not want more immigrants – especially as this free movement of labour could be of economic benefit. Europe worries about its own ageing population and declining fertility rate, but sees immigration of young persons from the southern Mediterranean as an unacceptable solution. The European policy of closing its doors to immigration while at the same time better integrating existing immigrants is self-contradictory. People who are deemed undesirable as immigrants for reasons of national origin are not suddenly transformed through the possession of a passport into first-class EU citizens. If, for instance, Somali refugees are excluded as immigrants, it requires an excessive leap of faith to imagine that legally-resident Somalis will not also be regarded by the European public as similarly undesirable.

The prospect of increased migration from the southern to the northern shore of the Mediterranean is frequently referred to by Commission officials, politicians and academics as a 'threat', a 'population bomb' or 'time bomb'. These latter phrases particularly hark back to the influential 1968 book by Paul Ehrlichs, *The Population Bomb*. But it is worth recalling that this book had significant racist and sexist undertones, and that its predictions that hundreds of millions of people would starve during the 1970s and 1980s proved wrong.[59] UNICEF, for example, found that in the last decade human fertility in most countries has fallen dramatically. In fact, the 'steepness of these falls in fertility is unprecedented in demographic history.'[60] Algeria, Tunisia and Morocco experienced an average decline of more than one child per woman between 1980 and 1991.

Europe's policy towards immigration from the Mediterranean

may be wrong on several counts. Population growth in that region may naturally decline as development increases, reducing the 'push' towards Europe. Europe's efforts in family planning and economic development in the service of reducing demographic growth may be ineffective. By excluding would-be immigrants from the Mediterranean, Europe may be missing out on a resource as well as avoiding a 'threat'. Finally, Europe may be repeating the mistakes of the USA in the 1960s and 1970s. For example, UK aid policy's emphasis on 'children by choice, not chance' in the developing world may be intended to benefit and empower women, but may have the opposite effects.[61]

Jaquette and Staudt found that the US aid programme's goal of giving women in developing countries more control over their reproduction was right, but in practice was not achieved. Power was given to developing countries' governments and the medical profession, not to women. Women were in fact manipulated to meet reproductive targets that were established without consulting them. They were not empowered to make their own decisions.

Traditionally, human migration has been an area of 'low politics'. It has been of more interest to demographers and geographers than to political scientists. The subject seemed particularly diffuse and difficult to understand in terms of social science.[62] However, more interest in the political and international relations aspects of migration is now developing. Migration in the Mediterranean and from Haiti and Cuba to the USA is taking on particular political salience. Studies of immigration have been undertaken at the Institute for Strategic Studies (London), the Institut Français des Relations Internationales (Paris), and the Royal Institute of International Affairs (London), among others.

It is to be hoped that better social scientific understanding of the subject of immigration will feed into a better European policy. Building up a 'fortress Europe' against immigrants is an unimaginative response. Using aid policy to meddle in developing countries with the objective of pre-empting emigration is a risky policy. It risks both failing to achieve its objective and appearing inhumane.

THE CONFERENCE ON SECURITY AND COOPERATION IN THE MEDITERRANEAN

It has recently been fashionable to ask whether the Mediterranean Sea constitutes a bridge or a barrier between the two shores. Adda Bozeman rightly considered that this formulation was too simple: the Mediterranean Sea has always been both.

> Southern Europeans gained a profound understanding of the Mediterranean Sea and its geographic function on the one hand as an irreversible link between Europe, Asia, and Africa, and on the other as a lasting divide between the numerous, strikingly divergent cultures and political systems that evolved on the edges of these three continents. Further, they were persuaded in the course of 800 well-chronicled years of close co-existence with various Islamic groups on both land and sea that while mutually tolerable, even agreeable terms of accommodation are possible in social and intellectual matters, Christianity and Islam are indeed antipodes when it comes to conceptions of political organization and warfare.[63]

Despite these historical divisions, at the end of the twentieth century it is both possible and necessary to build new bridges between the two Mediterranean shores. Trends towards democratization and economic liberalization in North Africa, as well as greater diffusion of Western ideas and greater understanding of Islamic cultures make the present time more amenable to political cooperation in the interests of preventing warfare. The trans-Maghreb gas pipeline to Europe, environmental cooperation, and the proposed 'fixed link' bridge or tunnel between Spain and Morocco are manifestations in practical terms of the benefits of cooperation.

The northern shore of the Mediterranean has a plethora of international institutions. These include the EU, the Conference on Security and Cooperation in Europe, the UN's Economic Commission for Europe, the Council of Europe, and the Western European Union.[64] The southern Mediterranean region has many fewer regional institutions and those which it has, such as the AMU, seem less effective. Furthermore, it could be said that, in lacking institutions which directly link the northern and southern shores, the Mediterranean region has an institutional deficit.

Since its inception in 1975, the Conference on Security and

Cooperation in Europe (CSCE) has had provisions for the involvement of the Mediterranean countries. The Helsinki Declaration's clauses on 'Questions Relating to Security and Cooperation in the Mediterranean' contained provisions for the 'non-participating Mediterranean states' to increase their cooperation with the thirty-five European (including Malta) and North American signatory states. In practice, cooperative relations with the Mediterranean states have expanded, with all non-member Mediterranean states being invited to meetings or parts of meetings specifically devoted to the Mediterranean. Egypt, Morocco, Tunisia and Algeria were invited to contribute to a ministerial CSCE meeting in 1994 at the political level. Israel, too, has indicated strong interest in increasing its links with the CSCE.[65]

Since 1991 the CSCE has admitted ten new member states, including six Asian successor states of the old USSR. This has led to some charges that the CSCE is no longer European but Eurasian.[66] So far, the CSCE has resisted the idea that the Mediterranean states might become full members, considering that it already has its plate full with seemingly insoluble crises such as Yugoslavia and Armenia–Azerbaijan without adding potential conflicts in the Mediterranean region. Turkey, Egypt and Jordan, for instance, have indicated their willingness to go to war over water resources.[67]

In addition, the decision-making process in the CSCE is by consensus among the member states, or in exceptional cases 'consensus minus one'. The existing members are unwilling to let Mediterranean states become full members and have in effect a veto over their activities.

Nevertheless, the increased dialogue between Mediterranean states and the CSCE – including participation in seminars on Human Dimension issues – is to be welcomed. The CSCE has been criticized for being ineffectual and under-resourced, and for lacking its own military force, but few criticize its role in promoting human rights or in disarmament and military confidence-building. The Director of the CSCE Secretariat, Nils Eliasson, has emphasized the success of the CSCE in promoting democracy, human rights and the rule of law in Central and Eastern Europe. Underlining the positive role of the CSCE, the President of Kazakhstan recently proposed the creation of a CSCE-type organization for Central Asia.

An alternative to including the Mediterranean states in the

CSCE was put forward by the Italian and Spanish foreign ministers in 1990. This is known as the Conference on Security and Cooperation in the Mediterranean (CSCM). Spanish Foreign Minister Francisco Fernandez-Ordonez argued that in the post-Cold War era the two shores of the Mediterranean were alarmingly polarized. Economic, religious, cultural and demographic differences were growing. The Mediterranean basin was a potential scene of conflict. A comprehensive system was needed to govern the 'Euro-Mediterranean space'. What was needed was a Conference on Security and Cooperation in the Mediterranean (CSCM), including the Middle East and Gulf states. This organization should cover security, cooperation, human rights, and ecological and trade issues. Its principles would be enshrined in a Mediterranean Act. Only a 'comprehensive system designed to promote the concerted development of all of the countries in the region' would succeed in guaranteeing their peace, security and prosperity.[68]

However laudable its objectives, the CSCM has not yet got off the ground. Italy's political scandals, including the trial of one of the founders of the idea, former Foreign Minister De Michelis, have hampered developments. Countries such as the UK favour the participation of the Mediterranean states in the CSCE but do not see themselves as having any particular interest in a pan-Mediterranean forum. France is unenthusiastic about CSCM, seeing the idea as over-ambitious.

The CSCM proposal is widely considered as moribund or dead. But it does have continuing support, for instance from Tunisia. As CSCE Secretariat Director Nils Eliasson recalled, the CSCE itself took some twenty years to establish.[69] Thus, it may be that the proposal for a Conference on Security and Cooperation in the Mediterranean to remedy the region's institutional deficit will be around for some time to come.

In addition to the proposal for the CSCM, there are other initiatives to enhance Mediterranean regional cooperation. These range from the idea of an Arab–Israeli security community to Egypt's 'Mediterranean Forum' of foreign minsters, to the Treaty for Co-Development and Partnership advocated by Tunisia's President Ben Ali in his speech to the European Parliament in June 1993. Tunisia has also proposed the establishment of a Mediterranean Council, with a permanent secretariat, as a broad forum for increasing dialogue, peace, and security in the region and for discussing transregional projects. The existence of these various plans suggests that there is a need for more cooperation in the Mediterranean basin on many levels.

CONCLUSION

The further enlargement of the EU into the Mediterranean region remains a possibility. The countries of the Mediterranean basin have powerful and ancient ties with Europe. Malta, Cyprus, Turkey and the Maghreb countries of Morocco and Tunisia are seeking stronger links – and even membership of the EU. But in political debates today, the issues of the entry of Eastern and Central Europe into the EU and into NATO figure prominently. The issues of enlargement to the south are less well known.

Up to the present, with the exception of the 1972 accession to the Community of the UK, Eire and Norway (which subsequently twice decided not to join), all of the subsequent enlargements have been Mediterranean. The accession of Greece in 1981, followed by Portugal and Spain in 1986, gave the Community a more Mediterranean outlook as well as considerable problems over agricultural products such as wine and olive oil. After observing that these countries obtained benefits from being inside the Community's external tariff and common agricultural policy, as well as receiving aid from the Community's regional funds, it is only natural that their neighbours, the Mediterranean applicant countries, want the same benefits for themselves.

Turkey has been waiting on the doorstep of Europe since 1963, having made a first formal application to join in 1987. The Commission has not so far accepted that the time is right for Turkish membership. Morocco also applied for Community membership in 1987, but has not been regarded as eligible. Malta and Cyprus applied to join in 1990, and are under consideration. The Commission's opinion on these two states called for Cyprus to resolve the problem of its internal division first and for Malta to institute financial and economic reforms, which it is doing.

To EU decision-makers Turkey seems too large, Malta too small, Cyprus too divided and Morocco too poor and too southerly to qualify for admission. Nevertheless, these countries have a strong desire to participate in the economic prosperity and political stability of the EU. Attempts to create an alternative community of nations on the southern littoral, the Union of the Arab Maghreb, have so far faltered.

Up to now, the EU's most successful relations with Mediterranean countries are with those it has admitted to full membership. Full integration of Spain and Portugal was completed by January 1996. The bilateral agreements with the other Mediterranean countries, including those under the so-called Global Mediterranean Policy and the New Mediterranean Policy, have been less satisfactory. If the Mediterranean region as a whole is to become a zone of prosperity rather than an 'arc of crisis', the EU needs to deal actively and consistently, positively and imaginatively with its Mediterranean neighbours.

Chapter 4

Europe and Africa
The Fourth Lomé Convention

This chapter is a study of the political economy of the fourth
Lomé Convention. It looks at how Lomé IV was negotiated and
the main provisions which were agreed. Next, the results of the
aid and trade cooperation system come under scrutiny. The
chapter then assesses the attitude of the European Commission
to its critics and the outcome of the mid-term review of Lomé
IV. Subsequently, the prevailing view that 'the writing is on the
wall' for the future of the Lomé system is examined. The conclusion argues that the winding-up of the Lomé Convention at
the end of the century is conceivable – even likely – but undesirable. The main accomplishment of the Lomé Convention is the
North–South dialogue it established, not its economic results.

The Lomé Convention is widely regarded as a trade and aid
agreement between the Community and ACP states. In fact,
the Lomé relationship is based upon a political decision by the
contracting parties to cooperate extensively, at levels ranging from
the construction of sewers to the support of import programmes,
from the preservation of ACP antiquities to the protection of
human rights. So wide is the purview of the Convention that an
enthusiastic Community publication proclaimed that it 'includes
all existing ways and means of promoting development'.[1] The
Convention, however, disposes of neither the financial means nor
the institutions to merit this description.

One notable aspect of the Lomé Conventions operating during
the 1980s, Lomé II and III, was their growing obscurity to the
press and the public at large. The signing of the Lomé IV Convention on 15 December 1989 followed this trend and was widely
ignored, for instance, by the UK press. The *Economist*, which
specializes in international news and has reported extensively on

earlier Conventions, signally failed to report anything at all about the fourth Lomé Convention in its December and early January issues.

The Lomé Conventions can be not only obscure but also confusing. Even experts on the Community may misunderstand some fundamentals of the Lomé relationship. Jonathan Story and Guy de Carmoy wrote in their 1993 article 'France and Europe' that 'the European Council presided over the initiation of the Lomé Convention, originally between forty-six former French and British colonies of Africa, the Caribbean and Pacific.'[2] In fact, Lomé was not involved with the European Council, formed in the mid-1970s to further Political Cooperation, but with the Council of Ministers of the European Communities, constituted under the Treaty of Rome.[3]

Neither were the forty-six African, Caribbean and Pacific states solely the ex-colonies of the UK and France; they included non-colonies such as Liberia and Ethiopia and ex-colonies of Portugal and the Netherlands. Story and de Carmoy argued that the Franco-German entente could be found at the centre of the Community's global web of diplomatic and trade relations. In the Lomé case they described, this was untrue: France was at the centre of Lomé but Germany was always a reluctant partner – for instance, even challenging the banana compromise which protected ACP states' interests. Lomé I represented mainly the accommodation of the UK's interests in African and Caribbean Commonwealth states with the interests of the existing African associates of the Community. Lomé was primarily a response to UK membership of the EC, not a development from the Franco-German alliance.[4]

Nevertheless, the first Lomé Convention, signed in 1975, was widely praised and was predicted to be a model for a new era in North–South relations. But in fact this kind of dramatic change never occurred. The 1980s were the decade during which the Lomé agreement, with its extensions in 1980 and 1985, became a convention in the broader sense. That is, the Lomé Convention became more than a legal contract or compact among the participating states and became a usual, customary or conventional, way of organizing the relations among the signatories. The implications of the functioning of the Lomé Convention as a system of international cooperation or 'regime' are discussed in Chapter 5. Within the four successive Lomé Conventions innovations and

THE AFRICAN, CARIBBEAN AND PACIFIC STATES, AND OVERSEAS COUNTRIES AND TERRITORIES

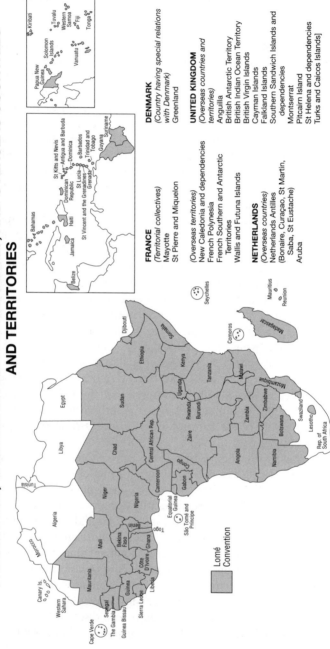

DENMARK
(Country having special relations with Denmark)
Greenland

UNITED KINGDOM
(Overseas countries and territories)
Anguilla
British Antarctic Territory
British Indian Ocean Territory
British Virgin Islands
Cayman Islands
Falkland Islands
Southern Sandwich Islands and dependencies
Montserrat
Pitcairn Island
St Helena and dependencies
Turks and Caicos Islands]

FRANCE
(Territorial collectives)
Mayotte
St Pierre and Miquelon

(Overseas territories)
New Caledonia and dependencies
French Polynesia
French Southern and Antarctic Territories
Wallis and Futuna Islands

NETHERLANDS
(Overseas countries)
Netherlands Antilles
(Bonaire, Curaçao, St Martin, Saba, St Eustache)
Aruba

Lomé Convention

The EU

Austria
Belgium
Denmark
Finland
France
Germany
Greece
Ireland
Italy
Luxembourg
Netherlands
Portugal
Spain
Sweden
United Kingdom

The 70 ACP states

Angola
Antigua & Barbuda
Bahamas
Barbados
Belize
Benin
Botswana
Burkina Faso
Burundi
Cameroon
Cape Verde
Central Africa Republic
Chad
Comoros
Congo
Côte D'Ivoire
Djibouti
Dominica
Dominican Republic
Equatorial Guinea
Eritrea
Ethiopia
Fiji
Gabon

Gambia
Ghana
Grenada
Guinea
Guinea Bissau
Guyana
Haiti
Jamaica
Kenya
Kiribati
Lesotho
Liberia
Madagascar
Malawi
Mali
Mauritania
Mauritius
Mozambique
Namibia
Niger
Nigeria
Papua New Guinea
Rwanda
St Kitts and Nevis

St Lucia
St Vincent and The Grenadines
São Tomé & Príncipe
Senegal
Seychelles
Sierra Leone
Solomon Islands
Somalia
Sudan
Suriname
Swaziland
Tanzania
Togo
Tonga
Trinidad & Tobago
Tuvalu
Uganda
Western Samoa
Vanuatu
Zaire
Zambia
Zimbabwe

Figure 4.1 The Lomé Convention, 1996
Source: European Commission

improvements occurred, but the basic aims of the Conventions and the main methods for achieving them remained unaltered.

NEGOTIATING LOMÉ IV

The negotiations for Lomé IV began officially in October 1988, and were scheduled to conclude by the end of 1989. The negotiations involved the then twelve member states of the European Community and the European Commission, and the sixty-nine African, Caribbean and Pacific countries. The French, holding the presidency of the Community until the end of 1989, were particularly eager to complete the signing of a new Convention during their term of office. They achieved this, with the signing of Lomé IV on 15 December 1989. This allowed the interim arrangements for the period between the expiry of Lomé III on 28 February 1990 and the ratification of Lomé IV to come into force.

The Community entered the Lomé IV negotiations with the view that the new Convention should not represent a major change, but should consolidate and adapt the experience of past Conventions. The main proposals for Lomé IV were made by the European side, with the ACP reacting to them.

As early as the ACP–Community ministerial meeting in June 1989, several texts were agreed for inclusion in the new Convention. The ministers resumed meeting in September and October 1989. But by the end of the October ministerial meeting, the only topics settled were the new ten-year duration of the Convention (replacing the succession of five-year agreements), the accession of new members, and the provisions for the Centre for Industrial Development, for rum, and for toxic waste. Another ministerial meeting was scheduled for November to finalize the text.

The ACP states' demand for 15.5 billion ecus in resources for the Convention was not accepted and the Community finally offered 12 billion ecus (10.8 from the European Development Fund and 1.2 from the European Investment Bank) for the first five years of Lomé IV (see Table 4.1). On 3 December the ACP accepted this and the final texts were prepared. This figure was slightly (4 per cent) less than the 50 per cent increase over Lomé III (8.8 billion ecus) which was widely reckoned to be needed to maintain the real value of aid in the face of inflation and increasing ACP populations, and which had been favoured by the European Commission and widely leaked. But the Community

Table 4.1 EU aid to the ACP countries, 1958–91

Convention (Fund)	Date of entry into force	Number of countries	Total population (millions)	EDF (non-reimbursable aid + special loans, incl. Stabex. Sysmin)	EIB own resources (loans)	Aid per caput (ecus)
Treaty of Rome – Part IV (1st EDF)	1.1.1958	31	55	581		
Yaoundé I (2nd EDF)	1.7.1964	18	69	666	64	10.6
Yaoundé II (3rd EDF)	1.1.1971	19	80	843	90	11.7
Lomé I (4th EDF)	1.4.1976	46	250	3,124	390	14.1
Lomé II (5th EDF)	1.1.1981	57	348	4,754	685	15.6
Lomé III (6th EDF)	1.5.1986	66	413	7,754	1,100	21.4
Lomé IV (7th EDF)	1.9.1991	69	±460	10,800	1,200	26.1

Source: Eurostat, *Europe in Figures*, Brussels and Luxembourg, 1992
Notes:
EDF   European Development Fund
EIB   European Investment Bank
Stabex/Sysmin   see pp. 118, 127–8

states, citing their own economic problems, were inclined to err on the stingy side.

In terms of aid, it was observed that the ACP states failed to produce serious alternative figures or counter-arguments to those of the Community. The usually restrained ACP–European Community *Courier* reported that, 'never since 1973 has there been so much criticism of the technical preparation of the negotiations on the ACP side, except for some subjects such as cultural cooperation and human rights'.[5] Proposals for the ACP Secretariat to take a leading role in a dialogue with the Community about debt were never realized. Indeed the ACP Secretariat was regarded by some analysts as underfunded, demoralized and ineffective.

It was true, as the Wurtz report on the European single market's effects on the ACP states argued, that the ACP countries wanted cooperation and not confrontation with the EC. However, the lack of preparedness to deal with the EC, to challenge it over the complex provisions of the Convention, was not in the ACP states' best interests. This will be seen again in the banana export dispute described on pp. 114–15.

The changes which emerged in Lomé IV were mainly those which the Community wanted, including a new ten-year duration for the Convention, with the funding levels reviewed after five years. The Community had long hankered after a Convention of unlimited duration, partly to address long-term problems such as desertification and rural development, and partly to affirm a political message of alliance. The ten-year duration was a reasonable step in this direction. But, with hindsight, the ACP states would probably have done better to have signed an unlimited Convention. As discussed on pp. 146–8 and in Chapter 5, the political events of 1989 meant that the ACP states would in future have less bargaining power with the Europeans.,

Three new states were admitted to the Convention: Haiti, the Dominican Republic and Namibia (in principle, pending its independence in March 1990). The importance of Namibia to the Community's Africa strategy was underlined by Commissioner Marin. He said in October 1989 that Namibia's accession to Lomé upon independence would be 'automatic'. Of course, an alliance with the Community, as a counterweight to its powerful South African neighbour, and Lomé aid and trade preferences were valuable to the fledgling Namibian government.

Haiti, supported by France, had long wanted to enter Lomé, but its Caribbean location – outside the Community's centre of interest in Africa – and its human rights record stood against it. Problems of smuggling between Haiti and its neighbour on Hispaniola were also cited by the Community as obstacles. The political problems of Haiti soon manifested themselves and the EU cut off aid in 1991 when the elected president was deposed.

However, with the application (encouraged by Spain) of the Dominican Republic (DR) for membership of Lomé, the change of regime in Haiti in 1986 and the approval of the Caribbean Community states, Haiti's membership was agreed. Haiti and the DR were granted a kind of second-class Lomé membership, without participation in the special concessionary trade protocols for sugar, rum or bananas.

The DR's plans to ship bananas to Europe outside of the banana protocol were the cause of considerable arguing among ACP banana exporters. Instead of negotiating with the Community to get more favourable terms or larger quotas for banana exports, it seemed these Caribbean countries argued with each other. Agreeing to share even a tiny proportion of the duty-free banana quota with the DR would have sent a more positive message to Brussels than the outright competition which occurred. The Caribbean exporters finally agreed that the DR could expand dutiable banana exports to parts of Europe outside traditional ACP markets such as the UK.

The whole EU banana import regime came under fire in the wake of the GATT Uruguay Round. The European Market, worth about £120 million per year, is vital to small ACP producers such as Belize, Dominica, Jamaica, and the Windward Islands. Without the Lomé preferences, they would lose an estmated 50 per cent of their banana exports.[6] Only the determination of the French and UK governments to protect their former colonies' trade preferences prevented their abolition. At the end of 1994, the GATT contracting parties agreed a waiver of GATT rules so that the EU could continue to give ACP producers trade advantages over more competitive Latin American banana producers such as Ecuador and Costa Rica.[7] However, the Lomé system of preferences clearly infringes the principles of free trade, and therefore will be vulnerable to attack in the future. For the small ACP countries the only alternative to their protected bananas market is getting more aid, or else being driven into the trade that is in the number one problem of the Caribbean – illegal drugs.[8]

Structural adjustment

Aid for structual adjustment is a major new feature of Lomé IV. The new Convention provides 1.5 billion ecus of aid for ACP countries which have introduced macroeconomic policies deemed appropriate to deal with their economic problems. According to Article 246(2) of Lomé IV, ACP states 'undertaking reform programmes that are acknowledged and supported at least by the principal multilateral donors [i.e. the IMF and World Bank]' are reckoned to have done this; for other ACP states, the Community will decide if their adjustment policies warrant Community aid for an import support programme. This aid can be drawn from a special import support fund or from the national indicative aid programmes set up for each ACP state. Unfortunately, the aid for structural adjustment is not additional funding, but a new use for the same money.

According to the World Bank, there is no alternative to the IMF and World Bank Group structural adjustment programme for developing countries. Structural adjustment means reducing demand in the economy – often at the expense of the poor – while increasing production, particularly for export. Other models, notably the UN Economic Commission for Africa's 1989 *African Alternative Framework to Structural Adjustment*

Programmes for Socio-Economic Recovery and Transformation (AAF-SAP) which aimed at a sustained development plan suited to Africa's particular conditions, have not been adopted by the donor community. The EU has chosen to accept the World Bank and IMF formulae, despite many economists' questioning of their value and ultimate effects.

The World Bank's 1989 claim that 'The evidence points to better overall economic performance in countries that pursue a strong reform programme than in those that do not' is unfortunately not justified by the evidence.[9] In fact, countries in Africa with strong structural adjustment programmes recorded an overall negative average annual growth rate (about 1.5 per cent) of GDP in 1980–87, whereas African countries with weakly adjusting and non-adjusting economies grew by 1.2 and 3.1 per cent respectively. Coupled with the harsh impact of structural adjustment on the most vulnerable groups – women, children, the poor, and the elderly – such figures give cause for concern. Moreover, the transitional effects of structural adjustment are potentially destabilizing. These effects include declining per caput incomes and real wages, dwindling social services, and falling educational and training standards, coupled with rising unemployment and under-employment, and increasing malnutrition and public health problems.

In their major 1991 study of the World Bank, development economists Mosley, Harrigan and Toye applauded the World Bank's move into policy-based lending despite the 'social costs of adjustment', that is, the costs to poor people of withdrawing social benefits such as healthcare. They envisioned the World Bank listening to criticisms and moving in a 'kinder, gentler and greener' direction. Nevertheless, the results of the structural adjustment programmes were mixed. Export growth and external accounts benefited, aggregate investment declined; the effect on national income and financial flows from overseas, and on the distribution of income was neutral although the poorest groups suffered falling living standards.

This study recognized that structural adjustment was more suited to some countries than others, and that Africa in general fell into the 'others' category:

> For both economic theory and the evidence of our case studies suggest that the Bank's chosen package of reforms have more

relevance to Thailand and Turkey, say, than to Ghana or Guyana. A policy of trade liberalization works better if industry is already competitive on export markets; price incentives to commercial farmers work better if those farmers have access to credit, fertilizer and good roads; privatization works better if their exists a private sector able and willing to take over the public sector's assets.

Mosely *et al.* then continued, damningly, 'The point is that structural adjustment policies of the Bank's chosen variety constitute in very poor countries a gratuitous obstruction.'[10] If the Bank's policies are indeed a 'gratuitous obstruction' or even just of unproven benefit to the ACP states, the EU ought to be cautious in recommending them.

Also worrying from a political perspective is the increased dependence that is entailed by relying on structural adjustment programmes designed in Washington. Adjusting countries rely on the economic policies of the IMF and World Bank and on loans from these institutions to implement the policies. Loxley and Campbell observed, 'The conditions under which African governments have had to respond to the global challenges of the early 1980s have had the effect of locking them into new forms of dependent relationship with western governments and international organizations.'[11] This new kind of dependency was not what the Lomé Convention was supposed to foster.

When President Yoweri Museveni of Uganda addressed the European Parliament in March 1991, he impressed the members with his frank admission that many of Africa's problems were of its own making. There is no doubt that African countries, in the first place, have to put their own houses in order because no-one else has the ability or the will to do so. The Lomé Convention, too, stresses that development is firstly the responsibility of the developing country. Lomé IV refers to the ACP countries as having responsibility in the first instance for all of the development programmes implemented under the Convention. Lomé IV states: 'The ACP States shall determine the development principles, strategies and models for their economies and societies in all sovereignty.'[12] The EU should recognize that undue influence by the World Bank policy-makers is not necessarily in keeping with the concept of ACP states taking on responsibility for their own development and excercising their sovereignty to the full.

ACP debt-distressed countries have little choice in the international system about whether to adjust, following World Bank and IMF guidelines. The EU is not offering them an alternative model.

Lomé's entry into structural adjustment was a topic of considerable debate in development circles. The proposals made by the Commission on this topic were questioned but not strongly opposed by the ACP states. At the Lomé IV signing ceremony, the president of the ACP Council of Ministers even mentioned aid to structural adjustment as a positive signal for future cooperation. In large part this new, overt, macroeconomic conditionality represents a pragmatic recognition by the Community of the relative failure of its project aid, its microeconomic approach. The Community's aid policy, of course, was not a complete failure: schools, roads and sewers have been built and forestry projects have been established which otherwise would not have been. Yet despite almost four decades of cooperation and billions of ecus of aid disbursed by the Lomé Conventions and by other donors, many African countries still face severe economic hardship.

Like other donors, the Community hoped for the success of its aid in priming the pumps of development. Like the World Bank, it aimed at creating self-sustaining development where aid would no longer be required. Nevertheless, this strategy failed to work in Africa. Lomé III dealt with this problem through setting up 'policy dialogues' aimed at creating food security. It also authorized aid for the first time for recurrent (or running) costs, eliminating the concept of 'turn-key' projects from which the donor walked away after completion. Five hundred million ecus of import support for the poorest ACPs countries were allocated under Lomé III, such as a petroleum import support programme for Equatorial Guinea to back up its structural adjustment programme.

Thus, venturing into macroeconomic policies is not entirely new in Lomé IV. Half of the ACP countries have recognized their need for structural or sectoral adjustment by taking loans for these purposes from the World Bank. The European Community has consistently maintained a close relationship with the IMF and the World Bank. Stabex (stabilization of export earnings), for instance, the Community's aid showpiece launched in 1975, can be traced to the IMF's Compensatory Financing Facility established in 1963. Likewise, IMF and other donors' disbursements have in practice long been considered in making ACP indicative programmes. In addition, the World Bank is a trusted project co-financing partner.

The Community's own development officials have had little experience in the field of structural adjustment and tend to rely on the Washington institutions as 'senior partners'. Thus, supporting their plans seemed to make sense. Whereas one developing country can entertain a variety of differently conceived and funded projects, it cannot aim at conflicting macroeconomic targets at the same time. Given that IMF and World Bank adjustment plans are likely to be a feature of the development scene for some time, coordinating the Community's programmes with them has some merit. The Community's aid might help to soften them at the margins, giving them something of the 'human face' they have lacked. Nevertheless, the Community should give serious consideration to monitoring the effects of structural adjustment, rather than just following the orthodoxy of the major donors. The EU should remain open to the possiblity that developing countries' criticisms of structural adjustment policies are well founded. It could even make sure that such views get a hearing in international forums.

The question of whether support for structural adjustment will ultimately be a more successful tool of development than project aid remains to be answered.

Trade

In the area of trade preferences, the Community entered the Lomé IV talks with the view that few concessions would be possible since the Community already had such a liberal trade regime with the ACP countries. Among all of the Community's trade partners, the ACP states were the most privileged. In the end, the Community agreed a range of limited improvements for access for some ACP agricultural products, such as rice, exported to the Community. But the sugar and banana quotas were not increased, and it was agreed to phase out rum quotas by 1995.

In terms of manufactured goods, ACP countries export very few products; and most enter the Community duty-free. ACP textile exports are not subject to the Multi-Fibre Arrangement, but in practice 'voluntary' export restraints operate. The major issue of dispute has been the rules of origin which require ACP manufactures to contain only limited amounts of non-ACP or non-Community inputs. The ACP states have long claimed that these rules require an unrealistically high percentage of value to be added by them. Many processes such as the washing, labelling or packaging of goods do not confer ACP-originating status and duty-free entry into the Community. In the Lomé negotiations, the Community reduced the value which has to be added by the ACP countries to 45 per cent and improved the procedures for granting derogations. Further hope for liberalization of the rules is also on the agenda. The Community agreed in February 1990 at the talks of the Uruguay Round of the GATT that it would accept general rules of origin established within the GATT framework. But so far the Community has wanted to make the Lomé Convention's rules of origin an exception to the GATT system.

Community Commissioner Ripa di Meana proposed in 1989 to put a quota on tropical wood, the ACP countries' fifth most important export, in order to conserve the rain forests. The Commission as a whole did not agree to this proposal which would have been a cause for a major dispute with the ACP states – even if it might ultimately have operated to their benefit in environmental terms. Under GATT rules, discriminating between timber which is sustainably raised and that which is indiscriminately harvested is not permitted.

In Lomé IV a double ban was imposed: on the import and export of toxic and radioactive waste to and from the ACP states. The ban may prove useful in practice, but the necessity for it reflects badly on the ACP states' ability to police their own borders. Since 1995, other international environmental agreements have similarly banned the dumping of toxic waste in developing countries.

Lomé IV: additional features

All disbursements from the stabilization of export earnings (Stabex) and mineral production support systems (Sysmin), which had been partly in the form of low-interest loans, were made into grants. This will benefit the ACP states, debt-ridden to a total of $US150 billion, in a small way, but it is not the kind of debt initiative which the ACP countries need and which the Community has said is solely the province of the member states. Gold and uranium were included as minerals eligible for support through Sysmin or, now, for aid for diversification. Also added were new texts on the environment, human rights, population, the role of women and cultural cooperation (although the legal incorporation of the Foundation for Cultural Cooperation was refused by the EC).

The ACP states, GATT and 1992

Two external influences overhung the Lomé IV negotiations. These were the Uruguay Round of GATT and the Community's programme for the completion of the single market in 1992. These influences created uncertainty about the implementation if not the conclusion of Lomé IV. The ACP Group were deeply worried about the effects that decisions in these contexts would have on them. This was not the first time that external factors had impinged on the Community's relations with developing countries. The Community's development policy has never been insulated from political and economic problems in other areas. For example, the 1963 signing of Yaoundé I was delayed for months by the furore over the unsuccessful UK attempt to join the European Economic Community at that time.

In terms of the single market, the Community made it clear that this was a programme undertaken by the Community for its own benefit. The effects on other countries were secondary in its thinking. Nevertheless, Community estimates are that the completion of the single market, that is, doing away with internal excise duties and barriers to trade, will increase the Community's GDP by some 200 billion ecus or 5 per cent of its gross domestic product.[13] This wealthier Community could then import more ACP goods. The removal of excise duties on products such as coffee could increase consumption in Germany and Denmark.

The Uruguay Round of GATT, which began in 1986 and concluded in 1994, is scheduled to abolish tariffs on tropical products. This will work to the disadvantage of ACP producers who have preferential access to the Community market. ACP coffee, for example, has a preference of 4 per cent over other suppliers while ACP bananas have a preference (within their quota) of 20 per cent. The overall trade effects of the Uruguay Round's reforms of tariffs on agricultural and manufactured goods are that, whereas developing countries as a group will benefit, sub-Saharan Africa and the ACP states will be losers. Page and Davenport calculated that because of the Uruguay Round, developing countries would increase their exports over 1992 levels by 1.3 per cent. For sub-Saharan Africa, there would be a loss of 0.7 per cent while the ACP states would lose 1.7 per cent of exports. This would arise mainly because of a loss of preference on beef, sugar and rice. Another model predicted that by 2005 Africa would lose 0.3 per cent of GDP because of falling exports and rising costs in food imports.[14] The most valuable ACP export, crude petroleum, was already non-dutiable and therefore unaffected by the new trade regime. Nevertheless, there is a strong argument in favour of compensating already-poor countries which suffer disproportionately from the trade liberalization under GATT which was designed to increase global trade and welfare.

Despite the selective use by the Community of discriminatory trade measures such as quotas in favour of ACP exports such as sugar and bananas, the medium and long-term prospects for ACP agricultural exports are not bright. Most face a low income elasticity of demand, so that rising European incomes will result in only small increases in imports. Products such as coffee (the ACP countries' second most important export after oil), tobacco and palm oil face questions over their effects on consumers' health. Levels of pesticide residues in cocoa, for instance, cause similar worries. Ecological concern in Europe may decrease demand for tropical timber. Juggling its own sugar mountain, the Community shows little sign of increasing prices or quotas for ACP sugar. Overall, agricultural prices at the end of the 1980s were over 20 per cent lower than during the 1981–2 recession.

THE RESULTS OF TRADE PREFERENCES

The practice of granting the exports of less developed countries lower tariffs than industrialized countries is well established. It was hoped that these preferences would help developing countries to increase their market share and compete more successfully with developed countries. Through exporting, their economies would grow and their standard of living rise. But the value of trade preferences as a tool of development is uncertain. Neither GATT's Generalised System of Preferences for developing countries nor the Lomé preferences for African, Caribbean and Pacific countries can be regarded as a resounding success. It could be argued that developing countries which have

Table 4.2 ACP trade with the EU (millions of ecus)

Year	Imports	Exports
1958	2,532	2,276
1970	5,715	4,142
1980	20,889	17,216
1990	20,195	16,649
1993	14,570	16,442

Source: Eurostat, *External Trade: Statistical Yearbook 1995*, Brussels and Luxembourg, 1995

the export capacity to benefit from preferences would export successfully in any case. But those developing countries without a successful export industry in operation cannot benefit from trade preferences.[15] A Commission official summarized the situation in 1990: 'The sad and solemn fact is that for very many ACP countries, the preferences accorded have little or no value, because a trade does not exist; or if it once did, it has now diminished.'[16]

In the Lomé case, only 35–45 per cent of all ACP exports benefited specifically from EU trade preferences. The value of these trade preferences was in any case dramatically reduced as a result of the general worldwide lowering of tariffs in the post-war period. ACP commodity exports, their main source of export earnings, faced a decline of 65.6 per cent in their margin of preference in the EU over the period 1958–86.[17]

Although trade between the ACP states and the EU during the post-war period grew six-fold (see Table 4.2), it grew less quickly than EU trade with developed countries. ACP–EU trade has also declined significantly since its high point in the early 1980s. Potentially, trade increments are much more valuable to the ACP states than the 2.4 billion ecus of grants and loans per annum allocated under Lomé IV. An increase of 15 per cent in ACP exports to the EU in 1993 would have been more valuable to them than Lomé aid. But in light of tough international competition in trade, and the difficulties in increasing preferences under a liberalizing GATT world trade regime, the ACP countries may well be unable to improve their export performance significantly.

Relative to other developed and developing countries, ACP trade with the EU has markedly diminished. Export shares have fallen by over 50 per cent during 1983–93 (see Table 4.3). On present trends, the European Parliament predicts that ACP trade

Table 4.3 EU imports from and exports to trading partners (per cent of total)

Imports	1983	1993
USA	17.2	17.3
Japan	6.4	9.7
Latin America	7.2	4.5
ACP countries	6.5	3.1
Exports		
USA	17.4	17.5
Japan	2.6	4.7
Latin America	4.1	4.8
ACP countries	5.9	3.4

Source: Eurostat, *External Trade: Statistical Yearbook 1995*, Brussels and Luxembourg, 1995

will account for less than 2 per cent of EU trade by 2000. So far, trade under the Lomé Conventions has not performed the development function that both sides wanted to see.

Trade in manufactures, often seen as an indicator of development, has not 'taken off' for the ACP states. In fact, during 1983–93, ACP exports of manufactures to the EU fell from 1.8 per cent to just 1 per cent of EU imports of manufactured goods.[18]

Trade with the EU has not been the 'engine of growth' leading ACP countries to wealth and self-sustaining development. Babarinde found that ACP exports to the EU received a short boost in 1976–8, growing faster than exports from non-ACP developing countries. But the general economic decline of the developing countries after 1975 counteracted the economic benefits from the Lomé Convention. Non-ACP countries were more successful at diversifying the destination of their exports than the ACP group in the 1980s. Thus, it was possible that the Lomé regime created an undesirable export dependence on the EU or discouraged the ACP countries from seeking new markets. Surprisingly, the growth of trade with the EU was correlated with negative economic development in the ACP countries, whereas for non-ACP countries it correlated with positive economic growth. Export growth for the ACP states was accompanied by a decline in infant mortality and an increase in life expectancy, but a reduction in food production. However, it is impossible to attribute either the improvement in social factors or the decline in growth and food production solely to Lomé. Social factors also improved in non-ACP countries, along with food production. Although there are many questions over the effects of the Lomé trade regime (including the reliability of many ACP trade statistics), few economists see any alternative for the ACP states but to increase their trade with Europe, taking advantage of whatever preferences the EU offers.[19]

The European Parliament has recommended that the EU take the path of trying to deepen, or improve, the value of the preferences received by the ACP countries. Although GATT approved the continuation of the Lomé preferences in late 1994, it would be unlikely to look favourably upon increasing them – a practice diametrically opposed to the goal of free trade. However, other measures which the EU could realistically undertake would be to relax the rules of origin of ACP products, relax or eliminate some agricultural quotas, remove or reduce internal taxes on tropical products, and help the ACP states not only with trade planning and development but also with creating trade infrastructure such as roads and ports.[20]

LOMÉ: THE RECORD OF PROJECT AID, STABEX AND SYSMIN

Serious questions have been repeatedly raised about the record of project aid under the Lomé Conventions. Putting together and implementing development projects is not an exact science and even those governments which claim that their aid programme is unsurpassed are still liable to extensive criticism.[21] The overall effectiveness of post-war development aid has not been proven. Overseas aid does not always bring about economic growth or social development. Trying to generalize about whether aid works or not may well be impossible. The only meaningful statement about aid is that it works in some cases, and fails in others.[22]

In the case of Lomé aid projects, there is considerable uncertainty about their overall effectiveness and value. To the ACP partners, the main source of discontent is the slow rate of disbursement of aid. At any one time, half a dozen countries have their aid packages held up because of political problems or civil unrest. Bureaucratic procedures in Brussels, such as in allocating a sum of aid for each country, and slow communication between Brussels and that ACP country slow down the disbursement of the rest. At the end of the third year of operation of Lomé IV (the seventh European Development Fund or EDF), only 15.5

per cent of funds had been disbursed. The fifth European Development Fund, (Lomé II) was closed in 1994, having paid out only 87.4 per cent of its resources.

Another problem of aid administration in general is shared by European aid. This is the issue of aid evaluation. EU aid projects are inadequately evaluated and the results of those evaluations are not sufficiently incorporated into subsequent projects. An Overseas Development Institute study of EU aid found that almost half of the projects were effective or very effective in preparation and implementation, but a quarter were distinctly ineffective in these respects.[23] The European Commission reckoned that 'around one-third of our projects and programmes go well, around one-third are satisfactory but not brilliant and about one-third are not good value for money.'[24] The sustainability of projects after the donor leaves, and the lack of incorporation of social and women's concerns are considered to be particular weaknesses of EU aid. The UK's Foreign Affairs Committee, dissatisfied with this state of affairs, called for greater monitoring and evaluation of projects by the Commission, the European Parliament, and the UK's National Audit Office and Public Accounts Committee, to supplement the reports already made by the European Court of Auditors. The wider dissemination of such evaluations would also improve the institutional learning of the EU aid programme. Although the World Bank is also estimated to have a project failure rate of around 30 per cent, the EU's development projects record is widely viewed as less successful. Because of this, the UK development minister Baroness Chalker argued in 1993 for an increased emphasis on policy reform in developing countries and a reduction of emphasis on traditional project aid.[25] This change of emphasis has already occurred under Lomé IV; whereas in the 1980s some two-thirds of European Development Fund resources were spent on projects, by 1994 this had declined to 42 per cent.[26]

Another issue of European development policy is the way in which funding is agreed at inter-governmental level in the Lomé Conventions. This negotiating process produces insecurity as European governments may try to reduce their individual contributions. One solution which has been proposed is the 'budgetization' of aid funding. If European Development Fund contributions were assessed on the basis of member states' GNP (in the same way as their contributions to the EU budget), it is argued that this would be fairer and more consistent. It would also bring Lomé aid under the budgetary scrutiny of the European Parliament, forcing it to become more efffective and more transparent – also more political. Under this system, Germany, Italy and Spain would pay more while France, the UK and Belgium would pay less.[27]

At present, budgetizing European aid is supported by the European Parliament but firmly opposed by the UK government which wants to keep control of its aid contribution. The UK's parliamentary Foreign Affairs Committee supported budgetization in principle, but argued that the administratively overstretched European Commission could not now manage it and the overstretched UK government could not afford it.[28]

The main disadvantage of budgetization would be to end the convention that the levels of EDF aid funding should be mutually agreed with the ACP countries, the partners. But in practice the ACP partners have no option but to accept the levels of aid which are agreed by the European states. Sharing out aid payments more fairly could reduce the element of post-colonial responsibility that the major former colonial powers, the UK and France, take for their former colonies. However, in principle nothing would prevent these powers from augmenting their bilateral aid programmes to compensate for any loss of influence they might incur through European aid policy.

One significant problem of the European Union aid programme has been its very comprehensiveness. European Commission staff find it difficult to do everything from aid allocation to structural adjustment to project evaluation. This overstretch was recognized by the UK's aid minister Chalker: 'I do not think you can be active everywhere and effective everywhere in the ways in which some people are pushing the European Union to be in development projects.'[29] For instance, the EU has been unable to solve problems in the operation of the Stabex (stabilization export earnings) system. Stabex was originally a quick-disbursing programme, but in the 1980s it experienced long delays in giving out funds.

Since its inception, Stabex has suffered from a chronic shortage of resources. It soon became apparent that Stabex could not do the job it was designed for: giving ACP developing countries some insurance against the problem of instability in world commodity markets. As commodity prices have fallen and fluctuated over the past two decades, Stabex has not kept up. In some cases Stabex funds were extremely useful to recipient governments, amounting to as much as 10 per cent of GDP. The moneys were used as a 'funding instrument' to support a variety of desirable public expenditures.[30] However, although Stabex remains popular with the recipients, its purposes and rules are unclear. The European Court of Auditors concluded that the Stabex accounts did not give a true view of its operations. The treatment of some countries – for example, Côte d'Ivoire and Cameroon – was much more generous than the treatment of others. The end use of Stabex funds was not carefully monitored.[31] Stabex failed to disburse any funds in 1993 and subsequently has been meeting only 40–50 per cent of requests.[32] Stabex urgently needs to be reformed so that it can either meet its original objectives or be transformed into a more workable scheme.

The smaller relative of Stabex, the mineral production support system Sysmin, has functioned even less well than Stabex. Under Lomé III only 35 per cent of the funds allocated to Sysmin were spent on minerals-related projects. The other funds were re-allocated. Of the few projects which were approved, many encountered serious problems. The Sysmin projects in Togo and Papua New Guinea, for instance, had to be suspended.[33] Given its track record, there seems to be little reason for the EU to maintain Sysmin as an independent programme. Any viable minerals projects could be funded from general project aid.

At present, the EU operates an aid programme which overlaps with those of its member states. The member states subscribed to common development objectives in the Treaty of Maastricht, but not to a common competence to execute them. EU aid is thus a sixteenth aid programme, supplementing or complementing those of the fifteen EU member states. However, it is possible that the EU should move to a different role, or find itself a niche where it can use its expertise to best advantage. Coordinating or managing the aid programmes of the member states is one possibility, but would face considerable national opposition. One niche which the EU ought to avoid is increasing food aid. Food aid already amounts to 20 per cent of the EU aid budget but has questionable effects on local food production and consumption patterns. It is also difficult to separate the developmental role of food aid from the EU's agricultural production interests.[34]

The EU has been an emergency aid donor since the 1960s.

Recently, emergency aid from the EU has dramatically increased. Over the period 1990–93 it grew six-fold, and a separate emergency aid department ECHO (EC Humanitarian Aid Office) was set up in 1992. In 1993 almost two-thirds of funds were spent on former Yugoslavia, while over half went to Rwanda in 1994. Although giving disaster relief aid to those in desperate need is highly commendable, the establishment of ECHO has given several causes for concern. In practice, increases in emergency aid may well mean decreases in development aid. Furthermore, ECHO is a separate department from the development directorate and not well coordinated with it. NGOs (non-governmental organizations or charities) and businesses have complained about ECHO's bureaucratic and slow procedures.

Ninety per cent of ECHO's resources are transmitted through NGOs and UN agencies. Little of the funding went through local (recipient country) NGOs. In 1993 the biggest recipient was the United Nations High Commission for Refugees (UNHCR) with 87 million ecus, followed by the World Food Programme. The Commission has maintained that the increase in ECHO's budget was driven by events and not by policy. But ECHO could compete for funding with long-term development aid or divert aid from Africa to South Eastern Europe and the former Soviet Union as emergencies arise there.

The immediate challenge for the EU is to make ECHO more efficient and better integrated with development programmes. As a second-tier provider of emergency aid and funding to UN agencies, ECHO could have a useful role to play, but any increase in ECHO's resources should be additional to long-term development aid. Equally, the existence of the EU-funded ECHO programme should not allow EU member states to cut their own bilateral allocations to disaster relief organizations such as UNICEF and UNHCR.

LOMÉ: THE REPLY TO CRITICS

On occasion the World Bank has been rather more forthright about acknowledging criticisms of its policies than has the Lomé system. In the 1989 *Annual Report* the Bank admitted that concerns about the effects of its adjustment policies had been raised: 'Little is known about the overall effect of adjustment programmes on poverty.'[35] The 1991 *Annual Report* contained a section entitled 'Lessons Learned', showing that the Bank realized that more ought to be done to help vulnerable groups, and it admitted that some projects such as the Sardar Sarovar Dam in India (later abandoned by the Bank) and the Carajas Iron Ore project in Brazil were environmentally controversial.

By contrast, the European Commission has traditionally taken a more trenchant tone, defending its policies even against criticism from other Community institutions. The majority of the Court of Auditors' criticisms of the Community's internal and Lomé sugar policy, for instance, were roundly rejected by the Commission in 1991, which even claimed (against all evidence) that Community sugar exports did not depress world prices. The UK's parliamentary Foreign Affairs Committee found that the Commission often responded to criticisms in an 'ad hoc and resentful' way.[36] However, in reply to the the 1993 Court of Auditors Report, the Commission did adopt a cooperative attitude, accepting that there were problems in its financial management which it was trying to sort out.[37]

The European Commission too often took the attitude that public criticisms of the Lomé policy only showed how well the policy in fact worked and how even more of it was needed. The policy was exemplary, a touchstone for other relations between industrialized and developing countries. Controversy within Lomé only highlighted the vitality of the institutions. Criticisms in general were made by rote and ill-informed: 'The result is a series of standard criticisms, some of which are trotted out regularly without any real thought as to whether they are well founded or not.'[38]

Because the Lomé package had been so ambitious, aiming at achieving a 'new, more just and more balanced world order' according to the Preamble to Lomé IV, the disillusion with the package was the more intense. As late as 1992, the European Commission still claimed that 'Stabex and Sysmin can be regarded as tangible elements of a new international economic order'.[39] But in view of the shortcomings of these two systems discussed on pp. 127–8, Stabex and Sysmin could better be described as tangible expressions of the fact that EU development policies sometimes did not work very well. It is true that Lomé has attracted more criticism than the Commonwealth Fund for Technical Cooperation, for instance, or even the USA's highly political Caribbean Basin Initiative. The Gabonese co-President of the ACP–EU Joint

Assembly in October 1994 was caustic but not untypical in his assessment of the instruments of the Lomé Convention: 'Today, we note with some bitterness, that none of these [development] policies has succeeded.'[40]

The European Commission and the EU member states only needed to consider the views of many ACP delegations or the general air of disappointment which surrounded the successive renegotiations of the Lomé Convention to realize that criticisms of Lomé had to be taken seriously.

It could be argued that the sensitivity about the Lomé Convention shown by the Commission stands in great contrast to the Commission's apparent willingness (described in the next section) to give up on Lomé altogether. This is perhaps best understood on a human level. If the Commission staff worked long and hard to produce a successful Lomé Convention, but instead of being applauded for their efforts were repeatedly criticized by the Court of Auditors and others, it is understandable that the Commission staff might – out of frustration – decide to give up on Lomé. Given the political and financial constraints upon it, the Commission could not put together a Lomé Convention which would satisfy all the signatories or even be substantially improved every five years. Thus, the feeling of some officials and politicians that they might as well give up is comprehensible. However, as the next section argues, the Commission and the EU member states should continue trying to improve Lomé to meet the needs and wishes of the now seventy ACP states and twenty dependent territories that are party to the Convention.

THE MID-TERM REVIEW OF LOMÉ IV

The context of the review

The fourth Lomé Convention was concluded in 1989 and designed to run for ten years, twice the duration of each of its three predecessors. Lomé IV provided for a mid-term review to be held to assess the provisions of the Convention and to allocate resources for the eighth European Development Fund. In view of the lack of donor interest in the Convention, which is discussed below, it was fortunate for the ACP states that they were facing only a mid-term review in the mid-1990s rather than a full-scale renegotiation of the Convention.

The mid-term review of Lomé was launched in May 1994. It should have been concluded by 1 March 1995, in time to replace the financial protocol which expired at the end of February of that year. But disagreements over the aid package delayed the conclusion of the review until the end of June. Originally, the review was envisioned as being primarily about the levels of aid to be given by the EU member states, but, under Article 366 of Lomé IV, additional measures could be reviewed if both sides agreed.

The Lomé mid-term review faced two conflicting tendencies. One was the general phenomenon of donor fatigue. Donors were discouraged about the long-term prospects of development aid and wondered whether their contributions did any good. A senior aid official described in 1994 how – when aid issues were on the agenda – the Commission chamber rapidly emptied. The Lomé mid-term review attracted almost no press coverage. The *Economist*, for instance, did not use the word Lomé and merely complained that the Cannes European Summit in June 1995 had got 'bogged down' with trivia such as aid to Africa.[41]

The other tendency notable in the review was the desire of the donors to have a major reformulation of Lomé. In the wake of the end of the Cold War, Europe wanted to have more control over the operation of the Convention. It was felt that the fundamental changes in the international political system which occurred following the demise of the socialist system called for a more far-reaching examination of the Convention than just re-valuing the aid package. Commissioner Marin was noted for cryptic statements saying such as 'things must change in order to continue' and for giving his officials rather vague instructions to 'modernize' the Lomé Convention without specifying how.

In the 1990s the Convention no longer had any competition from the socialist systems. Indeed, the large aid donors such as the World Bank, USAID and the EU seemed to have reached a consensus over the kind of liberal, free market policies that developing countries ought to follow. Developing countries had few alternative donors to turn to, giving the major donors more power to implement their economic and political prescriptions.

The European member states wanted Lomé to function better and more efficiently, without costing more. They were prepared to make significant changes in the Convention, shifting the balance of power within the EU–ACP partnership more in favour of the European partners. The EU–ACP Joint Assembly felt it necessary to remind the EU that there were limits on the changes it could make to the Convention: 'the mid-term review involves the review of the existing Lomé IV Convention and not the re-negotiation of a new Convention.'[42]

The results of the mid-term review

The amount of financial resources to be made available by the EU member states for the second five years of Lomé IV was the single most important issue under discussion. It was also the last issue to be resolved. The influence of the French presidency of the Union was brought to bear on the other member states to reach an agreement. To encourage the others, France increased its original aid offer by 100 million ecus, becoming the single largest donor to the eighth EDF (see Table 4.4).

The EU member states agreed to maintain the value of Lomé aid in real terms but not to increase it, despite the rise in the number of donors from twelve to fifteen. The 13.3 billions of ecus offered for the eighth EDF were described by the French Presidency as 'realistic and generous'. However, except for the contribution of France itself, the first adjective was more accurate than the second. The British were able to cut their EDF aid payments by 25 per cent in real terms, and hoped to make a 12 per cent cut in their overall aid budget. Analysts who had expected the new Scandinavian members of the EU to have a positive effect on the funding levels of the EDF were disappointed.

The Commission originally proposed that the ACP–EU Consultative Assembly should meet only once a year instead of six-monthly as it has always done. The expenses of the Consultative Assembly are charged to the regional funds of the Convention and it has been argued that the limited, consultative powers of the Assembly do not justify this expenditure. However, the Assembly serves as a forum of dialogue for the relationship. Its main effect is to influence and educate the members of the European Parliament, who do have power to affect EU policy-making and budget-making. In some cases its calls for ACP 'prisoners of conscience' to be released have been heeded. The objective of 'training the ACP members in democracy' is harder to evaluate. Pressure from the Joint Assembly led to the withdrawal of this proposal and the

Table 4.4 Contributions to European Development Funds – Lomé IV
(millions of ecus)

	7th EDF (1990–95)	8th EDF (1995–2000)
Belgium	433	503
Denmark	227	275
Germany	2,840	3,000
Greece	134	160
Spain	645	750
France	2,666	3,120
Ireland	60	80
Italy	1,418	1,610
Luxembourg	21	37
Netherlands	609	670
Portugal	96	125
United Kingdom	1,791	1,630
Austria		340
Finland		190
Sweden		350
Unutilized previous EDF funds		292
Extra humanitarian aid for ACP states from EU budget		160
Transformation of special loans into grants		15
Sub-total	10,940	13,307
EIB own resource funds for lending	1,200	1,658
Total	12,140	14,965

Source: D. Percival 'Agreement clinched at eleventh hour', *Courier* 153,
September–October, 1995, p. 7

review concentrated on the issue of ensuring as far as possible
that ACP states were represented by elected parliamentarians.

In a positive move, South Africa was allowed an 'automatic
entry' to the Lomé Convention, once the final terms of admission
were negotiated. The EU expressed solidarity with banana producers and concern about ACP debt problems. It agreed that the
uncommitted loan funds from previous Conventions could be
transformed into grants.

The next three sections evaluate new provisions agreed in the
mid-term review.

Trade provisions

Some improvements were made to the Lomé trade regime for ACP agricultural products. A number of customs levies on ACP goods which did not receive any preference were reduced by 16 per cent. Duties on cereals, pork, and rice were reduced while the treatment of sorghum, millet, sheep and poultry meat, meat preparations, milk products, fresh figs, pears, and strawberries was improved. But sensitive products such as olives, wine and lemons were not included in the new provisions.

With some exclusions, for the first time the ACP states were allowed to 'cumulate' up to 15 per cent of a product's value in a neigbouring non-ACP country and still qualify for an ACP preference under Lomé. Pending further discussion, this amount of value added could originate in South Africa.[43]

The broadening of human rights under Article 5 of Lomé

Lomé was the first aid convention to mention human rights. Article 5 'toughens up' human rights by making them an 'essential element' of Lomé. Further, Article 366 of the Convention now specifically states that if any essential human rights are violated, aid can be partly or totally suspended.

The ACP states are to be consulted about the suspension, except in cases of emergency. The provision for a mechanism of consultation on human rights has been thought to put ACP countries into a difficult position: having to pronounce on each other's human rights policies.

In practice, the Commission already takes decisions to halt aid on human rights grounds. The new provisions just formalize a situation which already existed *de facto*. It could be argued that the Commission's actions were previously *ultra vires* or beyond the powers it explicitly possessed under Lomé. In the 1970s the Community frequently assured the ACP states that Lomé funds were inviolable and outside of all political considerations. In the 1980s the EU operated political criteria without making them explicit. In the 1990s, the EU is making the conditions for receiving aid more transparent and more open to pressure, for example from the European Parliament, to halt aid to repressive regimes such as General Abacha's in Nigeria.

More flexible aid programmming

More flexibility in paying out aid is desired by the EU. The idea of annual tranches of aid was considered but abandoned by the Council of Ministers. Now 70 per cent of an ACP country's aid is to be allocated for three years on a firm basis, and then more aid is to be given depending on the situation. This is referred to as 'use it or lose it'.

In the past awkward situations arose regarding aid disbursement. For example, the Community sent a letter to Sudan detailing in 1990 funds to be allocated to it but saying that the Community could not enter into a dialogue with Sudan owing to its human rights record. Thus, the allocated money just sat uselessly, instead of being re-allocated to a deserving recipient. Under the new provisions, fewer development funds should sit idle.

Thus, in the important areas of paying out aid and enforcing human rights, the EU now has greater explicit powers of action than previously as a result of the mid-term review.

THE LOMÉ CONVENTION: HORIZON 2000 OR HORIZON 0?

In May 1992 the European Commission set out its view of 'Development Cooperation Policy in the Run-Up to 2000'. This document, popularly known as 'Horizon 2000', tried to assess what Community aid had so far achieved and where it was going in the future.

The report recognized the difficult conditions faced by the poorest developing countries and the at best mediocre record of aid in dealing with them. The loss of geo-strategic importance of developing countries to the donors meant that the donors could now apply ever more stringent criteria to assessing the efficiency of their aid. The report also dwelt on the desirability of greater Community coordination in aid policy to make it more effective and influential. 'Horizon 2000' acknowledged the expansion and proliferation of the Community's development policies since 1958, and the importance of a ' "contract" of true partnership between Africa and the Community' was emphasized.[44] However, the continuation of the Lomé Convention after the year 2000 was not mentioned. Indeed, the word 'Lomé' did not appear at all. This absence of any support for the Community's flag-ship development programme was striking.

Among development analysts there has been a consistently high degree of disappointment in and criticism of the Lomé system. There has been little academic support for the Lomé concept of European cooperation with the African, Caribbean and Pacific countries. Development specialists such as Professor R. H. Green and Laurence Tubiana questioned the continuing relevance of the Lomé framework. The Deputy Director of the Overseas Development Institute, Adrian Hewitt, wrote in 1986 that 'it looked as if the writing was on the wall' for the Lomé Convention and subsequently in 1991 considered Lomé 'a dying relationship'.[45]

The idea that the Lomé Convention was a failure also infiltrated the ranks of the European Commission, the body responsible for administering it. In the *Financial Times* of 3 November 1994, the European Commission Director-General for Development, Peter Pooley, was quoted as saying there would probably be no Lomé Convention by the end of the century. He said that Lomé could not continue in its present, exclusive form. Why should Uganda be included but not Bangladesh? Director-General Pooley argued that the fall of the Berlin Wall made Lomé less relevant. The EU's approach to development needed to be adjusted after the end of the Cold War, after the end of colonialism. The remarks of the Director-General caused considerable consternation amongst the ACP countries, particularly as they were aired without mentioning any alternative form which aid and trade preferences for these countries might take.

At present, there is a general belief in the European Commission and among the staff of some European development aid ministries that the Lomé Convention will not be renegotiated again. UK Foreign Secretary Douglas Hurd reiterated in 1995 the UK's consistent reservations about EU aid and publicly criticized the EU programmes, calling them 'haphazard' and 'diffuse', and arguing that no-one would have designed EU aid policies as they now exist.[46] Even France might be willing to reduce its traditional support for special aid to Africa – or it might be outvoted on this issue in future by its other European partners.

Although the Lomé Convention has many failings, letting it wither away at the end of the millennium is not a happy prospect for the African, Caribbean and Pacific states. The Lomé

Convention is not likely to be replaced with a bigger, better, more global aid policy, but with a more fragmented, low profile and low priority development policy. Without Lomé, the impetus for EU member states to enter into serious negotiations with the ACP countries over aid, and to maintain or increase their development aid expenditure, would diminish. Without the institutional framework of Lomé which has promoted almost forty years of dialogue on subjects ranging from human rights to project implementation, European–ACP cooperation would be in danger of drastically declining.

The effects on the South of the 'transition to democracy' in Europe

The fall of the Berlin Wall certainly affected Europe, but it is unclear why this event should fundamentally alter Europe's relations with Africa. 'Cooperation with Central and Eastern Europe' is discussed in Chapter 1; the political effects of the demise of socialism as a viable alternative system are examined in Chapter 4. This section looks at the results of the transition to democratic and market systems in Eastern and Central Europe in terms of their probable effects on aid and trade for the developing countries.[47] Most of the indicators so far suggest that the effects of the transition in Eastern Europe will be mildly negative, at least for some time to come. The small African aid programmes of the German Democratic Republic and Romania have now ceased, along with the Soviet foreign aid programme. In terms of international relations, there is a generalized fear among developing countries that the EU will be interested first in its internal development, its economic and monetary union, and second in the neighbouring Central and Eastern European states such as Poland, Hungary, the Czech Republic and Slovakia. The EU will therefore have little attention left to devote to developing countries.[48]

The effects of the Eastern European transition to democracy and to market economies are extremely difficult to predict in the short and medium term. Most economists consider that in the long term the transition to market economies in Eastern Europe is bound to generate economic growth and thereby benefit all members of the world economy. But the precise effects will depend on how fully the transition is accomplished: the commitment to economic reform in countries such as Romania is sometimes half-hearted.

The economic effects of changes in Eastern and Central Europe on the future of the developing countries will be complex and neither wholly negative nor wholly positive. There will probably be competition between Eastern Europe and developing countries for international capital in the form of aid, loans and (to a lesser extent) private investment. There will also be complicated repercussions on trade, which will be further affected by changes in EU tariffs and quotas, including not only the disruption of existing barter trade between Eastern Europe and developing countries but also the possible increase in demand for developing country products as Eastern European incomes rise. There could also be the partial replacement of developing country products in Western markets as Eastern European exports such as petroleum and petroleum products, wood, nickel, copper, coal and clothing become more available and competitive.[49] Finally, there are likely to be migration or labour-oriented effects as Eastern European migrants compete with those from developing countries for unskilled jobs in Western Europe.

Christopher Stevens' careful study of the economic effects of the reforms in Eastern Europe on developing countries recognized that so many factors were involved that any forecasts would be extremely speculative. He summarized his conclusions:

Middle income developing countries could be *adversely* affected if Eastern Europe competes with them for commercial bank loans, foreign direct investment, semi-concessional aid and markets for exports of manufactures. The outcome could be potentially *positive* for the poorer developing countries that are still heavily dependent on exports of primary commodities and may not experience serious competition for aid (official development assistance) since most of the assistance to Eastern Europe ought to be on quasi-commercial or only slightly concessional terms. But if the outcome of reform in Eastern Europe is only economic stagnation, its principal effect on the Third World may be migrant worker competition in the West European labour market and greater aid diversion (as the West seeks to mitigate social or political unrest in its neighbours).[50]

The arguments for continuing cooperation

Although European–African cooperation may no longer be based on Cold War considerations, on the need to line up developing countries as supporters of the 'free world' rather than as members of the Soviet bloc, all the other arguments for European–ACP cooperation remain valid. The development priorities of poverty alleviation, environmental protection and social development are still important. Europe still has economic, geopolitical, moral and historical interests in its former colonies and their neighbours.

The idea which many development specialists had at the time of the signing of Lomé I in 1975, that a global aid policy was superior to a regionally-based one, looks increasingly dated two decades later. The bloc-to-bloc or region-to-region development strategy is also practised by the fifty-member Commonwealth, an international discussion forum and an aid organization. Even the Nordic countries – Sweden, Norway, Finland, Denmark, and Iceland – have adopted a regional development strategy since 1986, focusing one-third of their total bilateral aid on a group of the poorest African countries.[51] Nordic–Southern African cooperation is primarily an aid relationship rather than a comprehensive restructuring of relations of production, as it was sometimes styled. Nevertheless, the region-to-region development approach, like the EU–ACP Lomé Convention, does have some positive examples to recommend it.

The failure or very limited success of global development strategies is widely acknowledged. The New International Economic Order, the Generalized System of Preferences, the Integrated Programme for Commodities, and the Common Fund for Commodities failed to make major changes in the international system or to solve the problems of the poorest countries. The UN's aid target for developed countries to give 7 per cent of their GNP in development aid is given only lip-service by the USA, the UK and most of the EU states. In October 1995, world leaders met in New York not only to celebrate the fiftieth anniversary of the United Nations but also to point out that the institution was in political and financial crisis. The UN's progressive trade and development organization, UNCTAD, is under particular threat. In this uncertain global environment, abandoning any development policy, such as the Lomé Convention, is hazardous. It risks worsening the conditions of the developing

countries involved without having any concrete, positive alternative to offer them.

The idea that a successful development policy, as noted above,
must be global is unrealistic in the present international climate.
A post-modern perspective on the variety of the human condition, on the importance of acting and responding locally,
dovetails better with the Lomé Convention's philosophy than
with an aspiration to modernist, global development plans. Such
global development plans, like the proposals of the Brandt
Report, may themselves never be implemented or may become
the sole province of the free market orthodoxies of the IMF and
World Bank. The immediate challenge for the European and ACP
states is to build a regional development policy that works, not
to wait for a global panacea.

The negotiations for the Lomé Convention to be entirely
revised are scheduled to begin in late 1998. At present, the Lomé
Convention is not likely to be replaced with a 'kinder, gentler,
greener' and more global development policy. If Lomé is abandoned, its replacement would be a watered-down policy resulting
from disappointment with Lomé's economic results. Such a policy
would not reaffirm the aspirations for cooperation which created
the Lomé Covention. Within the Lomé relationship, there remain
opportunites to utilize the lessons of past experience, to incorporate current human rights standards, and to benefit from the
changes within the EU which increase the political input of
the European Parliament.

CONCLUSION

The African, Caribbean and Pacific states face bleak economic
conditions in the 1990s. Prospects for their traditional exports
are poor, and their ability to attract sufficient private or public
investment flows to support major growth in new sectors is questionable. Wars, internal instability, and the epidemic of HIV and
AIDS threaten the future of the African continent.

Lomé IV, despite its range of instruments from structural
adjustment support to export earnings stabilization, was limited
in its ability to tackle development problems. It did not dispose
of the means to solve ACP countries' debt problems, ensure their
self-sufficiency in food production or achieve industrial development. However, within the limitations of the Lomé framework,

both the ACP states and the EU have taken a flexible and largely realistic approach to their relations. They did not let their varying development philosophies up to 1990, or their often acrimonious debates about the apartheid regime in South Africa, disrupt the Lomé dialogue. The ACP states have accepted since 1985 the importance of the private sector and private investment, at least in principle, in fuelling development. They have also accepted in many cases the need for structural adjustment, food security and respect for the mechanisms of the market. From the Community side, positive changes such as aid for recurrent costs in projects, aid for structural adjustment, aid for human rights projects and for small-scale 'microprojects' have been made.

For the medium term future, the Community needs to think about fundamental reforms to improve the Lomé instruments, including project aid, Stabex, and Sysmin. Every effort should be devoted to improving the record of ACP–EU trade. The Community needs to ensure that its almost four decades of independent development cooperation do not become merely a footnote to IMF and World Bank policies. In the analysis of the Lomé Conventions, the importance of maintaining the dialogue, the habits of cooperation and conciliation between partners and their continuing determination to achieve 'the more balanced and self-reliant development of the ACP States' outweigh the so far modest results of the aid and trade provisions.

Chapter 5

Lomé IV and the breeze of change

LOMÉ IN CONTEXT

President Omar Bongo of the West African state of Gabon was widely quoted in 1990 when he referred to the 'wind from the East that is shaking the coconut trees'. That wind from the East, marking the end of the socialist system as a viable alternative to Western-style democracy, brought profound changes to Africa. On the one hand, by 1991 over half of the forty-five sub-Saharan states had, with greater and lesser conviction, committed themselves to democracy. This was a welcome step forward from the era of widespread personal, military and often corrupt rule which followed decolonization. On the other hand, changes in Eastern Europe and the former USSR preoccupied West Europeans, allowing development in general and Africa in particular to slip further down their agenda.

This chapter investigates some of the political issues and the international context surrounding Lomé IV. The sources of the marginalization of development policy, of Africa and of the Lomé Convention are uncovered. Chapter 5 argues that despite the marginalization of the Convention, there are also solid reasons to consider that it may have the ability to withstand the current phase of pessimism and neglect. The 'fallacy of transposition' holds that developing countries cannot replicate the integrative experience of the EU. But neither developing nor European countries are convinced of this. Finally, Chapter 5 looks at the possible expansion of the membership of the Lomé Convention. It scrutinizes the rapidly developing relations beween the EU and South Africa. These set a precedent for a qualified form of Lomé membership, which could be applied to another country under-going social upheaval: Cuba.

The fourth Lomé Convention was signed in 1989 by the then twelve members of the European Community and sixty-eight countries of the African, Caribbean and Pacific Group of States. Changes within the series of Lomé Conventions are noticeable, but the changes are not so far of the hurricane proportions experi-enced in Europe or in various countries in Africa. Changes in the developing world in the 1990s will be likely to be in the direction of the Western liberal democratic model. The influence of internal advocates of democracy such as trade unions and the 'good governance' policies and stricter aid conditionality of the UK, German, French and other governments have had a marked effect on the direction that change in the developing countries can be expected to take. No longer is it possible to predict, as Bill Freund did in 1984, that a storm would sweep aside African regimes throughout the continent and replace them with socialist governments.[1] In fact, the storm has replaced socialist governments with apparently liberal–democratic ones.

In the early 1990s European Commission President Jacques Delors insisted that the increasing pace of change within Europe had caused history itself to accelerate. This acceleration is now being felt in the Lomé relationship in the wake of the mid-term review which ended in June 1995. Both parties, the European Community and the African, Caribbean and Pacific (ACP) states, have tried to protect what Lomé IV called the *acquis* of their relations, the acquired benefits and consensus on many policy issues. But increasing uncertainty has recently crept into the relationship, as described in Chapter 4. The voices which defend Lomé, such as that of ex-President Mitterrand at the UN Social Summit in Copenhagen in 1995, are so far fairly isolated.[2] More arresting was the view of the Tanzanian representative to the Joint ACP–EU Assembly in October 1994 that 'The vision of partnership [between Europe and Africa] seems to grow dimmer every day.'[3]

Lomé I was signed in 1975 on the high-tide of developing countries' expectations for the future. The UK was taking seriously its post-colonial responsiblities to Commonwealth Africa, the Caribbean and Pacific. There was a period of rising commodity prices and optimistic and imaginative thinking about the world order and how to change it to benefit poor countries.

The friendship and allegiance of the developing countries was eagerly sought by Washington, Moscow and the European capitals. The Lomé Convention seemed to offer developing countries a package which included political recognition, aid, trade preferences and new instruments of commodity stabilization. It was disappointing that in practice these instruments failed substantially to better the conditions of the developing countries.

The demise of the French Community in the early 1960s left a gap which was largely filled for France by the Community's development policy. This situation, combined with the international environment when the UK acceded to the European Community in 1973, made Lomé a special case.[4] It would not be replicable in today's international environment. Despite the significant shortcomings of the Lomé Convention, it is hard to imagine that, in the tougher international atmosphere of the 1990s, the developing countries could negotiate a more generous or far-sighted deal with Europe than they did in 1975.

Even if some of Lomé's instruments, such as Stabex, the system for stabilizing export earnings, have not been justified in practice, the ACP countries have little option but to continue to take advantage of and where possible improve the structures there are. The outcomes of global-level initiatives have often been disappointing. For instance, the UN's special session for Africa in 1986, and the 1975–85 UN Decade for Women (commonly referred to as 'invisible') produced minimal results.[5] By comparison to these UN initiatives, the Lomé Conventions were successful; they did produce concrete results. Like the Tibetan story of the blind man who fell from a cliff on to the back of a wild horse, and then held on as long as possible to take advantage of the opportunity, the ACP countries need to take full advantage of the opportunity presented by their historically-conditioned relations with Europe.[6]

Tanzania's ex-president Julius Nyerere argued that the North–South dialogue ended at the Cancûn summit in 1982. To many observers, the global development negotiations of the 1980s were signposted 'dead end road'.[7] At the global level, results in the decade following the Cancûn summit were few and disappointing. But the North–South dialogue of the 1980s and early 1990s was not completely dead; a substantial section of the South continued to talk to a substantial section of the North in the form of the Lomé Conventions. It may be the case that at times the Lomé dialogue was, as former ACP states' Secretary-General Edwin Carrington called it, a dialogue between the deaf and the dumb. It was true that the Community was deaf to ACP states' requests for increased sugar quotas, substantial funds for industrial development, comprehensive sanctions against South Africa in the apartheid era or overall debt relief. The ACP countries were likewise sometimes 'dumb' in respect of their lack of technical preparation for negotiations or the taking of initiatives. But the Lomé Conventions offered at least the foundations of a dialogue. As discussed in Chapter 4, the current prospects for the demise of the Lomé system by the end of the century are at least fair.

In an ideal world no development policy would be necessary to eradicate what Lomé IV aptly calls 'causes and situations of misery unworthy of the human condition and deep-rooted economic and social inequalities'.[8] In a slightly less ideal world there would be no need for a selective development policy in which, to build on the achievements of the past, some poor countries such as Bangladesh were excluded from some development programmes. Of course, if a better development policy were on offer from the international community to all less developed countries (LDCs), the ACP states would do well in their own interests, and in the interests of equity and solidarity with other LDCs, to accept it in place of Lomé. But in the current situation of widespread human misery, the marginalization of Africa and the unstable world political environment, the time is not right to terminate the Lomé Convention.

SOURCES OF MARGINALIZATION

Development policy in general and the Lomé Convention in particular have declined in importance to the EU in the 1990s. Since the accession of Spain and Portugal to the Community in 1986, and the installation of the Spaniard Manuel Marin as Development Commissioner in 1988, there has been increased emphasis on Community relations with Central and South America. The extension of the stabilization of export earnings system (Stabex) in 1987 to Bangladesh, Bhutan, Haiti, Laos, the Maldives, Nepal, the Yemen Arab Republic and the People's Republic of Yemen showed additional broadening in the Community's interests. As early as 1988 the incumbent Development Commissioner, Natali, when trying to get the ACP countries to agree to sign a Lomé Convention of indefinite duration, argued that this would hold the Community's wandering attention on them.

The broadening of the Community's development interests coincided with the international marginalization of Africa. The 1980s have seen Africa slip down the development agenda. While some other developing areas, notably South East Asia, have experienced economic success, Africa has suffered economic failure. Famines rather than economic growth have been the order of the day. Africa was the continent that during the 1980s could hardly do anything right. Per caput incomes fell over the decade by as much as 25 per cent. The African, Caribbean and Pacific states since 1981 have suffered decreasing imports, decreasing export earnings and increasing external debt.

Another more recent factor leading to the marginalization of the Lomé Convention has been the increased interest in Eastern Europe since the momentous events of late 1989. This was noted, for instance, in the ACP–Community Joint Assembly meeting in September 1989 and in ACP countries' demands for funds for themselves in line with aid to Eastern Europe. By early 1990 the Community was helping to found an East European Bank for Reconstruction and Development, as well as granting large European Investment Bank loans to Eastern Europe. In October 1991, the European Council of foreign ministers refused to forgive 3 billion ecus of ACP countries' debts while at the same time approving 2 billion ecus of aid for the post-Soviet Union. The Community's order of priorities was clear. By contrast, the ACP countries have never been able to establish a development bank or an industrial development fund, the latter being a proposal going back to the 1960s.

In summary, the principal factors leading to the marginalization of the Lomé policy are:

- *The Community's diversion of attention towards Eastern Europe.* With the fall of the Berlin Wall and the end of Soviet domination in Eastern Europe, the Community's prime focus became its relations with these neighbouring states.
- *The steady expansion of the Community's external interests.* Since the early 1970s, the Community directed more attention to developing countries in Asia. In the 1980s, the Community became more interested in non-ACP states in Latin America.

The Community–Andean pact ratified in 1987 and the current EU interest in the Southern Cone Common Market (Mercosur) are evidence of this new interest in Latin America. Community membership expanded to include states such as Spain and Portugal which have strong ties to Latin America. Also, some Community members have never been enthusiastic about the Community's emphasis on Africa.

- *The disastrous economic performance of Africa in the 1980s and its consequent marginalization in the world system.* As Samir Amin put it, 'Today Africa is already beginning to be excluded from the international division of labour, by the system which has confined the continent to agriculture and mining and forces it to exploit its land to exhaustion, and by the technological revolution which cuts down on the need for some raw materials.'[9]

However, as well as these marginalizing forces, there are factors which work to foster the stability and continuity of the Lomé system. The next section analyses the sources of stability in the Lomé relationship.

SOURCES OF STABILITY

The marginalization of the Lomé Convention is a considerable problem. Attracting new financial resources or bringing new ideas to a marginalized Convention is not easy. Even keeping the Convention functioning becomes more difficult.

But, despite its diminishing importance in the Community's external relations, the Lomé Convention cannot yet be written off. EU Commissioner Marin made a point of telling the ACP states at the signing of Lomé IV that progress in relations with the South would not cease but would proceed in parallel with progress in relations with the East. Moreover, it is not inconceivable that changing international circumstances, such as a new wave of attention to the developing countries, would again put the Convention to the forefront of EU policies. There is considerable reason to predict that the fourth Lomé Convention may not be the last.

Eight sources of stability and continuity in the Lomé relationship are outlined below. Taken together, these suggest that the foundations of the Lomé Convention are reasonably strong. The sources of stability are:

- the existence of a long tradition of interaction between Europe and its ACP partners;
- the tendency towards inertia in international institutions;
- the political support for Lomé in EU member states, especially France;
- the favourable public opinion in the EU towards overseas aid-giving in general;
- Europe's interest in Africa's resources;
- the EU's global political ambitions;
- Lomé's role as an alliance;
- Lomé's functions as an international regime.

The long (colonial) tradition of EurAfrican relations

As an association between Africa and the European Community, the Lomé relationship stretches back to the Treaty of Rome Association. This was established in 1957 for the dependencies of the then six Community member states. It could be argued that if the traumas of decolonization in the 1960s and the economic disappointments of the 1980s failed to disrupt the EurAfrican association, the neglect of the 1990s will not be likely to do so.

Furthermore, from the point of view of political utility, as long as the Lomé Convention remains a club which everybody (including Namibia, Eritrea and South Africa) wants to join, the EU will remain interested in it.

Institutional inertia

The long history of the Convention, its well-established institutions and its role in national foreign ministries mean that major changes such as the abolition of the Convention would be difficult to accomplish. According to decision-making theory, it is more likely that there will be incremental changes in this decades-old relationship, rather than a complete policy review or break with tradition. Policy-makers find it much easier to make adjustments in existing institutions than to start completely afresh.[10] International organizations such as UNESCO, the International Labour Organization or the Southern African Development

Coordination Conference are rarely wound up, even when their *raison d'être* disappears or they face considerable opposition. The sheer complexity of the Lomé framework and the number of states and officials involved in operating it means that Lomé would be administratively difficult to abolish or to reorganize efficiently.

Political support

Another reason for the staying power of the Lomé Convention is its importance in French foreign policy. The Convention serves as the French counterpart of the Commonwealth; the Lomé Convention inherited the French Community which dissolved in the late 1950s.

As discussed in Chapter 1, Africa has always been of vital interest to France. Africa is also the location of the majority of ACP countries and thus the focus of European Community interest. France's continuing interest in the Lomé Convention was shown in French insistence on mentioning Lomé in the Maastricht treaty and by the ACP–Community Joint Assembly meeting in 1989 which was addressed by the president of the national assembly, the minister for cooperation and President Mitterand.

More recently, it has been possible to question the depth of French support for Africa. Under Prime Minister Balladur, Africa seemed to become less important to France. France cut the link between the Central African franc and the French franc in 1994, causing the former to plunge in value. France may have been bowing to economic necessity, but it also created the impression of handing fiscal responsibility for French-speaking Africa over to the IMF. Nevertheless, there is a long habit of 'EurAfrican' thinking in France which will tend to support Lomé. In the 1995 mid-term review, it was French pressure and French financial commitment which clinched the agreement (see Chapter 4).

Another source of political support for the Lomé Convention is the European Parliament. European parliamentarians meet jointly with the ACP states in the Lomé Consultative Assembly. Many of the Europeans find this extremely valuable. The Parliament's Development Committee takes a profound interest in the the operation of the Lomé Convention. Although the Parliament's powers in respect to Lomé are limited to consultation,

European governments cannot completely ignore the Parliament's wishes.

Public opinion in the EU

Although public opinion in liberal democracies is not always directly or quickly translated into government policies, there is strong support in Europe for the idea of giving foreign aid to less fortunate areas in general, and to the developing countries in particular.

The Development Studies Association took a pessimistic view of the 1990s: 'So successful was the Reagan–Thatcher decade in making the uncaring pursuit of personal affluence respectable that the prevailing climate of Western opinion is opposed or at least indifferent to the notion of helping the poor and disadvantaged in the world, especially if it involves any hint of personal risk or sacrifice.'[11] As well as the concrete evidence of billions of ecus of public donations to development charities, surveys show that public opinion in Europe is not as unfavourable to aid as the above view suggests. Recent public opinion surveys by the European Commission's *Eurobarometer* give a more sanguine picture of a European public for whom aid has an important if not unassailable degree of support. For instance, the 1987 survey found that those who supported third world aid strongly or fairly strongly amounted to 89 per cent of respondents, including 87 per cent of those from the UK. Of Europeans who had a positive view of the United Nations in 1989, 45 per cent did so because of reasons related to development and famine relief. In 1990, *Eurobarometer* surveyed Community citizens on their views of aid to Eastern Europe and the former USSR. Sixty-nine per cent favoured allowing Eastern Europeans to benefit from Community programmes and resources, with 62 per cent still in favour when this necessitated a Community budget increase. Supporting aid to the former USSR was a similar 62 per cent, rising to as much as 73 per cent in Denmark. In the UK, a 1995 Harris poll found that only 10 per cent of the public supported cuts in overseas aid.[12]

These polls do not not prove that the European public would favour the relatively unknown Lomé system *per se*, but giving aid in general does have strong popular backing in the Community.

Small increases in the aid programme or living up to the 0.7 per cent of GNP aid target could well attract public support.

Europe's interest in Africa's resources

There is continuing interest by the EU, especially by France, in Africa's primary products, notably minerals. Imports from the ACP states into the Community reached a high of over 20,000 million European currency units (ecus) in 1990 while Europe's exports to the ACP countries in that year were over 16,000 million ecus.[13] ACP countries' exports are mainly of primary products; Europe's are mainly of manufactures. While Europe may not be particularly interested in preserving its supplies of ACP tropical products such as coffee, the EU has a special interest in African minerals. In the words of a Community publication: 'Nature has not spoiled the European Community, which will always depend on the formidable mineral resources of the South. Africa, especially well-endowed, possesses reserves of primary products which are largely intact.'[14]

Although Europe is not exclusively reliant on African primary products, and fears rather than seeks an influx of labour, the image of Africa as a reservoir of oil, minerals, timber and other resources for the future is still attractive to European policy-makers. Some World Bank policy-makers have even suggested that Africa could play another resource-oriented role: as a receptacle for Europe's overflowing waste.

The global political strategy of Europe

It used to be fiercely maintained by the Community that it had no strategy towards the developing countries, no foreign policy, and no political interests. The former Community Development Commissioner, Edgard Pisani, forcefully expressed this position: 'it [the Community] has no strategic interest and little or no commercial interests, it has always been solely concerned with development up to now.'[15] This non-political image was portrayed as one of Lomé's main strengths in the 1970s and 1980s. Lomé was said to be politically neutral and completely non-judgemental of its partners' internal affairs. Lomé's respect for their sovereignty was absolute: 'It [Lomé] is non-aligned in that it respects each partner's freedom to choose its economic system, political

regime and development model. It embraces countries represented by governments of varying political tendencies.'[16]

In practice, this political neutrality was a convenient fiction.
Political disputes over, say, the diplomatic recognition of East
Germany by ACP countries, the abuses of dictators such as Idi
Amin and the apartheid regime in South Africa did intrude on
the Lomé relationship. But following the demise of the alternative
Soviet model of development and the major aid donors' new
emphasis on democracy, even the appearance of political neutrality was less to the forefront in Lomé IV. The 1980s were an
era of intense economic conditionality as the World Bank and
IMF tried to get developing countries to balance their budgets
through structural adjustment plans. By 1989 Lomé, too, was
supporting structural adjustment for indebted and impoverished
ACP countries.

The Community has always had a plethora of political, strategic, and commercial interests in the Lomé Convention,
including those outlined on p. 152. In the 1980s, the emphasis on
respecting human rights (and women's rights) grew within the
Lomé system. By the 1990s the 'second wave' of international
aid conditionality had washed over the Lomé system.[17] The 1995
mid-term review made aid explicitly dependent on ACP countries' observance of human rights and 'good governance'
standards.

Despite widespread acceptance of political conditionality by
donors ranging from the USA to Switzerland and the EU, the
application of it is fraught with problems. Double standards,
where sanctions are applied according to the importance rather
than the virtue of the recipient, are almost impossible to avoid.
Cases where suspending aid harms the poor instead of the government, causes the regime to 'dig in' rather than undertake reforms,
or leads to embarrassing splits among the donor community are
not infrequent. However, the existence of flexibility within the
donor's requirements and the use of positive support measures
for civil society – such as aid to trade unions or women's movements – instead of just punitive sanctions has reduced some of
the original concerns of the recipients.[18]

More extreme versions of Western conditionality or intervention have not come about. In September 1992 UK Foreign
Secretary Hurd urged the UN to adopt an 'imperial role', taking
over the governance of countries which were in a state of collapse

such as Cambodia or Somalia.[19] Foreign Secretary Hurd even recommended the early use of troops by the UN to prevent warlords from taking power. However, this 'new imperialism' was not adopted by the USA or the UN, and even Hurd's deputy minister, Lynda Chalker, called his use of the term 'imperial' mistaken. The United Nations in the 1990s does not have sufficient resources, power or political support to engage in the role of policing the world, even if it had the wish to do so.

In the Lomé Convention and elsewhere, political conditionality, because of the difficulty of implementing it in any consistent way, remains chiefly at the level of declaration and exhortation. But it also operates at the level of aid for projects supporting democracy and temporary stoppages of aid to countries which violate human rights or good governance standards. Whether transferring the donors' model of good government and administration to developing countries can be successfully achieved or can be achieved without crippling the recipients' ability to formulate their own policies, however, remains to be seen.[20]

Lomé as an alliance

Overtly, the Lomé Convention is not a diplomatic alliance. It is also not an alliance in the traditional sense of a military defence or security pact.[21] Nevertheless, by analysing the Lomé Convention in the context of the sometimes hostile external environment described below, it can be regarded as an alliance. As in many alliances, the parties to it are not of equal power. The Lomé Convention is an alliance directed against poverty, underdevelopment, and political marginalization both for Europe and for the ACP countries.

The longevity of the Lomé Convention can be attributed to internal factors such as the signatories' shared histories of colonialism (as colonizers and colonized), shared hopes of economic benefits from increased trade, or – as the Community sometimes claims – its own altruism. But in analysing the Lomé Convention as an alliance, external factors, or threats, become more significant. That is, in maintaining an alliance the perception of a common threat is the most significant factor in ensuring the survival of the relationship.[22]

In terms of the Lomé Convention, the relevant threats are not primarily those of military conquest, but others which are equally real. These include the fear by the ACP countries of isolation from Europe, or – as in the case of Guinea (Conakry) before 1975 – isolation from other ACP members.[23] The ACP states also face the fear of an unstable world economy with declining commodity prices, rising interest rates, and growing foreign debts. There is the fear – in the absence of the soft loans and grants of Lomé – of having to turn to 'harder', more demanding donors such as the World Bank and IMF. The ACP countries also see as a threat a world dominated economically and politically up to the present by the superpowers – or more recently by the USA alone.

For the Europeans, the alliance with the ACP states is based on the fear of being relegated to third-rate powers without global influence, and without power in the developing world. They also fear that their traditional influence over the former colonies will be usurped by others, and that they will have no guaranteed access to the raw materials or markets of their former dependencies. The Lomé alliance responds to the threats which are perceived by both the ACP countries and the EU to their international political and economic standing.

Lomé as an international regime

Forms of international cooperation have become a key focus of interest in international relations and political science. The question of how the units, the states, in an anarchical system manage to co-exist and cooperate most of the time in a peaceful fashion is central to this study.

Regime theorists observed that there was neither the constant conflict of a Hobbesian 'war of all against all' internationally nor a condition of order and cooperation based on the adherence of states to international law or subjection to a world government. Instead there existed intermediate structures – termed regimes – which mediated conflict and performed specialized functions. The nature and functioning of these international regimes has spawned a considerable literature, particularly in the USA.

According to the classic definition, regimes were 'principles, norms, rules and decision-making procedures around which actor expectations converge in a given issue area'.[24] Regimes were networks which regularized and controlled a state's international behaviour.[25] Countries did not just exercise power, they followed rules. The successive Lomé Conventions are a good example of four decades of rule-based international cooperation, involving over eighty sovereign states.

Although some scholars have disputed that the Lomé Convention constitutes a regime, close analysis shows that it does fulfil the major criteria of an international regime.[26] It demonstrates the following defining characteristics of a regime:[27]

- *It stabilizes mutual expectations as regards behaviour.* A senior UK diplomat characterized Lomé in just these terms in 1991. He noted that the UK did not particularly like Lomé, but at least it meant that all parties knew the rules and what to expect from the relationship. Both the text of the Lomé Convention and the habits of behaviour and interaction which have grown out of it over decades give the relationship considerable predictability and stability.

- *It reduces transaction costs.* The Lomé regime may also increase costs in some areas, such as the expenses for ACP states to send representatives to the Joint Assembly. But the cost of EU delegations in ACP countries are now charged to the Community budget and not to aid funds. If trade preferences are included here, the costs of doing business with the EU are definitely decreased by the existence of the Lomé regime.

  Moreover, the ACP and European partners receive considerable value from the trade and business information provided within the Convention system by *inter alia* the Centre for Industrial Development (CDI) and the Technical Centre for Agricultural and Rural Cooperation (CTA).

- *The flow of information is increased.* One of Lomé's indisputable effects has been to increase the flow of information, communication and interaction between the respective parties. The levels of interaction between developing countries in different regions, which now participate in the ACP Group, and between the developing countries and European countries which were not their former colonizers have been greatly expanded.

  The ministerial and ambassadorial committees, the Joint Assembly and the ACP Secretariat contribute to this flow. Lomé even has institutions largely devoted to disseminating information, such as the CDI and CTA mentioned above, as well as a variety of occasional publications and its own bi-monthly journal, *The Courier*.

- *Interactions are repeated frequently enough to perpetuate them-selves.* Up to the present the Lomé regime has successfully perpetuated and expanded itself for nearly four decades. This is not to say that other events cannot overtake a regime's tendency to perpetuate itself. To regime theorists, any of a variety of factors can lead to a regime's downfall.[28] For instance, European governments' desire for cost-cutting or the French wave of Afropessimism might one day signal the end of the Lomé regime, just as the East–West regimes of cooper-ation were swept away by events in 1989.

All regimes have some internal inconsistencies between the components or between the norms of the regime and the regime's actual behaviour. The Lomé regime is no exception. Incoherence among the components can be seen in the dif-ferent interests of the European member states, and in the divisions between African and non-African ACP countries. Inconsistencies also exist between the Lomé Convention's stated equality of partners and the reality of European prepon-derance, between the stated aims of helping to eliminate situations of misery unworthy of the human condition and the widespread persistence of such conditions in many ACP countries.

Lomé is far from meeting all of the ACP countries' develop-ment needs, but it has satisfied some of them. For instance, in 1992 the Côte d'Ivoire's Minister of Health declared: 'Overall, I think we are satisfied with the fields of Community assistance and particularly with the medicines supply operation where Community aid is very effective.'[29] On a larger scale the 1990 *Annual Report of the ACP–EEC Council of Ministers* reported that 'both parties agreed that the results of cooperation could be regarded as positive on the whole and that the objective of the Convention has broadly been achieved.' The Report did go on to highlight problems in the area of slow payment of aid in particular. But, in terms of the main Lomé goal of creating a North–South alliance focused on Europe and Africa, the regime has been quite successful.

In summary, the Lomé Convention can usefully be considered as an international regime. Like other international regimes it is an orderly arrangment which regulates and strengthens the interactions among participants, acts in some respects towards attaining its goals and reducing conflict, and perpetuates itself.

In the next section Lomé is considered not as a regime, but as an example of regional integration. Like the EU member states, many developing countries have sought to maximize their political stability and economic prosperity by entering into regional groupings with neighbouring states. Whereas regime theorists point out the processes of cooperation among disparate states within international regimes, the regional integration theorists emphasize that the participants of regional organizations should be similar in political outlook and economic development, as well as contiguous in geographical location.

THE FALLACY OF TRANSPOSITION

Rolf Langhammer and Ulrich Hiemenz argued that the experiences and gains of European integration in 1957–8 were unique and not replicable by developing countries. The high level of intraregional trade, similarities in income and industrialization levels, political congeniality in foreign affairs, and capacity and willingness to compensate those adversely affected were unique to Europe. This meant, they contended, that developing countries could not copy the European model. They termed this theory, that the gains which had accrued to the Community from integration could not be repeated elsewhere, as 'the fallacy of transposition'.

Furthermore, Langhammer and Hiemenz argued that developing countries themselves had adopted this view and accepted the so-called 'fallacy of transposition': 'It has taken quite a long time for developing countries to accept the fallacy of transposition and to draw lessons.'[30] It is indisputable that those developing countries which have tried to replicate the European model of integration and cooperation have had problems. The Community itself has suffered from budgetary, economic and political problems, as well as successive crises.

Langhammer and Hiemenz rightly point out that actors have not always distinguished between regional integration as a means to economic betterment or as an end in itself. This, however, has been as true in Europe as elsewhere. In Europe the underlying argument for regional integration was based on the need to keep the peace, twice destroyed by wars in this century. Economic integration measures followed from this political necessity. Furthermore, it is by no means clear that developing countries or other policy-makers have accepted that regional integration will not provide some of the benefits to LDCs that Europe has enjoyed.

It is correct that many efforts up to now to foster regional cooperation and integration in developing countries have not had the desired effects. The Latin American Free Trade Association (LAFTA), founded in 1960, even seemed to have produced mainly negative economic consequences of trade diversion and lower levels of absolute trade.[31] Yet even in Latin America the impetus for other regional groupings such as the Andean Pact and the Latin American Integration Association has not diminished. There are still high hopes for positive results in terms of trade creation and economic growth for the North American Free Trade Association (NAFTA) between Mexico, Canada and the USA.

In Africa, there are many failed examples of regional cooperation, most notably the now-defunct East African Community. Another example of a grouping which is generally admitted not to have lived up to its ambitions is the Economic Community of West African States (ECOWAS). The ECOWAS experience has been one of slow implemenation of liberalization measures, incomplete observance of ECOWAS rules, and extremely small trade effects. Based on the problems of fifteen regional organizations, Langhammer and Hiemenz judged that regional integration among developing countries (covering customs unions, common markets, and joint investment planning) has not proved viable. 'There seems to be no alternative to trade liberalization on a non-discriminatory basis,' they conclude.[32]

However, the problems of getting global trade liberalization through the General Agreement on Tariffs and Trade (GATT)[33] are well known. The Uruguay Round began in 1986 and dragged on until 1994, missing a succession of deadlines since 1990. Major trading countries have often negotiated or imposed agreements to their advantage outside of the GATT framework. Despite GATT's free trade rules, the GATT secretariat listed 284 known restrictive trade agreements. Developing countries are often disadvantaged in the international marketplace by the power of multinationals, their own lack of capital and resources and the declining terms of trade of primary commodities. Furthermore, while international trade remains a power-based rather than a rules-based system, where the most powerful countries can force 'voluntary export restraint' on the weak, global trade liberalization cannot be relied upon to benefit developing countries.[34]

The analysis of the problem by developing countries and most development specialists calls for more regional integration, not less. The experience of the European Community remains an incentive. A recent study of ECOWAS noted, 'A battle has been lost for regional cooperation within the framework of ECOWAS, but the war was still to be won.'[35] Former Nigerian president Obasanjo argued eloquently that Africa needed more regional cooperation and should look for inspiration to Europe: 'we can rekindle our flickering African flame from the European torch.'[36] European Parliamentarian and former prime minister of Portugal, Maria Lourdes Pintasilgo, even derived specific lessons from European integration which were applicable to the West African experience: to cooperate beyond the nation state; to develop leadership at all levels; and to abandon old, idealized concepts of development, building from the bottom up.

In the context of the Lomé Conventions, the value of regional integration and solidarity was not lost on African leaders. The successes gained by the ACP in negotiating Lomé I and subsequently inserting declarations condemning 'apartheid which constituted a violation of human rights and an affront to human dignity' into the third and fourth Lomé Conventions were largely due to their solidarity (Annex II, Lomé III). Former President Olesegun Obasanjo rightly noted that the LDCs needed regional unity in order to get fair treatment in their trade relations: 'If we do not in our turn achieve meaningful economic integration, it is unrealistic to hope in our disunity to secure a square deal from our trading partners.'[37]

Of course, each type of regional grouping must find its own appropriate structure and functions. The lessons outlined above may be necessary but not sufficient for integration among countries which have not yet built nation states and which vary widely in size and levels of economic development. Yet LDCs – encouraged by the European example and the regional cooperation provisions of the Lomé Convention – will continue to look to regional organizations to offset their political and economic marginalization. It is far from clear that they should not do so. Thus, we can refer to 'the fallacy of the fallacy of transposition'.

The vitality of the regional ideal can be seen in the new regional organizations which continue to be established. Some of them, such as the Union of the Arab Maghreb discussed in Chapter 3, or the Indian Ocean Zone of Peace (still under discussion after twenty years), may not have a bright future. But the prospects for Mercosur in Latin America, for instance, are good. The transformation of the Southern African Development Coordination Council (SADCC), an organization originally designed to counter South African domination and destabilization of southern African countries, is a demonstration of how strongly countries seek regional cooperation. SADCC has been transformed into the Southern African Development Community (SADC), an organization now including South Africa. Obeying the principle that international organizations are rarely disbanded, SADC sees a new vocation for itself in economic development. Although questions have been raised about its continuing usefulness, SADC may well find a positive new role.

The current vigour and influence of the European construction gives the idea of regional integration new strength. Europe certainly regards itself and recommends itself (as shown in the following section) as a model of cooperation which other regions should follow. It could be argued that the next century will be the century of the Europeans. If Europe can achieve economic and monetary integration and incorporate Central and Eastern Europe, then its economic power will be greatly enhanced. Based on its well-educated population, huge productive base, and efficient capital markets, Europe is likely to set much of the world economic agenda for the twenty-first century.[38]

Developing countries in the African, Caribbean and Pacific Group need a united approach to this European economic superpower. At the same time, carefully constructed, effective regional cooperation among developing countries has the potential to provide them with economic benefits and political strength.

ENLARGING LOMÉ

The New South Africa and the EU

Since becoming a fully democratic country after the 1994 elections, South Africa has normalized and increased its international relations. Its serious economic and social problems have also

started to be tackled by the government. According to government figures, after years of stagnation South African GDP grew
by 1.3 per cent in 1993 and by 2.7 per cent in 1994. The government hopes for growth of 3.5–4.0 per cent in 1995.

At present important negotiations are taking place between
South Africa and its largest trading partner, the EU, which takes
40 per cent of South Africa's exports. The broad framework of
these negotiations is greatly to be welcomed and seems likely to
be of substantial benefit to both sides.

Although its economy and export potential dwarf those of
other African countries – South African exports to Europe
amount to over 50 per cent of those of the seventy African,
Caribbean and Pacific countries associated with the EU – South
Africa is far from developed. According to the United Nations
Development Programme, South Africa is the 80th richest
country in the world, but only 95th in terms of its human
development, ranking below many developing countries. Its
manufacturing industries are not internationally competitive and
its export earnings are dependent on a few products such as gold,
metal products and precious stones. Thus, there is a good argument for saying that South Africa is more like a middle income
developing country than a developed one.[39]

To its credit, the EU has been extremely active in the new
South Africa and flexible in its approach to the country. Unlike
the USA, which tends to take a 'task force' approach to Africa,
undertaking a mission and then decamping, the EU is aiming at
a long-term relationship. The head of the EU delegation in South
Africa stressed the moral underpinnings of European interest: 'It
is this same vision for peace and social justice which unites us
with South Africa as it sets out on the road of reconstruction and
development, an effort to which the EU is deeply committed.'[40]

As early as 1990 the Community unblocked new investment in
the Republic of South Africa, and in 1992 it began to dismantle
the sanctions on the country – starting with oil, sports and culture
– which it had never imposed very enthusiastically. In the early
1990s the EU was non-committal regarding the form of its future
relations with a democratic South Africa. At the end of 1993 the
prospects for South Africa to participate in the Lomé Convention,
Europe's most generous aid and trade agreement, looked bleak.
It was claimed that South Africa's proposed membership of the
Southern African Development Community would be economi-

cally incompatible with the Lomé relationship. South African goods would pour into Europe at unacceptably high levels through other SADC members, threatening the survival of the Convention. Furthermore, getting approval for South African membership of Lomé from the then twelve European Community and sixty-nine African, Caribbean and Pacific member states would be very difficult.[41] At a meeting in Paris in early 1994, the South Africans were told that it would be impossible for them to join Lomé. The existing members thought that the Lomé 'cake' was too small for South Africa to get a share.

On the South African side, some advisers believed South Africa should hold out for the whole Lomé package of aid and trade preferences and accept nothing less. But during the visit of European Development Commissioner Pinheiro in May 1995, the South Africans agreed to the 'Lomé minus' option. It is this option which is currently being negotiated. According to the 'minus' programme, South Africa can accede to the Lomé Convention but will be excluded from most of its provisions. Thus, South Africa will not be admitted to the commodities stabilization scheme, the minerals production support scheme, the aid facility, or the trade preferences, including the provisions for sugar, beef, rum and bananas. What South Africa is likely to get under Lomé will be limited to participation in tendering for aid project contracts on the same terms as EU member states and the ability to 'cumulate' its exports with those of neighbouring Lomé signatory countries. South Africa will also be admitted to the Lomé political institutions. But in addition to 'Lomé minus', South Africa will get a separate aid programme and a trade agreement. This is known as the 'twin-track' approach.

The aid programme

While this 'twin-track' approach may seem to involve a drastic curtailment of Lomé benefits, South Africa will continue to receive aid under a special European budget line which has been operating since 1985. The European Programme for Reconstruction and Development (EPRD) will disburse 500 million ecus of aid over the period 1995–99. This is by far the EU's largest and most generous aid programme for a single country. Led by the Nordic countries, the Netherlands, the UK and Denmark from the donors' side, there was a remarkable degree of consensus about putting extra effort into supporting the new South Africa.

Concerning the operation of EU aid, there are plans to prioritize key aid sectors and reduce the 600 projects currently operating to a more manageable number. The sectors to be targeted are: health; rural development and water supply; urban development; economic cooperation, trade promotion and support for small and medium enterprises; good government and democratization.

To some observers, the EPRD has been the only recipient-driven rather than donor-driven aid programme in Africa. South Africa wants to set its own priorities and make sure that the 'policy dialogue' with the EU is a two-way dialogue, not one-way conditionality. The EU, for instance, proposed to use some aid funds for the 'trade promotion' or marketing of its own products. This was not well received.

Following the signing in October 1994 of a framework agreement emphasizing human rights and democracy, the EU has stepped up its activities in South Africa. The European Investment Bank was authorized to lend 300 million ecus in South Africa over two years and the smaller European Community Investment Partners scheme to help joint ventures has selected seven projects.

Free trade?

Both South Africa and the EU see their trade relations as more valuable than the aid programme; and the negotiations on trade have been more controversial. South Africa is classified as a developed country under GATT – and the USA and others have opposed its reclassification. Nevertheless, in 1994 the USA, Japan, Canada and the EU gave South Africa access to the Generalized System of Preferences (GSP) – which is supposed to be limited to developing countries. In the European case, the letter announcing the giving of GSP preferences indicated that they were being offered despite the fact that South Africa was neither a developing nor a transitional (from Communism) economy. The GSP is a welcome step, but only 14.4 per cent of South Africa's industrial exports to the EU are dutiable. Of these dutiable products, 86.3 per cent receive GSP concessions.[42] Some officials have suggested that extending the GSP to South Africa is a prelude to tightening the conditions on the Asian 'tigers'.

The negotiations on the trade agreement designed to run in parallel with Lomé are aimed at establishing a free trade area in industrial products between South Africa and the EU. As a member of the World Trade Organization, South Africa is in principle in favour of free trade. Nevertheless, the negotiations – which may continue for twelve to eighteen months – have to deal with some difficult issues.

One issue is the timetable for establishing the free trade area. Although the EU has discussed an asymmetrical timetable where it opens its markets faster than South Africa does, it has still urged that the free trade area be in place after five years. Ten years might be more realistic. In the Asia Pacific Economic Cooperation forum, for instance, current discussions involve creating a free trade area for developed countries by 2010 and for developing countries by 2020.

South Africa is already reducing its average tariffs from 20 per cent to 12 per cent. Following over two years of negotiation under GATT, some duties will fall dramatically. Tariffs on cars will fall from 65 per cent to 40 per cent; clothing duties will fall from 90 per cent to 40 per cent by 2004. But there is considerable concern that cheap imports will cause the loss of many jobs in a country where unemployment is estimated at 40–50 per cent.

As well as problems with employment, South Africa is concerned about the effects of a free trade area with Europe on its four partners in the Southern African Customs Union (SACU): Botswana, Lesotho, Namibia, and Swaziland. They would effectively be brought into free trade with the EU. At present customs duties finance the running of SACU; other funds would have to be sought. The EU is fond of extolling its experience as a model of regional integration. Commission President Jacques Santer declared that the success of Europe served as an inspiration to others. But in practice the Europeans may not have fully assessed the effects on SACU of their plan for a free trade area with South Africa. Although the US and the South Asian NICs do not regard the proposed EU–South African free trade area as a political threat, they may find commercial objections and respond accordingly.

Cuba and the EU?

It has been said that Cuba's problem is that it is a small country too far from God and too close to the USA. Up to now it has also been politically and economically quite far from the EU. Since 1962 the USA has had a trade embargo on Cuba and finds Cuba, one of the world's last vestiges of socialist ideology, a persistent thorn in its flesh.

Despite some signs in the 1990s that US policy-makers recognized that 'constructive engagement' with Cuba was more appropriate than the long-running embargo, there has been little change. In 1992 the embargo was further tightened on the residual trade in food and medical supplies between the two countries. President Clinton did relax restrictions on visits and news-gathering in Cuba in 1995, but 'Cuba-bashing' remains a popular way for US domestic politicians to win votes. The Helms–Burton bill of 1995 was designed to tighten the Cuban embargo again and has passed through the US Senate, albeit without the original draconian proposals to punish anyone who handled expropriated Cuban property or any foreign country which imported Cuban sugar.

Traditionally, Europe has been less ideologically opposed to the Cuban system than has the USA. Few votes in Europe depend on events in Cuba. But, so far, official European contacts with the regime of Fidel Castro have been tentative. The EU, which does not see itself as having a vital interest in the Caribbean or in Cuba, has deferred to the USA which does. For example, an airport construction project in Grenada in the early 1980s was long delayed owing to US fears about possible Cuban military use of the facility.[43] Nevertheless, the UK for instance never severed trade relations with Cuba. A visit by UK Trade Minister Ian Taylor in 1994 led to the signing of an investment protection and promotion agreement. In 1995 the UK's Commonwealth Development Corporation, which lends money to enterprises in developing countries, made plans to start to operate in Cuba.

The European Community established formal relations with Cuba in 1988, but tangible progress in their relations since then has been slow. The European Parliament in 1993 called in the strongest language (but unsuccessfully) for the USA to abandon economic sanctions against Cuba. The Parliament resolved that because there was no Community legislation discriminating against Cuba, it should be included in regional aid programmes for the Caribbean.[44] Since then, the UN General Assembly, the Ibero-American summit, and the non-aligned movement all decisively rejected the embargo on Cuba.

In April 1994, Development Commissioner Marin opened a branch of the Community Humanitarian Office (ECHO) in Havana. In 1993 ECHO made a commitment of 7.8 million ecus to Cuba to combat a local epidemic, and further humanitarian aid in cooperation with non-governmental organizations was envisioned. However, the Commissioner indicated that no wider agreement could be negotiated until Cuba had transformed its political and economic situation.[45] This type of strict conditionality, where political and economic reforms are required before aid is given, is called 'front-loading'. By late 1995 the EU approved a modest humanitarian aid package of 15 million ecus for medical supplies and improvements to sanitation on the island.

Cuba is still not a liberal–democratic polity or a market economy, but strides have been taken in both directions. In 1993 Cuba held one-party elections and began to turn the parliament into a centre for debate. In the economic sphere there has been even more change. Cuba has received economic advice from former Spanish finance minister Solchaga and from the IMF. There has also been speculation that Cuba would join the World Bank and IMF. Recent economic reforms include reducing subsidies to state enterprises, increasing prices, reforming currency regulations, decentralizing authority, raising taxes and trying to reduce the budget deficit. The partial privatization of state farms and the acceptance of some foreign investment, private businesses and services has moved Cuba further towards a market economy.

At present the situation seems to be at stalemate, with Europe moving a little way towards assisting Cuba and Cuba moving a little way towards establishing the kind of free market, liberal–democratic system the West requires. If the two sides could come together, there could be immense benefits for political stability in a region where Haiti in particular is in turmoil and many countries face severe economic problems. For Cuba, European aid and trade links would be invaluable: Cuba lost 60 per cent of its export earnings between 1989 and 1992. Sugar harvests in the 1990s were repeatedly disappointing, and half of the formal economy disappeared.[46] But by 1995 the sugar harvest and nickel production had significantly recovered and the government estimated economic annual growth for the year at 2.5 per cent.[47]

The increasing political conditionality of the Lomé Convention may make it more difficult to consider Cuba for membership while it preserves the structure of its revolution. But the policy of isolating Cuba has so far created more problems, for the USA in particular, than it has solved. A European policy of constructive engagement might well be more successful in encouraging a 'new Cuba' to emerge.

While the EU might not want to allocate the necessary resources or risk offending GATT by offering Cuba access to Lomé provisions such as Stabex or the sugar and banana trade regimes, it could follow the South African precedent. That is, the EU could negotiate with Cuba a 'Lomé minus' or associate membership option. This would enable Cuba to receive European development aid, participate in regional development projects and in the Lomé political dialogue.

CONCLUSION

This chapter has examined the political issues surrounding the contemporary Lomé Convention. It found that changes in EU policies and in the international position of Africa led to the increasing marginalization of the Convention. Nevertheless, there are also significant sources of strength and stability in the Lomé relationship, which can be considered as both an alliance and an international regime. The EU continues to inspire developing countries with its model of integration, even if the process of European integration cannot be exactly replicated or transposed to other regions.

At a time when the existence of UN organizations for development, including the United Nations Industrial Development Organization (UNIDO) and the United Nations Conference on Trade and Development (UNCTAD) are under threat of closure, the Lomé Convention remains a significant avenue for North–South dialogue between regions. Just as history 'accelerated' for Europe as it developed further momentum for integration after the mid-1980s, Europe's relations with developing countries are now poised to accelerate as Europe tries to support the transition to democracy and development in South Africa and elsewhere, and tries to reconstruct its development policy for the twenty-first century.

The old, apartheid government of South Africa projected an image of the country as efficient and developed. This may have caused Europe unduly to worry about South Africa's competitive potential and to see South Africa as a profitable market for their exports. A free trade area with Europe may be the only outcome South Africa can negotiate, but there is little doubt that European exporters are better positioned to take advantage of such an arrangement than are the South Africans. For other developing countries, this new agreement could be a worrying sign that the non-reciprocal preferences they have hitherto received are gradually to be replaced by free trade areas.

For the EU, translating the political goodwill of the member states into a fair trade agreement covering both agricultural and industrial exports will be a particular challenge. As European Commissioner Pinheiro stated: 'South Africa is a special case that deserves a special effort from our side. South Africa deserves the best possible arrangement we can offer for future relations.'[48] If the EU develops a free trade area with South Africa, it will need to monitor it with care to ensure that the benefits are not just one-sided.

The EU's new opening up towards South Africa raises the question of opening up new relations in the Caribbean. In the wake of the Cold War, Cuba has been cut adrift politically and economically from its former sponsors in the USSR and Eastern Europe. Thus there is now a good opportunity for the EU to establish closer, development-oriented relations with Cuba. This initiative could, like the South African one, allow Cuba to negotiate a limited type of Lomé membership without access, for instance, to the sugar protocol or Stabex. Such an arrangement would serve the objectives of fostering Cuban social and economic development while improving Caribbean regional cooperation among the existing Caribbean Lomé member states.

Chapter 6

Conclusion
The EurAfrican construction

The relations between Europe and Africa date back to beyond recorded history. As explained in Chapter 2, the fossil record of human remains in Kenya's Rift Valley and recent genetic evidence strongly suggest that human beings originated in Africa.[1] They then diffused throughout the world in the original diaspora. Relations between Europeans and Africans are thus relations between close relatives, but relatives who have not always understood each other well. The earliest map-makers considered that Africa was the same size as Europe – or smaller – and comparable misunderstandings have persisted up to the present.[2]

With the exception of the case of the Kongo described in Chapter 2, the relations between Europe and Africa in the modern era were largely those of slavery, inequality, exploitation and colonialism. These relations and their justifications by Europeans appear so strange to contemporary observers that it may be difficult to understand how human beings held such views and carried out such actions. Yet as the nineteenth-century liberal philosopher John Stuart Mill observed, each generation finds some of the beliefs of the previous generation to be not only wrong but absurd. Despite the emphasis by revisionist historians on the atrocities of the African ruler Menelik I or the participation of Africans in the slave trade, the underlying concept of these exploitative relations, including colonialism, was the failure of Europeans to respect those who were different, who represented the 'other'.[3] The persistent legacy of the colonial experience was outlined in Chapter 2.

There is no doubt that the current state of EurAfrican relations, however skewed politically and economically in Europe's favour, is far superior to the not-so-distant era of colonial domination.

The Portuguese colonies in Africa, for instance, only attained independence in the mid-1970s. The ideals of national and, subsequently, human equality have developed and expanded in the context of relations between the European Community (more lately Union) and the African, Caribbean and Pacific Group of States. Nevertheless, as shown in Chapter 4, in practice their relations frequently did not live up to the ringing declarations signed by governments.

The Treaty of Rome declared optimistically in 1957 that it would lead the dependencies of the then six member states to the 'economic, social and cultural development which they expect'. Just as General de Gaulle had told the Algerians that he understood them ('Je vous ai compris'), the Community made a similar promise to its developing country partners for almost twenty years before the signing of Lomé I. And, in truth, the Community has usually well understood – though not necessarily responded to, or subordinated its own interests to – the concerns of developing countries. The Yaoundé I convention of 1963 between the Community and its developing country partners recognized the developing countries as equal, sovereign states, while Lomé IV's 'respect for and promotion of all human rights' reflects some of the latest ideals in development thinking. At the Rio Summit of the UN Conference on the Environment and Development in 1992, the European Commission took a very progressive line on aid. It tried to get the twelve member states to agree to set a firm date to meet the UN's target of 0.7 per cent of GNP for aid disbursements. Although France and Denmark supported the European Commission, the UK opposed the measure and killed it. The final agreement weakly called for the 0.7 per cent target to be met as soon as possible. The inadequacy of such loose targets was subsequently demonstrated in the November 1995 UK budget which cut development aid by a full 5.4 per cent.

In view of the progression of objectives, if not always of achievements, in their relations and the lack of viable alternatives to this relationship, Europe and Africa should undertake to continue and improve their linkages. They should build a 'EurAfrican construction' to complement the Europeans' own 'European construction', the EU. This EurAfrican construction should also incorporate the Caribbean and Pacific Lomé member states. At the same time it should not preclude the development of trans-

Mediterranean agreements (see Chapter 3) or closer relations with other developing regions such as Latin America (see Chapter 1).

In spite of some negative historical connotations, I have chosen the term 'EurAfrican' as both apposite in view of Africa's centrality to the Lomé system, and, like 'partnership', susceptible to a positive interpretation.[4] 'EurAfrica' is a specific geopolitical idea which stems from the colonial period and refers to a particular model of international relations. (The term 'France–Afrique' expresses a similar idea about the relations between France and Africa.) Before the 1980s when the Brandt report brought into popular focus the idea of international interdependence, 'EurAfrica' expressed an earlier form of the same concept. It was not the kind of balanced and equal interdependence that the political economists of the 1980s discussed, but a skewed relationship where decisions were to be made in Europe. These decisions were then supposed to work to the benefit of both parties, but not necessarily to an equal degree.

EurAfricanism stemmed from the French view that Europe and Africa were, like the partners in a lichen, naturally complementary. This complementarity was more than economic; it was also political, social and cultural. What the Africans lacked in political and technical expertise, in social and cultural development, Europe could provide. What Europe lacked in labour, land and natural resources could be provided by Africa. According to Anton Zischka, a leading exponent of EurAfricanism, this complementarity did not end with decolonization; it was based on 'the permanent coexistence of organisms of different natures which sustain each other mutually'.[5] It is interesting to note that in the original concept of EurAfrica, African labour was regarded as a valuable resource; today the possible displacement of African and other labour to Europe is more commonly perceived as a threat (see Chapter 3).

As well as an internal dimension where Europe and Africa shared their complementary factors of production to their mutual advantage (France was always especially interested in African minerals), EurAfrica had an equally important external dimension. It was a geopolitical super-region. Its *de facto* existence enabled Europe, notably France, to be a 'great power', to act on the world stage with authority. The political significance of Africa to France, to French self-esteem, can hardly be overestimated.

As François Mitterrand put it in 1957, 'Without Africa there will not be any history of France in the 21st century.'[6] As explained in Chapter 1, the European Community's external policy was often French policy writ large (and sometimes German in the case of Eastern Europe); therefore Africa was important in making the Community a world actor, especially in the latter's early days.

Since the second decade of the nineteenth century the USA – with UK support – propounded the Monroe Doctrine, a kind of 'hands off' sign for the Western hemisphere directed towards Europe. Thus, European powers with world ambitions had to look elsewhere. 'Elsewhere' was Africa, conveniently to the south of Europe and apparently available for colonization and exploitation. Even after decolonization, the system of continental bilateralism persisted. That is, the USA considered its client states in Latin America as its 'backyard' while Europe concentrated its influence on Africa.[7] As Tony Chafer observed, decolonization did not mean that France adopted a policy of isolationism or the withdrawal of its military, economic or political power from Africa. On the contrary, in Africa after formal colonialism ended, 'traditional French concerns with grandeur and international status' reasserted themselves.[8]

In the context of the Community's external relations, the international importance of the connection with Africa continued. Former Community Development Commissioner and French foreign minister Claude Cheysson wrote exuberantly in 1975, after signing the first Lomé Convention, about the relative merits of US–Latin American and Community–African relations. He claimed that the Lomé Convention, which united all of Africa with Europe in a single agreement negotiated through a single spokesperson for Africa, surpassed the US–Latin American connection.[9]

In French eyes particularly, Europe and Africa still have a natural affinity. During the 1980s and early 1990s a variety of criticisms were made of French policy towards Africa. France had given generous aid to Africa, but the situation of increasing poverty and dictatorial and corrupt regimes warranted serious concern. In a keynote 1990 speech at La Baule in France, President by Mitterrand began by insisting on greater political reforms in Africa in return for French aid. None the less, in keeping with the complexities underlying the practice of placing political conditions on aid and the common divergence between theory and practice (see Chapter 5), some analysts calculated that French aid to authoritarian regimes in the 1990s actually increased while aid to democratizing regimes declined.[10]

One French commentator argued that the deterioration of the effectiveness of French policy towards Africa meant 'France no longer has a policy towards Africa, only had habits'.[11] France certainly has a habit of close relations with Africa, leading to the conclusion by the powerful and secretive adviser on French African policy under de Gaulle and Pompidou, Jacques Foccart, that it was indeed true 'that the interest of my country and that of the former colonies which became its partners merged'.[12] In practice, it was often the case that the interests of the French government and business community were assumed to be African interests, rather than that they were.

Despite debates within French government circles, France has officially maintained its commitment to Africa and to the EU's development policy. In January 1994 France abandoned its support of the over-valued Central African franc but later in that year, at the Franco-African summit, President Mitterrand reiterated France's commitment to development and democracy as 'a grand human adventure'. It could be argued that the French Afropessimism of the 1980s which resulted in a wave of closures of French enterprises in Africa has been replaced with an Afro-realism of the 1990s. This Afrorealism recognizes not only the longstanding problems of Africa but also the importance of Africa as a market for French industrial goods, as a source of oil and other primary products, and as the largest area of concentration of French capital investment in the developing countries.[13] Africa remains the one continent where France can continue to act as a great power.

The European Community (now Union) too has maintained its support for developing countries, although less impressively than France has expressed its commitment to Africa. The European Commission's programme for 1992 stated:

> The Community's commitments to its partners in Africa, Latin America and Asia remain a central plank of its external policy. It would be unthinkable for the Community to reduce its effort at a time when debt and the growing threat of instability demand a strong political presence and continued economic support.[14]

Nevertheless, the erosion of support for the continuation of the Lomé Convention (described in Chapter 4) may call the EU's future commitment to its developing country partners into question. The desperate needs of Africa – where as many as 40 million of the inhabitants in the south and in the Horn are estimated by the UN to be in danger of starvation, and where in 1990 the overall rate of growth of GDP for the region was just over 1 per cent – calls for a new concept of European responsiblity and a new and invigorated European response.

The Community has been able to put its relationships with developing countries into new clothes where this seemed appropriate. Thus, the 1963 and 1969 Yaoundé Associations became the Lomé Conventions, officially 'partnerships' in order to distance themselves from the colonial theory of association. Statements resembling the language of the UN's New International Economic Order have appeared in the Lomé Conventions, but without the more controversial substance. In a similar way, the old theory of EurAfrica could be put to good use. 'EurAfrica' could be used to express a new, egalitarian conviction that there is an underlying political, economic and cultural interdependence between Europe and Africa. This kind of orientation already exists in the minds of many Africans and Europeans. For instance, the Lomé Conventions owe much of the rationale for their existence to the concept of 'EurAfrica'. When Commission President Jacques Delors referred to the priority Europe would have to give to 'a fruitful partnership with Africa, her natural companion',[15] this was a clear exposition of nothing other than the EurAfrican idea.[16] Without such a EurAfrican orientation, Africa risks remaining at the bottom of the international agenda and Europe risks the purposelessness described in the following section.

At a time when many analysts in the USA are searching for new enemies, seeking to replace the old bi-polar East–West divisions with visions of North versus South or civilizational conflict, the Europeans' approach is one to be welcomed. The Lomé Conventions show a steadfast European commitment, up to the present, to the development of Africa, the Caribbean and Pacific. This contrasts favourably with the Americans' 'task force' mentality towards Africa as demonstrated in their abortive attempts in 1992 and 1993 to reconstruct Somalia. Within the Lomé system, the new infusion of European conditionality, of programmes of support for structural adjustment and sometimes superficial declarations of support for democracy, and the abandonment of the politically neutral appearance of Lomé are changes whose benefits remain to be seen in the long term. Changes within the organization of the EU, including the increasing power of the European Parliament, may also result in dramatic changes in Europe's relations with developing countries. The European Parliament, for instance, has been reluctant to approve aid for countries such as Morocco and Turkey whose respect for human rights is deemed unsatisfactory.

THE EURAFRICAN CONSTRUCTION: THE SPIRITUAL DIMENSION

A constructive dialogue between the EU and the developing countries is necessary and beneficial for both parties. Without an attempt by Europe to position itself as a global partner, fostering prosperity, stability and democratic values in developing countries, Europe may end up lacking any purpose other than trying to match the power of the USA. In the run-up to the French presidential election of 1995, Jacques Delors argued that the construction of Europe was 'the only great collective adventure turned towards the future that is now on offer to France'.[17] In this statement M. Delors was certainly wrong: not only the construction of Europe but also the construction of a cooperative regime or regimes with the developing countries is now on offer to France and its European partners (see Chapter 5 for a discussion of regime theory). Its relations with developing countries are as important to Europe now as the relations with the ex-colonies were in the 1950s.

There is considerable vagueness about the project of European integration. No one is quite sure what its end point will be or how integrated Europe will finally become. Which countries of Central and Eastern Europe and beyond will eventually gain EU membership is not yet known. Modifying the internal institutions of the EU, rectifying the 'democratic deficit', creating economic and monetary union and cultivating a favourable image among the populations of the member states remain serious problems for the foreseeable future. Moreover, as discussed in Chapter 1, the creation of a common foreign and defence policy is slow and uncertain.

The lack of a cultural and spiritual dimension to the project of

European construction has been widely deplored. Czech President Vaclav Havel admired the technical content of the Treaty of Maastricht, but observed the dearth of any spiritual, moral or emotional content. Europe could thus, he feared, degenerate into 'a cast of fools, fanatics, populists and demagogues . . . determined to promote the worse European traditions. And there are, unfortunately, more than enough of those.'[18] It is hard, for instance, to find a single European country without a tradition of religious persecution, anti-semitism, intolerance of immigrants, and discrimination against women.

The eminent US political scientist Stanley Hoffman wrote caustically in 1994 about a Europe with no sense of direction and no purpose or goals: 'In 1964 I wondered about Western Europe's spiritual vitality. I still do.'[19]

For Hoffman Europe had no great leaders, no underlying shared values and no spiritual force. Parliaments were in decline while unaccountable bureaucracies expanded. The political process and political parties remained national, not European.[20] With twelve national languages, the EU institutions resemble a modern day Tower of Babel.

But by increasing and renewing its contacts with its roots in Mediterranean civilization, and with the former colonies of Africa, Latin America, the Caribbean and beyond, Europe could revitalize itself and find a positive role to play in the world. The new EurAfrican construction is certainly a project that could keep Europe usefully employed for many decades. Such a project of development for the poorer regions of the world would not bring Europe into conflict with the USA, Russia or the emerging powers of East Asia. But it could contribute to global peace and prosperity.

Notes

INTRODUCTION

1 Okri, Ben, 'An African Elegy', in *An African Elegy*, London, Jonathan Cape, 1992, p. 41.

1 THE EU AND FOREIGN POLICY

1 Puchala, Donald, 'Europe: Super-state or Bag of Marbles?', *Journal of Common Market Studies* 12 (1), 1973.
2 Henig, Stanley, 'From External Relations to Foreign Policy', *Journal of Common Market Studies* 12 (1), 1973.
3 Smith, Hazel, 'The Foreign Policy of the European Union', Lecture at the University of Bradford, 26 January 1994.
4 Smith, S., 'Foreign Policy Theory and the New Europe', in Carlsnaes, W. and Smith, S. (eds) *European Foreign Policy*, London, Sage, 1994.
5 Allison, Graham, *Essence of Decision*, Boston, Little Brown, 1971; also, Scott, Len and Smith, Steve, 'Lessons of October: historians, political scientists, policy-makers and the Cuban Missile Crisis', *International Affairs* 70 (4), October, 1994.
6 Strange, Susan, 'Wake up Krasner! The World has Changed', *Review of International Political Economy* 1 (2), Summer, 1994.
7 Zolo, D., *Complexity and Political Theory*, Cambridge, Polity Press, 1992.
8 Pfetsch, F., 'Tensions in Sovereignty', in Carlsnaes and Smith, op. cit., p. 121.
9 Petersen, Nikolaj, 'The European Union and Foreign and Security Policy', in Norgaard, O. Pedersen, T. and Petersen, N. (eds) *The European Community in World Politics*, London, Pinter, 1993.
10 For example, see Carlsnaes and Smith, op. cit.
11 Soetendorp, B. 'The Evolution of the EC/EU as a Single Foreign Policy Actor', in Carlsnaes and Smith, op. cit.
12 Ibid. p. 118.
13 Not having a coherent foreign policy is also an attribute of many states. A US ambassador, for instance, at a private meeting in London

expressed the opinion that the USA had only a weak, insufficient policy towards the former Soviet Union and no policy towards Eastern Europe. It could be said that Poland, for example, has a well-defined foreign policy towards Europe, but Europe has a much less well-defined policy towards Poland.

14 The official introduction of the term 'Union' to replace Community caused considerable confusion. Commissioner Leon Brittan remarked that he would drop any title and just give his name, hoping people would know who he was (Carvel, John, 'EC it may be, but EU it will be, if the meaning is clear', *Guardian*, 9 November 1993). The term Union may indicate a stronger desire by Europeans to imitate the example of the *United* States of America, but it lacks the legitimacy which twenty-five years of practice conferred on 'Community'. The 'Community' eponym also conveyed the idea of a social or people-based Europe which 'Union' fails to express.

15 The UK, of course, has long functioned as a nation state without a codified, written constitution. Nigel Haigh reckoned that the Community lacked statehood because *inter alia* it had no 'constitution adapted for dealing with all eventualities'. No constitution, even the especially successful US example, has been able to deal with all eventualities. See Haigh, N., 'The European Community and International Environmental Policy', in Hurrell, A. and Kingsbury, B. (eds) *The International Politics of the Environment*, Oxford, Clarendon, 1992. Haigh also compares EU and US federal systems.

16 *Treaty on European Union* (Maastricht), Luxembourg, Office of Official Publications of the European Communities 1992, 'Preface'.

17 Holsti, K. J., *International Politics* (4th edn), Englewood Cliffs, NJ, Prentice Hall, 1983, Ch. 4.

18 Regelsberger, E., 'European Political Cooperation', in Story, J. (ed.) *The New Europe*, Oxford, Blackwell, 1993, p. 272.

19 Goodwin, G. L., 'A European Community Foreign Policy?', *Journal of Common Market Studies* 12 (1), 1973.

20 Haigh, op. cit., pp. 240, 244.

21 Alker, H. and Russett, B., *World Politics in the General Assembly*, New Haven, Conn., and London, Yale University Press, 1965.

22 Moynihan, D., 'Party and International Politics', *Commentary*, February, 1977.

23 Hovet, Thomas, *Africa in the United Nations*, London, Faber and Faber, 1963.

24 Alker and Russett, op. cit.

25 Smyth, D. C., 'The Global Economy and the Third World: Coalition or Cleavage?' *World Politics*, July, 1977.

26 Buchan, David, *Europe the Strange Superpower*, Aldershot, Dartmouth, 1993, p. 49.

27 The *Independent* rated Commissioner Marin as one of the EU Commissioners 'to ignore'. It considered him ineffective, devoted to Spanish interests and wielding little influence outside of his own department (Helm, Sarah, 'Chastened Brussels Treads Softly', 3 May 1994).

28 European Commission, *Europe: World Partner*, Brussels, 1991, p. 18.
29 Beregovoy, P., speech of 3 September 1992.
30 George, Stephen, *Politics and The European Community* (2nd edn), Oxford, Oxford University Press, 1991, p. 16; Ross, G., *Jacques Delors and European Integration*, Cambridge Polity Press, 1995.
31 Delors, J. *Le Nouveau Concert Européen*, Paris, Odile Jacob, 1992, pp. 332–3. Also, Delors and Clisthène, *Our Europe*, tr. B. Pearce, London, Verso, 1992.
32 Delors, *Nouveau Concert*, p. 333.
33 Editorial, 'A Waste of a Useful Moment', *Guardian*, 2 June 1994.
34 Bocey, Pierre, 'Europe: une Diplomatie Commune en échec', *Le Figaro*, 2 February 1995.
35 European Commission, *European Security Policy in the Run-up to 2000*, Brussels, 1995.
36 I have argued elsewhere that the Union's lack of a military dimension is desirable. The member states' quest to save money through joint military production and procurement is, like the post-Cold War peace dividend, likely to prove illusory. Moreover, by adding a military capability the EU would lose its appeal as a non-threatening, civilian organization. The development of a European-level military capacity is likely only to lead to the duplication of NATO functions without offering Europe any more security. See Lister, Marjorie, 'European Security Cooperation', *New European*, Spring, 1989.
37 Buchan, op. cit., p. 139.
38 Lamassoure, Alain, 'L'Europe, un nain politique', *Le Figaro*, 12 May 1992.
39 Galtung, Johan, *The European Community: A Superpower in the Making*, London, Allen and Unwin, 1973.
40 von Habsburg, O., 'New Admissions', *New European* 4 (6), 1991.
41 Beedham, Brian, 'European Unity? Let's Be Clear About the Purpose', *International Herald Tribune*, 25 May 1992.
42 Thurow, L., 'Why the Next Century Will Belong to the Europeans', *International Herald Tribune*, 20 April 1992.
43 European Commission, *Europe*.
44 Editorial, 'How Europe Can Compete', *Financial Times*, 9 March 1994.
45 'Power' here refers to the Community's capacity 'to make its will felt within the decision-making process of another state or any other organization within the international system' or, more concisely, 'to control the behaviour of others'. See Northedge, F., *The International Political System*, London, Faber, 1976, p. 20; or Holsti, op. cit., note 2, p. 145.
46 Article C of Title 1 of the Maastricht Treaty called for the Union 'to ensure the consistency of its external activities as a whole in the context of its external relations, security, economic and development policies'.
47 However, Pfetsch, op. cit., might classify relations with Rwanda as 'high' or inter-governmental politics. In late 1996 the crisis in Rwanda and Zaire led to disputes among the Europeans.

48 Cooper, Glenda, 'Britain to cut aid via Europe', *Independent*, 16 February 1995.
49 Kohl, Helmut, 'Europe's Security and Germany's Role', Munich Conference on Security Policy, 5 February 1994.
50 Van Eekelen, W., 'Defence and Security in a Changing World', in *Defence Yearbook*, London, Rusi and Brassey's, 1992.
51 Rosenthal, A. M., 'A Scream of Agony falls on Deaf European Ears', *International Herald Tribune*, 23 May 1992.
52 Hill, Christopher, 'The Capability–Expectations Gap, or Conceptualizing Europe's International Role', in Bulmer, S. and Scott, A. (eds) *Economic and Political Integration in Europe*, Oxford, Blackwell, 1994. Hill reached a similar conclusion to mine, namely that the Community had external relations rather than a foreign policy. He argued that furthermore 'political cooperation' was a more desirable term than 'common foreign and security policy'.
    Professor Hill considered that the gap between EU aspirations to foreign policy and the reality of its weakness was 'dangerous'. But this would only be the case if non-European policy-makers believed that Europe had a coherence which even a cursory examination of press reports would show that it lacked.
53 Lister, Marjorie, *The European Community and the Developing World*, Aldershot, Avebury, 1988, repr. 1990, Ch. 6.
54 Keeting, William, 'Non-aligned defer to rich nations' summit', *Financial Times*, 30 June 1993, p. 4.
55 Hill, op. cit.
56 Lomé II was to many observers a disappointing sequel to the first Lomé Convention. See Lister, op. cit.
57 Hill, op. cit., p. 105.
58 Pelkmans, J., 'ASEAN and EC–1992' in Mayes, D. (ed.) *The External Implications of European Integration*, Hemel Hempstead, Harvester Wheatsheaf, 1993.
59 Riche, André, 'L'Europe se partage le monde', *Le Soir*, 6 January 1995.
60 Regelsberger, E., 'The Relations with ASEAN as a "Model" of a European Foreign Policy', in Schiavone, G. (ed.) *Western Europe and South-East Asia*, London, Macmillan, 1989.
61 Quinlan, J., 'Latin America: one of the most vibrant emerging regions of the world', in *The Global Investor*, Dean Witter Reynolds, November 1994.
62 Duran, Esperanza, *European Interests in Latin America*, London, Boston (Mass.) and Henley-on-Thames, Royal Institute of International Affairs and Routledge, 1985, p. 101.
63 Catholic Institute for International Relations, 'Solidarity with Central America', Briefing Paper, London, 1995.
64 Eurostat figures.
65 Grilli, Enzo, *The European Community and the Developing Countries*, Cambridge, Cambridge University Press, 1993, p. 227.
66 Ibid., p. 248.
67 Grabendorf, Wolf, 'Latin American and Western Europe', in Pearce,

J. (ed.) *The European Challenge*, London, Latin America Bureau, 1982.
68 Fidler, Stephen, Growth Late in Latin America may top 6%', *Financial Times*, 12 June 1995 p. 7.
69 European Commission, 'Background report: The European Community and Mercosur', Brussels, ISEC/B22/ 94.
70 Grilli, op. cit., p. 245.
71 Foster, Angus, and Pilling, David, 'Car curbs row ends Mercosur honeymoon', *Financial Times*, 21 June 1995.
72 Nester, William, *European Power and the Japanese Challenge*, Basingstoke and London, Macmillan, 1993.
73 Delors, *Nouveau Concert*, p. 236.
74 Lehmann, Jean-Pierre, 'Japan and Europe in Global Perspective', in Story, J. (ed.) *The New Europe*, Oxford, Blackwell, 1993.
75 Durkins, William, 'Tokyo leads aid donors at $US13 bn', *Financial Times*, 31 May 1995.
76 Hewitt, A., 'Japanese Aid', London, Overseas Development Institute, Briefing Paper, March 1990.
77 Ibid.
78 European Commission, *Europe*.
79 Schwok, R., *US–EC Relations in the Post-Cold War Era: Conflict or Partnership?*, Boulder, Colo., Westview, 1992.
80 Gill, Stephen (ed.) *Atlantic Relations*, Hemel Hempstead, Harvester Wheatsheaf, 1989, p. 7.
81 Nau, H., 'Europe and America in the 1990s', in Story, J. (ed.) *The New Europe*, Oxford, Blackwell, 1993, p. 88.
82 Gill, Stephen, 'American Perception and Policies', Gill, Stephen (ed.) *Atlantic Relations*, Hemel Hempstead, Harvester Wheatsheaf, 1989, p. 21.
83 Cockburn, Patrick, 'Germany tops the US global pecking order', *Independent on Sunday*, 4 July 1993.
84 Chase, James, 'Look here, the United States isn't a superpower any longer', *The Times*, 8 July 1993.
85 Quoted in Coffey, P. *The EC and the United States*, London, Pinter, 1993, p. 280.
86 Munchau, W. and Pittman, J., 'Clinton puts Asia at heart of American concerns', *International Herald Tribune*, 19 March 1992; and 'Pax Americana' (editorial) *Wall Street Journal*, 23 March 1992.
87 Martin, Jurek, 'Clinton urges European unity', *Financial Times*, 10 January 1994.

2 EUROPE'S COLONIAL HISTORY

1 Nicolson, Harold, *The Congress of Vienna*, New York, Viking, 1969, p. 273.
2 White, Jack, 'In African–American Eyes', *Time International* 40 (10), 7 September 1992, pp. 40–41; and Anyao-ku, Chief Emeka, 'The Image of Africa', *West Africa*, 27 April – 3 May 1992 pp. 718–19.

3 Thompson, Leonard, *The Political Mythology of Apartheid*, New Haven, Conn., Yale University Press, c. 1985, p. 73.

4 Ibid., p. 94.

5 Okri, Ben, 'Lament of the Images' in *An African Elegy*, London, Jonathan Cape, 1992.

6 Ruddick, Sara, *Maternal Thinking*, London, Women's Press, 1990.

7 Davidson, Basil, *Africa in Modern History*, Harmondsworth, Penguin, 1978.

8 Bozeman, Adda, *Conflict in Africa*, Princeton, NJ, Princeton University Press, 1976, Ch. 20.

9 Ridley, Hugh, *Images of Imperial Rule*, London, Croom Helm, 1983, pp. 119, 141.

10 Some US states and Canada, as well as Taiwan, have apologized for their treatment of their indigenous peoples, but apologies from sovereign states are rare. The Emperor of Japan, for instance, avoided giving a direct apology for wartime atrocities in Korea. But the Japanese Prime minister did make apologies for Japanese wartime actions in August 1993 and again in 1995, although on the latter occasion confusion surrounded whether the statement was intended as an apology or whether it had been withdrawn.

11 Hazel Walters, 'Introduction', *Race and Class* 33 (3), January–March, 1992.

12 Searle, C., 'Unlearning Columbus', *Race and Class* 33 (3), January–March, p. 69.

13 Cowell, Alan, 'Pope Celebrates Indigenous People', *The New York Times*, 12 August 1993, p. 20.

14 Carr, Matthew, 'The Aftermath', *Race and Class* 33 (3) January–March, p. 94.

15 Mannoni, Otare, *Prospero and Caliban*, tr. P. Powesland, New York and Washington, Praeger, 1964, p. 108.

16 Sorlin, Pierre, 'The Fanciful Empire: French Feature Films and the Colonies in the 1930s' in *French Cultural Studies* 2, 1991, pp. 135–51.

17 Thomas Pakenham, for instance neglects women in his prize-winning book, *The Scramble for Africa* (London, Abacus, 1993).

18 Bush, Barbara *Slave Women in Caribbean Society, 1650–1838*, London, Currey, 1990.

19 Stone, Elizabeth, *Women and the Cuban Revolution*, New York, Pathfinder, 1981.

20 See also Ransby, Barbara, 'Columbus and the Making of Historical Myth', *Race and Class* 33 (3), January–March, pp. 79–86.

21 Sjoo, M. and Mor, B., *The Great Cosmic Mother*, San Francisco, Harper, 1987, p. 291.

22 For example, Shreiner, Olive, *An English South African's View of the Situation* (2nd edn), London, Hodder and Stoughton, 1899.

23 Stroble, M., 'Gender and Race in the Nineteenth and Twentieth Century British Empire', in Bridenthal, R., Koonz, C. and Stuard, S. (eds) *Becoming Visible*, Boston, Houghton Mifflin, 1987.

24 Perham, Margery, *Native Administration in Nigeria*, London, Oxford

University Press, 1937, and *The Colonial Reckoning*, London, Collins, 1963.

25 Stott, Rebecca, 'The Dark Continent', in *Feminist Review* 32, Summer, 1989.

26 Lister, Marjorie, 'The European Community and the African, Caribbean and Pacific States: L'Entente Discrète', D. Phil. thesis, University of York (UK), 1985, p. 4.

27 Davis, L. and Huttenback, R., *Mammon and the Pursuit of Empire*, Cambridge, Cambridge University Press, 1988.

28 See, for instance, Waltz, Kenneth, *Theory of International Politics*, New York, McGraw Hill, 1979.

29 Deschamps, H., *Methodes et Doctrines Coloniales de la France*, Paris, Armand Colin, 1953.

30 Baran, P. and Sweezy, P., *Monopoly Capital*, Harmondsworth, Penguin, 1966.

31 Packenham, Robert, *The Dependency Movement*, Cambridge, Mass., Harvard University Press, 1992.

32 Lictheim, George, *Marx and the Asiatic Mode of Production*, London, St Anthony's Papers, no. 14, 1963; also Avineri, S., 'Marx and Modernization', in *Review of Politics* 31 (2), April, 1969.

33 Dos Santos, T., 'The Structure of Dependence', *American Economic Review* 60, 1970.

34 Galtung, Johann, 'A Structural Theory of Imperialism', in *Journal of Peace Research* 8 (2), 1971, pp. 81–117.

35 Cardoso, F., and Faletto, E., *Dependency and Development in Latin America*, tr. M. Urquidi, London, University of California Press, 1979, p. xx.

36 Packenham, R., op. cit., 'Introduction'.

37 Barrett, R. and Whyte, M., 'Dependency Theory and Taiwan: A Deviant Case', in *American Journal of Sociology*, 87 (5), March, 1982.

38 Packenham, R., op. cit., p. 244.

39 Adrian Hewitt refers to the 'Washington consensus' in 'Progress and Pitfalls in Popularising Trade', *Development Policy Review* 11 (2), June 1993.

40 Headrick, D., *The Tools of Empire*, Oxford, Oxford University Press, 1981, p. 4.

41 Shaeffer, B. B., 'The Concept of Preparation', in *World Politics* 18, October 1965, pp. 42–67.

42 Pakenham, T., op. cit., pp. 675–6.

43 Frisch, Dieter, 'The European Community's Development Policy in a Changing World', Second Bradford Development Lecture, University of Bradford, 22 October 1992.

44 Zartman, I. W., (ed.) *Europe and Africa: The New Phase*, Boulder, Colo., Lynne Rienner, 1993, p. 4.

45 Huntington, Samuel, 'The Clash of Civilizations?', *Foreign Affairs* 72 (3), July/August, 1993.

46 Huntington, Samuel, 'If Not Civilizations, What?', *Foreign Affairs* 72 (5), November/December, 1993.

47 In fact, it can be argued that the Cold War is not yet fully over.

Europe is still divided into the EU and the former Warsaw Pact members. Korea remains separated and Cuba is still isolated by the USA.

48 Zysman also makes this assumption; see Zysman, John, 'US Power, Trade and Technology', *International Affairs* 67 (1), 1991.

49 Huntington, 'Clash', p. 48.

50 Emmott, Bill, *Japan's Global Reach*, London, Century, 1992.

51 Wilson, Kevin and van der Dussen, Jan (eds) *The History of the Idea of Europe*, London and Milton Keynes, Routledge and the Open University, 1995, p. 11.

52 den Boer, Pim, 'Europe to 1914: the making of an idea', in Wilson and van der Dussen, op. cit., p. 15.

53 Bugge, Peter, 'The Nation Supreme: The idea of Europe 1914–1945', in Wilson and van der Dussen, op. cit., p. 125.

54 Bozeman, Adda, *Politics and Culture in International History*, Princeton, NJ, Princeton University Press, 1960.

55 Roy, Olivier, *The Failure of Political Islam*, London, I. B. Tauris, 1994.

56 Halliday, Fred, *Islam and the Myth of Confrontation*, London, I. B. Tauris, 1996.

57 Huntington, 'Clash'.

58 For further analysis see Tarock, Adam, 'Civilizational conflict? Fighting the enemy under a new banner' and O'Hagan, Jacinta, 'Civilizational Conflict? Looking for cultural enemies', *Third World Quarterly* 16 (1), March, 1995.

59 Hoefte, R. and Oostindie, G., 'The Netherlands and the Dutch Caribbean: Dilemmas of Decolonisation', in Sutton, P. (ed.) *Europe and the Caribbean*, London, Macmillan, 1991.

60 'Suriname: promoting young leadership', *The Courier* 151, Brussels, May–June 1995, pp. 34–5.

61 David, Steven, 'Why the Third World Still Matters', *International Security* 17 (3), Winter, 1992/3.

62 Ibid.

3 EUROPE AND THE MEDITERRANEAN

1 Hamilton, Alastair, *Europe and the Arab World*, Dublin, Arcadian Group with Azimuth Editions and Oxford University Press, 1994, p. 3.

2 Khader, Bichara, *Le Grand Maghreb et L'Europe*, Paris, Publisud–Quorum–Cermac, 1992.

3 Compare Said, Edward, *Orientalism*, Harmondsworth, Penguin, 1978.

4 Braudel, Fernand, *The Mediterranean* (first pub. 1949) 2 vols, tr. S. Reynolds, London, Collins, 1972, p. 14.

5 Gadant, Monique (ed.) *Women of the Mediterranean*, London, Zed Books, 1986, p. 1.

6 Fabre, Thierry, 'The Birth of the Mediterranean', *Contemporary European Affairs* 4, part 2–3, 1991.

7 Galtung, J., *On the Future of the Mediterranean*, Conflict and Peace Research Papers 58, University of Oslo, c. 1977.

8 Hager, Wolfgang, 'The Mediterranean: a European *Mare Nostrum*', *Orbis* 28 (1), Spring, 1974.

9 Packenham, Robert, *The Dependency Movement*, Cambridge, Mass., Harvard University Press, 1992, Ch. 4.

10 O'Donnell (a dependency theorist) quoted in Packenham, op. cit., p. 128.

11 Quoted from Said, op. cit., p. 310.

12 Gardner, David, 'EU turns strategic eyes to south', *Financial Times*, 17 May 1995.

13 Buchan, David, *Europe the Strange Superpower*, Aldershot, Dartmouth, 1993.

14 Tovias, Alfred, 'The EC's Contribution to Peace and Prosperity in the Mediterranean and the Middle East', *Jerusalem Journal of International Relations* 14 (2), 1992.

15 Schlie, Ulrich, 'The Mediterranean Challenge: Europe and North Africa', *Libertas Europäische Zeitschrift* 1–2, Stuttgart, 1992.

16 European Commission, 'Memorandum on the Community's Development Policy', Com (82) 640 final, Brussels, p. 36.

17 European Commission, *The Europe–South Dialogue*, Brussels, 1988.

18 Lister, Marjorie, *The European Community and the Developing World*, Aldershot, Avebury, 1988, repr. 1990.

19 Shlaim, A., and Yannopoulos, G. (eds) *The EEC and the Mediterranean*, Cambridge, Cambridge University Press, 1976, 'Introduction'.

20 European Commission, *Dialogue*, pp. 39–40, 47.

21 Tsoukalis, L., 'The EEC and the Mediterranean: is "Global Policy" a Misnomer?', *International Affairs* 53 (3), July 1977.

22 European Commission, 'Memorandum', p. 38.

23 Joffe, G., 'The North African Dimension', Lecture to the Royal Geographical Society Conference, *The Mediterranean at the End of the Millennium*, London, 28–30 April 1993.

24 Quoted in Buchan, op. cit., Ch. 9.

25 Pomfret, R., 'The European Community's Relations with the Mediterranean Countries', in Redmond, J. (ed.) *The External Relations of the European Community*, London, Macmillan, 1992.

26 This intriguing theory is as widely disbelieved as believed.

27 European Commission, *Dialogue*, p. 38.

28 Pomfret, R., *Mediterranean Policy of the European Community*, London, Macmillan, 1986, p. 20.

29 European Commission, *Dialogue*, p. 41.

30 Giving meaningful trade preferences has been difficult for all developed countries. See Kiljunen, K. (ed.) *Region-to-Region Cooperation Between Developed and Developing Countries*, Aldershot, Avebury, 1990, esp. Chs 7 and 15.

31 Pomfret, *Mediterranean Policy*, p. 24.

32 Pomfret, 'Community's Relations', p. 79.

33 European Commission, *Dialogue*, p. 44.

34 Marks, Jon, 'New kids on the Eurotrading bloc', *Financial Times*, 2 February 1996.

35 Bollaert, B., and Lorrieux, C., 'Les fantômes de Barcelone', *Le Soir*, 28 November 1995.

36 Fox, Robert, *The Inner Sea*, London, Sinclair-Stevenson, 1991, p. 308.

37 Buchan, op. cit., p. 105.

38 Libya withdrew earlier, in 1970. President Gadhafi then negotiated unsuccessful 'unions' with Egypt and Tunisia, and a brief alliance-union with Morocco.

39 Boyer, Y., 'Europe's Future Strategic Orientation', *Washington Quarterly* 16 (4), 1993.

40 Khader, Ch. 3.

41 Pomfret, 'Community's Relations', p. 86.

42 Schlie, op. cit.

43 Pomfret, 'Community's Relations'.

44 List, M. and Rittberger, V., 'Regime Theory and Environmental Management', in Hurrell, A. and Kingsbury, B. (eds) *The International Politics of the Environment*, Oxford, Clarendon Press, 1992.

45 European Commission, *Eurobarometer* 37, June, Brussels, 1992.

46 European Commission, *Background Report: The European Environment Agency*, London, SEC, 11 February, 1994.

47 Haas, Peter, *Saving the Mediterranean*, New York, Columbia University Press, 1990, p. xx.

48 Ibid., p. 66.

49 Nonneman, G., 'Environmental and Socio-cultural Cooperation in the Gulf', in Nonneman, G. (ed.) *The Middle East and Europe*, London, Federal Trust, 1993.

50 Haas, op. cit., p. 231.

51 Gomel, Giorgio, 'Migrations Toward Western Europe', *International Spectator* 27, April–June, 1992.

52 Buchan op. cit., p. 124; also 'Background Report: Immigration', Commission of the European Communities, London, ISEC/B23/93, 29 September 1993.

53 Boyer, op. cit.

54 'Development Cooperation Policy in the Run-up to 2000', Communication from the Commission to the Council and Parliament, Brussels, 15 May 1992, SEC (92) final.

55 'Background Report: Immigration'.

56 Gomel, op. cit.

57 Buchan, op. cit., Ch. 9.

58 Gomel, op. cit.

59 Jaquette, J. and Staudt, K., 'Politics, Population, and Gender', in Jones, K. and Jonasdottir, A. (eds) *The Political Interests of Gender*, London, Sage, 1988.

60 UNICEF, *The Progress of Nations*, New York, UNICEF, 1993, p. 36.

61 Chalker, Lynda (Baroness), 'Priorities in Development for the European Community', Speech to the House of Commons All Party Group on Overseas Development, London, 25 November 1992.

62 Collinson, Sarah, *Europe and International Migration*, London, Pinter and Royal Institute of International Affairs, 1993.

63 Bozeman, Adda, *Strategic Intelligence and Statecraft*, Washington, Brassey's, 1992, p. 233.
64 Aliboni, Roberto, 'Europe Between East and South', *International Spectator* 27, April–June, 1992.
65 In a letter from Director Nils Eliasson, CSCE Secretariat, Prague, dated 5 January 1994.
66 Pick, Hella, 'A diplomatic test of credibility in Eurasia', *Guardian*, 2 April 1992.
67 Caligaris, Luigi, 'Security Challenges in Alliance: the Southern Periphery', *International Spectator* 27 (4), October–December, 1992.
68 Fernandez-Ordonez, Francisco, 'The Mediterranean: Devising a Security Structure', *Nato Review* 5, October, 1990.
69 Since 1995 the Conference on Security and Cooperation in Europe has been known as the Organization for Security and Cooperation in Europe (OSCE).

4 EUROPE AND AFRICA

1 European Community, *The Lomé Convention*, Brussels, undated pamphlet c. 1986.
2 Story, J. and de Carmoy, G., 'France and Europe', in Story, J. (ed.) *The New Europe*, Oxford, Blackwell, 1993.
3 General Secretariat of the Council, *Guide to the Council of the European Communities*, Brussels, 1992.
4 See Lister, Marjorie, *The European Community and the Developing World*, Aldershot, Avebury, 1988, repr. 1990, Ch. 3.
5 'News round-up: the ACP–EEC negotiations for Lomé IV', *The Courier* 117, September–October, 1989, p. I.
6 Farmers' Link, *Just Green Bananas*, Norwich, 1995.
7 *GATT Newsletter*, Geneva, December, 1994.
8 Lewis, J. 'The European Community and the Caribbean', in Sutton, Paul (ed.) *Europe and the Caribbean*, London, Macmillan, 1991.
9 United Nations Economic Commission for Africa, *African Alternative Framework to Structural Adjustment Programmes for Socio-Economic Recovery and Transformation*, 1989, p. 22–3.
10 Mosley, P., Harrigan, J. and Toye, J., *Aid and Power*, London, Routledge, 1991, p. 304.
11 Campbell, Bonnie and Loxley, John, *Structural Adjustment in Africa*, London, Macmillan, 1989, p. 1.
12 'The Fourth Lomé Convention', *The Courier* 120, Brussels, March–April; 1990, Part One, Ch. 1, Article 3, p. 12.
13 European Community *Europe Without Frontiers*, European Documentation, Period 2/89, Brussels, April 1989.
14 Page, S. and Davenport, M., *World Trade Reform: Do Developing Countries Gain or Lose?*, London, Overseas Development Institute, 1994.
15 Svetlicic, M., 'Investment Promotion Measures', in Kiljunen, K. (ed.)

Region to Region Cooperation Between Developed and Developing Countries, Aldershot, Avebury, 1990.

16 'Symposium: trade issues in the context of Lomé IV and 1992', *The Courier* 123, Brussels, September–October, 1990, p. 7.

17 Grilli, Enzo, *The European Community and the Developing Countries*, Cambridge, Cambridge University Press, 1993, pp. 165–6.

18 Eurostat, *External Trade: Statistical Yearbook 1995*, Luxembourg and Brussels, 1995.

19 Babarinde, Olufemi, *The Lomé Conventions and Development*, Aldershot, Avebury, 1994.

20 ACP–EU Joint Assembly Resolution, *Official Journal of the European Communities C*, 381.22, 31 December 1994.

21 For instance, World Development Movement, *The Great Aid Robbery: How UK Aid Fails the Poor*, London, 1995.

22 Dreze, J. and Sen, A., *Hunger and Public Action*, Oxford, Clarendon Press, 1989, p. 274.

23 Foreign Affairs Committee, *Monitoring of the European Community Aid Programme*, London, HMSO, 1994.

24 Ibid., p. xxxi.

25 Chalker, Lynda (Baroness), 'Britain's Aid Strategy in the Changing World', Speech to the Royal Institute of International Affairs, London, 18 October 1993.

26 European Commission, *EU–ACP Cooperation in 1994*, Brussels, 1995.

27 Foreign Affairs Committee, op. cit., p. xxxii.

28 Ibid., p. xxxiii.

29 Ibid., p. xiv.

30 Launder, A. and Nixon, F., 'Stabex Conditionality and Economic Diversification', Paper to Development Studies Association Annual Conference, Nottingham, September 1992.

31 European Court of Auditors, Report, *Official Journal of the European Communities C*, Luxembourg, 16 November 1993.

32 'The Joint Dakar Assembly', *The Courier* 150, Brussels, March–April, 1995 p. 8.

33 European Court of Auditors, op. cit.

34 Foreign Affairs Committee, op. cit., p. xxvii. There is an extensive literature on the problems of food aid. See Singer, Wood and Jennings, *Food Aid*.

35 World Bank, *Annual Report*, Washington, 1989, p. 81.

36 Foreign Affairs Committee, op. cit.

37 Court of Auditors, 'Report on the European Development Funds', *Official Journal of the European Communities C*, Luxembourg, Office of Official Publication of European Communities, 2 November 1994

38 European Commission, Brussels, *The Europe–South Dialogue*, 1988, 1991, p. 33.

39 Eurostat, *Europe in Figures*, Brussels and Luxembourg, 1992.

40 'Lomé partnership goes under the microscope again', *The Courier* 148, Brussels, November–December, 1994 p. 6.

41 'No Cannes do', *Economist*, 1 July 1995, p. 37.

42 'Resolution on the Lomé IV mid-term review', *Official Journal of the*

European Communities C, Luxembourg, Office of Official Publications of European Community, 31 December 1994.

43 Percival, D., 'Agreement clinched at eleventh hour', *The Courier* 153, Brussels, September–October, 1995, pp. 6–8.

44 European Commission, 'Development Cooperation Policy in the Run-up to 2000', Communication to the European Council and Parliament, Brussels, 15 May 1992.

45 Hewitt, A., 'The EEC's Year in Africa', *Africa Contemporary Record* 18, pp. A208–15.

46 Cooper, Glenda, 'Britain to cut aid via Europe', *Independent*, 16 February 1995.

47 The discussion here does not extend to the former USSR, but in Chapter 5 the devastating effects of the loss of Soviet support for the Cuban economy are outlined.

48 Stevens, Christopher, 'The Impact of Europe 1992 on the South', *IDS Bulletin* 21 (1), 1990. He makes a similar point about the diversion of attention from external affairs.

49 These exports (excluding clothing) accounted for almost 50 per cent of Eastern European exports to the Community in 1989. See note 46.

50 Stevens, Christopher, 'The Implications for Developing Countries', in Stevens, Christopher and Kennan, Jane (eds) *Reform in Eastern Europe and the Developing Country Dimension*, London, Overseas Development Institute, 1992.

51 Green, R.H., 'The NIEO and North–South Relations', in Kiljunen, K. (ed.) *Region to Region Cooperation Between Developed and Developing Countries*, Aldershot, Avebury, 1990.

5 LOMÉ IV AND THE BREEZE OF CHANGE

1 Freund, Bill, *The Making of Contemporary Africa*, Bloomington, Indiana University Press, 1984.

2 Interview with François Mitterrand, *The Courier* 151, Brussels, May–June, 1995, p. 49.

3 'Lomé partnership goes under the microscope again', *The Courier* 148, Brussels, November–December, 1994, p. 12.

4 For details of the establishment of Lomé I, see Lister, Marjorie, *The European Community and the Developing World*, Aldershot, Avebury, 1988, repr. 1990.

5 Ashworth, G. and Bonnerjea, L. (eds) *The Invisible Decade*, Aldershot, Gower, 1985.

6 Gyatso, Geshe K. (eds Lister, R. and Lister, M.) *Buddhism in the Tibetan Tradition: a Guide*, London, Arkana, 1988.

7 Green, R. H., 'The NIEO and North–South Relations', in Kiljunen, K. (ed.) *Region to Region Cooperation between Developed and Developing Countries*, Aldershot, Avebury, 1990.

8 'The Fourth Lomé Convention', *The Courier* 120, Brussels, March–April, 1990, Chapter 1, Article 5, p. 12.

9 Amin, Samir, 'Europe and North–South relations', *Contemporary European Affairs* 2 (3), 1989, p. 125.

10 Lindblom, Charles, 'The Science of "Muddling Through"', in Clower, R. (ed.) *Monetary Theory*, Harmondsworth, Penguin, 1969.

11 'Editorial,' *Development Studies Association Forum* 40, May 1992, p. 1.

12 *Spur* (Newspaper of the World Development Movement), November–December, 1995. Even so, the UK government went ahead in late 1995 to cut the aid budget by 5.6 per cent.

13 Eurostat, *External Trade Statistical Yearbook 1995*, Brussels and Luxembourg, 1995.

14 Commission of the European Communities, *The Europe–South Dialogue*, Office for Official Publications of the European Community', Luxembourg, 1989, p. 9.

15 Pisani, Edgard, 'Warning', in *Lomé Briefing* (Liaison Committee of NGOs to the European Communities) 2, Brussels, September 1988.

16 European Commission, *Southern Africa and the European Community*, Brussels, 1990, p. 5.

17 Stokke, O. (ed.) *Aid and Political Conditionality*, London, Frank Cass, 1995.

18 Robinson, M. and Moore, M., 'Can aid promote good government?', *The Courier* 151, Brussels, May–June, 1995, pp. 77–9.

19 *Independent*, 21 September 1992.

20 Doornbos, M., 'State Formation Processes Under External Supervision', in Stokke (ed.), op. cit.

21 The Community became involved in security issues when it decided in 1987 to provide 'non-lethal' aid to protect development projects in Mozambique. Similarly, it allowed aid funds to be used for security purposes during the Western intervention in Somalia in 1992. For a defence of the pragmatism of this action see, Lister, Marjorie, 'Using Aid to Pay Troops', *Spur* (World Development Movement newspaper), November–December, 1992.

22 Holsti, K. J., *International Politics* (4th edn), Englewood Cliffs, NJ, Prentice-Hall, 1983, pp. 106–8.

23 For details of Guinea's isolation, see Lister, op. cit.

24 Krasner, Stephen, 'Structural Causes and Regime Consequences', *International Organization* 36 (2), Spring, 1982.

25 We can also find very broad concepts of regime where international and national regimes are insufficiently distinguished. For example, Puchala and Hopkins' conception of a regime is something like an underlying Platonic form: 'For every political system, be it the United Nations, the United States, New York City, or the American Political Science Association, there is a corresponding regime.' Quoted from *International Organization* 36 (2), Spring, 1982.

26 Herbst, Jeffrey, 'Theories of International Cooperation: the Case of the Lomé Convention', *Polity* 19 (4), Summer, 1987, pp. 637–59.

27 Rittberger, V. (ed.) *International Regimes in East–West Politics*, London, Pinter, 1990.

28 Young, O. *International Cooperation*, Ithaca and London, Cornell University Press, 1989.
29 Interview with Professor Alain Ekra, *The Courier* 133, Brussels, May–June, 1992, p. 14.
30 Langhammer, R., and Hiemenz, U., *Regional Integration among Developing Countries*, Kieler Studien 232, Tübingen, J. C. B. Möhr, 1990, p. 3.
31 Ibid., p. 23.
32 Ibid., p. 74.
33 Since 1995 the GATT treaties have been administered by the World Trade Organization (WTO).
34 Jackson, John, *Restructuring the GATT System*, London, Pinter, 1990.
35 Obasanjo, O. and d'Orville, H., *The Impact of Europe in 1992 on West Africa*, New York, Crane Rusak, 1990, Preface p. xiii.
36 Ibid., p. 6.
37 Ibid., p. 7.
38 Thurow, Lester, 'Why the Next Century Will Belong to the Europeans', *International Herald Tribune*, 20 April 1992.
39 Page, S. and Stevens, C., *Trading with South Africa: the policy options for the EC*, London, Overseas Development Institute, 1992.
40 Ambassador Erwan Fouéré, quoted in *European Union: Official Newsletter of the Delegation of the European Commission in South Africa* 1, 9 May 1995, p. 1.
41 'News round-up: the Convention at work', *The Courier*, 142 Brussels, November–December, 1993, p. VIII.
42 *European Union: Official Newsletter of the Delegation of the European Commission in South Africa* 1, Pretoria, 9 May, 1995.
43 Lister, Marjorie, op. cit., p. 135.
44 European Parliament 'Resolution on the embargo against Cuba and the Torricelli Act', 16 September 1993.
45 'Mr Marin visits Cuba', *The Courier* 146, p. x Brussels, July–August, 1994.
46 Dominguez, Jorge, 'Cuba's switch from state economy', *Financial Times*, 26 January 1994.
47 Fletcher, Pascal, 'Cuba's big earners stage a recovery', *Financial Times*, 8 December 1995.
48 *European Union: Official Newsletter of the Delegation of the European Commission in South Africa* 1, Pretoria; 9 May 1995, p. 4.

6 CONCLUSION

1 Other recent theories are that humans arose from a mixture of African, Asian and other ancestors, or from marine ancestors. But the theory of African origins is the dominant paradigm. See Morrow, Lance, 'Africa: the Scramble for Existence', *Time International* 40(10) 7 September 1992, pp. 28–39.
2 den Boer, Pim, 'Europe to 1914', in Wilson, Kevin and van der

Dussen, Jan (eds) *The History of the Idea of Europe*, London and New York, Routledge, 1993, p. 23.

3 Mannoni, Otare, *Prospero and Caliban*, tr. P. Powesland, New York and Washington, Praeger, 1964.

4 See Lister, Marjorie, *The European Community and the Developing World*, Aldershot, Avebury, 1988, repr. 1990, for a discussion of partnership and association.

5 Zischka, A., *Afrique, Complement de l'Europe*, Paris, Laffont, 1952.

6 Quoted in Chafer, Tony, 'French African Policy', *African Affairs* 91, 1992, pp. 37–51.

7 Curzon, G. and Curzon, V., 'Neo-colonialism and the European Economic Community', *Yearbook of World Affairs*, London, 1971; a similar view was expressed by Jean-Pierre Prouteau in 'J'ai finalement choisi de dire toute la verité', *Jeune Afrique* 1598–99, 14–27 August 1991, p. 148.

8 Chafer, op. cit.

9 Lister, op. cit., p. 192.

10 Martin, Guy, 'Continuity and Change in Franco-African Relations', *Journal of Modern African Studies* 33 (1), 1995.

11 Quoted in Chafer, op. cit.

12 Jacques Foccart, *Foccart Parle: Entretiens avec Phillipe Gaillard*, Paris, Fayard and *Jeune Afrique* 1995, p. 467.

13 Dorée, F., 'Le hit-parade africain', *Jeune Afrique* 1598–99, 14–27 August 1991, pp. 172–3.

14 European Commission, *Bulletin of the European Communities* Supplement 1/92, 1992, p. 24.

15 In French the term *compagne* implies more than 'companion', also 'mate' or 'mistress'. This reference shows a deep psychological link between Europeans and Africa. For the implications of this terminology see Lister, Marjorie, 'Uncovering the Female State', *Baetyl: The Journal of Women's Literature*, Issue 2, Winter 1993, pp. 104–23.

16 Delors, Jacques, *Le Nouveau Concert Européen*, Paris, Odile Jacob, 1992, p. 263.

17 Frankland, M., 'Star contortionist set for test of skill under European spotlight', *Observer*, 14 May 1995.

18 Vaclav Havel, Address to the European Parliament, *EP News*, 7–11 March, 1994.

19 Hoffman, S., 'Europe's Identity Crisis Revisited', *Daedalus* 123 (2), Spring, 1994.

20 Ibid.

Index

Africa: colonial relations with
Europe 149; first links with
Europe 43–5; French support for
150–1; history 45–6; and
independence 60–2; Kongo
model 46; Lomé Convention see
Lomé Convention (Fourth);
marginalization of 146–8;
resources, Europe and 152
African, Caribbean and Pacific
countries (ACP) 112–13; map of
110–11; trade with EU 123–4. see
also Lomé Convention (Fourth)
aid programmes: ACP countries
113, 115, 125–9, 153; and human
rights 136; South Africa 163–4
Albania 78, 84
Algeria 74–5, 78–80, 81; aid to 87–8;
GNP 83; and Maghreb 92–3; and
security 104
Alker, H. 12
Allison, Graham 8
Amin, Samir 148
Andean Pact 32, 148, 159
Andreotti, G. (Italian PM) 11
Anguilla 67
Arab League 87
Arab unity 77
Arab world and Europe 82
Argentina 30, 32, 34
Asia Pacific Economic
Cooperation (APEC) 67
Association of South-East Asian
Nations (ASEAN) 29–30
Atlantic Alliance 25, 37–8
Australia 99

Austria 134

Babarinde, O. 124
Baker, James 39
Balladur, E. (French PM) 150
Bangladesh 22, 146
Baran, P. 55
Barcelona Conference and
Declaration 88–90, 97
Barrett, R. 57
Belgium 42, 134
Belize 115
Bellow, Saul 46
Ben Ali (Tunisian President) 86, 95,
105
Beregovoy, P. (French PM) 15
Bermuda 67
Bhutan 146
Bongo, Omar (Gabon President)
143
Bonino (EU Commissioner) 15
Bosnia 65
Boyer, Yves 92
Bozeman, Adda 46, 65, 103
Braudel, Fernand 71
Brazil 30, 32, 34, 58
Brittan, Leon 14, 15, 30
Buchan, David 77, 91, 100
Burton, Richard 45
Bush, Barbara 51

Cambodia 154
Campbell, Bonnie 117
Canada 99
Cancún Summit (1982) 145
Canning, George 43

Cardoso, F. 55, 57, 76
Carrington, Edwin 146
Central Europe 28–9
Centre for Industrial Development
    (CDI) 156
Chafer, Tony 173
Chalker, Lynda 126–7, 154
Cheysson, Claude 173
Chile 30
China 30, 66, 99
Claes, W. (NATO Secretary
    General) 75
Clinton, Bill (US President) 34, 35,
    39–40
Cold War 78, 81, 132
colonial history of Europe 42–69;
    in Africa 43–6, 60–2; age of
    colonialism 47–9; and clash of
    civilizations 64–9; and
    dependency 55–8; economic
    explanations of 53–8; legacy of
    62–3; and the 'other' 49–51; and
    technology 58–9; and women
    51–3
Columbia 99
Columbus, Christopher 48–9
Common Agricultural Policy
    (CAP) 31, 33, 34, 85
common foreign and security
    policy (CFSP) 7, 8
Commonwealth Development
    Corporation 166
Community Humanitarian Aid
    Office (ECHO) 129, 167
Conference on Security and
    Cooperation in Europe (CSCE)
    103–4
Conference on Security and
    Cooperation in the
    Mediterranean (CSCM) 103–6
Costa Rica 22, 115
Côte d'Ivoire 22, 99
Council of Europe 103
Court of Auditors 128, 130
Cousins, Margaret 52
Cuba 58, 102; and Lomé
    Convention 165–8
Cuban Missile Crisis 8
Cyprus 74, 78, 80, 83–4

Davenport, M. 122

David, Stephen 68
Davidson, Basil 48
de Carmoy, Guy 109
de Gaulle, Charles (French
    President) 62, 171
De Michelis, G. 105
de Silguy (EU Commissioner) 15
de Tocqueville, A. 65
decolonization of Africa 60–2
Delors, Jacques 16–18, 20, 24, 35,
    144; on Africa 175–6; and
    European Commission 14–15; on
    Mediterranean 91
dependency theory: and
    colonialism 55–8; and
    Mediterranean area 74–7
Deschamps, Hubert 54
Development Studies Association
    151
Dominican Republic 114
Dos Santos, T. 56
Duran, Esperanza 31

Eastern Europe 28–9, 147
Economic Commission for Europe
    103
Economic Community of West
    African States (ECOWAS)
    159–60
economic explanations of
    colonialism 53–8
Ecuador 115
Eelter, Dennis 43
Egypt 66, 74, 78, 84, 104; aid to 88;
    GNP 83
Ehrlichs, Paul 101
El Salvador 31, 99
Eliasson, Nils 104, 105
Engels, F. 55, 56
environmental problems:
    Mediterranean area 95–9
Eritrea 149
Ethiopia 22, 45
EUROMARFOR 75
European Commission 35–6; and
    European integration 16–18;
    Horizon 2000 100, 136; on Lomé
    Convention 130–1, 137; on
    project aid 126; structure of
    13–16
European Court 11, 20

European Development Fund 112, 126–7, 133–4
European Environment Agency (EEA) 96
European Investment Bank 28, 112, 147
European Parliament 20
European Political Cooperation (EPC) 11, 15, 29
European Programme for Reconstruction and Development (EPRD) 163–4
European security and defence identity (ESDI) 23, 83
European Union: and African resources 152; bilateral relations 34–41; colonial relations with Africa 149; development policy of 22–3; as economic superpower 20–1; exports 21, 123–4; external and internal policies 24–5; foreign policy of 17, 18–20; global political strategy 152–4; and Lomé Convention *see* Lomé Convention (Fourth); and Mediterranean area *see* Mediterranean and Europe; multilateral relations 27–34; as political dwarf 18–20; role of 25–7; security policy of 23; as a state 10–13; trade 123–4
exports: of ACP 123–4; of European Union 21; of Mediterranean 74

Fabre, Thierry 72
Faletto, E. 55, 57, 76
Fernandez-Ordonez, Francisco 105
Fitzgerald, Garrett (Irish PM) 24
Foccart, Jacques 174
Fourth Lomé Convention *see* Lomé Convention (IV)
France: and Africa 42, 50–1, 61–2; EDF contributions 134; foreign policy 19, 150–1; GNP 83; and Lomé Convention (Fourth) 109, 114–15, 150; and Mediterranean 78, 79, 82, 91, 97; migration to 99; sovereignty of 15–16; and United Nations 11
Franco, General Francisco 49

Frank, Andre Gunder 55, 56, 57, 76
Frenssen, Gustav 47
Freund, Bill 144

Gabon 143
Gadant, Monique 72
Galtung, Johan 7, 20, 57, 73
Gardner, David 77
General Agreement on Tariffs and Trade (GATT) 10, 18, 38, 122, 168; and Mediterranean 81, 84, 94; Uruguay Round 115, 120, 121–2, 159
Generalized System of Preferences (GSP, GATT) 31, 84, 122, 140, 164
Germany: EDF contributions 134; and Lomé Convention (Fourth) 109; migration to 99; security policy 23; and USA 39
Ghana 37, 45–6
Ghessous, Azeddin 90
Gibraltar 82
Giscard d'Estaing, V. (French President) 73
Global Mediterranean Policy (GMP) 83–7
Goodwin, Geoffrey 11
Greater East Asia Co-Prosperity Sphere 73
Greece 80, 86; GNP 83; and Macedonia 19–20; and Mediterranean 73, 83, 90
Green, R.H. 137
Grenada 166
Grilli, Enzo 31
Gross National Product, Mediterranean states 83
Group of Seven 26, 35
Guatemala 34
Guinea, Republic of 62
Gulf War 36, 66, 87, 92
Gummer, John 21
Guyana 34

Haas, Peter 96
Hager, W. 73, 74
Haiti 34, 102, 114, 146, 167
Halliday, Fred 66
Hamilton, Alastair 73
Harrigan, J. 116

Hassan II (Morocco) 90, 92–3
Havel, Vaclav (Czech President)
    177
Headrick, Daniel 58–9
Hegel, G.W.F. 45
Helsinki Declaration 104
Henig, Stanley 7
Herodotus 65
Hiemenz, Ulrich 158–9
Hill, Christopher 26–7
Hobson, J.A. 53–4
Hoffman, Stanley 177
Holsti, K.J. 11
Hondius, Jacobus 44
Hong Kong 57, 76, 99
human rights under Lomé
    Convention 135–6, 153
Huntington, Samuel 64–8
Hurd, Douglas 23, 137, 153–4
Hussein, Saddam 40, 66

imperialism 47–8; economic
    motives 53–5
India 55–6, 99
International Labour Organization
    149
International Monetary Fund
    (IMF) 26, 27, 87, 141, 150, 155,
    167; structural adjustment
    programmes 115–17, 153
Ireland 134
Islam 66, 71, 75
Israel 74, 78, 86–7; aid to 88; GNP
    83
Italy: and Africa 42; EDF
    contributions 134; GNP 83; and
    Mediterranean 97

Jamaica 115
Japan: and EU 35–7; trade 124
Jaquette, J. 102
Joffe, George 81
John Paul II (Pope) 48–9
Jordan 74, 77, 78, 84; aid to 88;
    GNP 83

Kelleher, C.M. 39
Kenya 37, 43
Kohl, Helmut (German
    Chancellor) 23

Kongo model of Europe–African
    relations 46
Kuwait 99

Lamassoure, Alain 19
Land-Based Sources Protocol
    (1980) 97
Langhammer, Rolf 158–9
Laos 79, 146
Latin America: and EU 30–4; trade
    with EU 124
Latin American Free Trade Area
    (LAFTA) 159
Latin American Integration
    Association 159
Lebanon 74, 78, 84, 88; migration
    from 99
Lehmann, J.-P. 36
Lenin, V.I. 54, 55, 56, 76
Leys, Colin 57
Libya 74, 78–9, 81; aid to 88; GNP
    83; and Maghreb 92–3
Lisbon Declaration 75
Lomé Convention (I) 12, 27, 62,
    109, 113, 144, 160
Lomé Convention (II) 27, 108, 113
Lomé Convention (III) 108, 113
Lomé Convention (IV) 108–42;
    additional features 120–1; and
    African resources 152; as alliance
    154–5; context of 143–6;
    continuing cooperation 140–1;
    criticism of 129–31; and Cuba
    165–8; and democracy in Europe
    138–9; enlarging 161–8; and
    European public opinion 151–2;
    and French foreign policy
    150–1; and global political
    strategy 152–4; and Horizon
    2000 136–41; human rights under
    135–6; institutional inertia
    149–50; as international regime
    155–8; marginalization, sources
    146–8; mid-term review of 131–6;
    negotiating 112–22; project aid
    in 125–9; and relations with
    Europe 149; and South Africa
    161–5; stability, sources 148–58;
    structural adjustments in
    115–19; trade preferences of
    119–20, 122–5; and transposition

fallacy 158–61; and Uruguay
    Round 121–2
Loxley, John 117
Luxembourg 134

Maastricht, Treaty of 10, 16, 22,
    24–5, 96, 150
Macedonia (Former Yugoslav
    Republic of) 19–20
Maghreb see Union of the Arab
    Maghreb (UMA)
Maldives 146
Mali 45
Malta 74, 78, 80, 81, 84; GNP 83
Mannoni, Otare 42, 49, 50
marginalization and Lomé
    Convention 146–8
Marin, Manuel (EU
    Commissioner) 14–15, 132, 146
Marx, Karl 45, 55, 56, 57, 76
Mashreq 88
Mauritania 88, 92–4
Mediterranean Action Plan (Med
    Plan) 97
Mediterranean and Europe 70–107;
    and Barcelona Conference
    88–90, 97; Conference on
    Security and Cooperation in
    103–6; and dependency 74–7;
    environmental problems 95–9;
    exports 74; global policy for
    83–7; GNP of 83; Mediterranean
    ideal 71–4; and migration 99–102;
    and Morocco 90–1; new policy
    for 87–8, 100; relations between
    77–90; security issues 81–3;
    trade preferences 78; and Union
    of Arab Maghreb 91–5
Menelik I 170
Mercosur (Mercado de Sur) 32–4
Mexico 26, 99
migration from Mediterranean
    99–102
Mill, John Stuart 47, 170
mineral production support
    systems (Sysmin) 120–1, 125–9
Mitterand, François (French
    President) 16, 24, 144, 150,
    173–4
Mor, B. 52
Morocco 70; aid to 87–8; and EU

78–9, 90–1; exports 74; GNP 83;
    and Maghreb 92, 94; and security
    104
Mosley, P. 116–17
Moynihan, Daniel 12
Mozambique 22
Multi-Fibre Arrangement 119
Museveni, Yoweri 117

Namibia 114, 149
Natali, Lorenzo (EU
    Commissioner) 146–7
National Audit Office (UK) 126
Nau, Henry 38
Nepal 146
Netherlands 25, 99
Netherlands Antilles 67
New International Economic
    Order 140
New Mediterranean Policy (NMP)
    87–8, 100
newly industrialized countries 30,
    57, 76
Nicaragua 34
Nigeria 37, 135
North Africa 75, 77, 81
North American Free Trade Area
    (NAFTA) 26, 32, 34, 67, 159
North Atlantic Treaty Organization
    (NATO) 19, 37–8, 40, 67, 75
Nyerere, Julius (Tanzanian
    President) 145

Obasanjo, Olesegun 160
Okri, Ben 5, 44–5
Organization for Economic
    Cooperation and Development
    (OECD) 27, 36
Organization of American States
    (OAS) 26
Organization of Petroleum
    Exporting Countries (OPEC) 12
'other', concept of in colonialism
    49–51

Packenham, Robert 57, 58, 76
Page, S. 122
Pakenham, Thomas 61
Pakistan 66, 99
Paleokrassas, Ioannis 14

Palestine Liberation Organization 87
Paraguay 34
Partnership for Peace (NATO) 15, 40, 67
Perham, Margery 52
Peru 32, 34
Petersen, Nikolaj 8
Phare programme 28, 100
Philippines 99
Pinheiro (EU Commissioner) 15, 163
Pintasilgo, Maria Lourdes 160
Pisani, Edgard 152
Pisani Memorandum 78–9
political power, European 16–18
Pomfret, Richard 94
Pooley, Peter 137
Portugal 86, 146; and Africa 42, 45–6; EDF contributions 134; and Mediterranean 77
Prebisch, Raul 55
preferential trade agreements: in Lomé Convention 119–20, 122–5; Mediterranean 78, 85–6
Public Accounts Committee (UK) 126

Regelsberger, Elfriede 11, 30
Rhodes, Cecil 50
Rio Summit 27, 36, 95, 171
Ripa di Meana, C. 120
Ritchie-Calder, Lord 97
Rome, Treaty of 11, 22, 62, 79, 95, 171
Rosenberg, Alfred 65
Rosenthal, A.M. 24
Roy, Olivier 66
Russett, B. 12
Rwanda 22

San José dialogue 31, 32
Santer, Jacques 14, 17–18, 165
Saudi Arabia 66, 99
Schreiner, Olive 52
Schumpeter, Joseph 53
Schwok, René 37
security policy: of European Union 23; in Mediterranean 75, 81–3
Shein, E. 82
Shlaim, A. 79–80

Singapore 76
Single European Act 16, 24, 96
Sjoo, M. 52
slavery 48
Slovenia 65
Smith, Hazel 7
Soetendorp, B. 9
Solchaga, Luis 167
Somalia 154
Sorlin, Pierre 50
South Africa: aid programme 163–4; and free trade 164–5; and Lomé Convention 149, 161–5
South Korea 57, 76, 99
Southern African Customs Union (SACU) 165
Southern African Development Community (SADC) 161, 163
Southern African Development Coordination Conference (SADCC) 149–50, 161
Southern Cone countries 31, 32, 33, 148
Spain 86, 146; and Africa 42, 45, 48–9; EDF contributions 134; GNP 83; and Lomé Convention (Fourth) 114; and Mediterranean 97
Sri Lanka 99
Stabex (stabilization of export earnings) 118, 120, 125–9
Staudt, K. 102
Stevens, Christopher 139
Stone, Elizabeth 51
Story, Jonathan 109
Stott, Rebecca 52
structural adjustment in Lomé Convention 115–19, 153
Sweden 134
Sweezy, P. 55
Syria 74, 78, 84; aid to 88; GNP 83
Sysmin (mineral production support systems) 120–1, 125–9

Taiwan 57–8, 76
Tanzania 144, 145
Taylor, Ian 166
Technical Centre for Agricultural and Rural Cooperation (CTA) 156
technology and colonialism 58–9

Thurow, Lester 21
Toye, J. 116
trade: ACP with EU 123–4;
  preferences *see* preferential
  trade agreements; with South
  Africa 164–5
Trans-Atlantic Free Trade Area
  (TAFTA) 32–3
transposition fallacy and Lomé
  Convention 158–61
Tubiana, Laurence 137
Tunisia 74, 86, 89; aid to 87–8; and
  EU 78–9, 80; GNP 83; and
  Maghreb 92, 94; and security 81,
  104–5
Turkey 74, 78, 80; GNP 83

Uganda 61, 117
Union of the Arab Maghreb
  (UMA) 70, 82, 88, 91–5;
  objectives and prospects 93–5
United Arab Emirates 99
United Kingdom: and Africa 42–3,
  54, 61; EDF contributions 134;
  and India 55–6; and Lomé
  Convention (Fourth) 115; on
  project aid 127, 134, 137; tied aid
  25; and United Nations 11
United Nations Conference on
  Environment and Development
  (UNCED) 27, 171
United Nations Conference on the
  Human Environment 95
United Nations Conference on
  Trade and Development
  (UNCTAD) 140, 168
United Nations Development
  Programme 162
United Nations Educational,
  Scientific and Cultural
  Organization 149
United Nations Environment
  Programme (UNEP) 96–7, 98
United Nations General Assembly
  12–13
United Nations High Commission
  for Refugees (UNHCR) 129
United Nations Industrial
  Development Organization
  (UNIDO) 168

United Nations International
  Children's Emergency Fund
  (UNICEF) 101
United Nations Security Council 11
United States: and Asia 30; and EU
  37–41; and Latin America 30–2;
  migration to 99; trade with EU
  124; and United Nations 11
Uruguay 34
Uruguay Round (GATT) 115, 120,
  121–2, 159

van den Broek, Hans 14, 15
van der Dussen, J. 65
van Eekelen, W. 23
Vietnam 79
von Habsburg, Otto 20–1

Warren, Bill 57
Waters, Hazel 48
Western European Union 23, 75,
  103
Western Hemisphere Free Trade
  Area (WHFTA) 34
Whyte, M. 57
Wilson, K. 65
Windward Islands 115
women: and colonialism 51–3; in
  Mediterranean 72
World Bank 27, 31, 33; and Lomé
  Four 115–17, 129, 141, 152, 155,
  167; and Mediterranean 87, 99
World Food Programme 129
World Health Organization
  (WHO) 44
World Trade Organization (WTO)
  67
Wurtz Report 113

Yannopoulos, G. 79–80
Yaoundé Conventions 62, 113, 171
Yemen, People's Republic of 146
Yemen Arab Republic 146
Yugoslavia 74, 78, 84, 129; crisis 19,
  24, 65; GNP 83

Zambia 37
Zartman, William 63
Zimbabwe 46
Zischka, Anton 172